DATE DUE

WITHDRAWN

PRAISE FOR *MATSUSHITA LEADERSHIP*

"A compelling discourse on a fascinating man and his legacy. The writing is both engaging and lucid. Kotter shares anecdotes that enable readers to discover insights for themselves. The businessman will learn a great deal from a man who affirmed that idealistic goals are both achievable and compatible with humanistic beliefs. The lay reader will be inspired by a model of a man who never ceased in his quest to learn."

—Stephan Roche, Consultant, Bain and Company

"Easy to read, well researched, and inspirational. Its basic messages are powerful and persuasive, especially regarding the importance of lifelong learning, having a positive view on human nature, and the need for humility. Overall, I cannot praise it enough."

—Pam Merrell, Vice President and Secretary, The Montana Power Company

"The single best biography of a business leader who helped change the world. A great story of a man, an organization, an industry, and a nation."

—Professor Warren Bennis, Founder of the Leadership Institute
at the University of Southern California and author of *Organizing Genius*

"I loved the book, especially the stress on humility and serving others."

—Kenneth MacKenzie, Chairman, The Mentor_I Group Ltd.

"A compelling book which puts so many things in perspective, especially about continuous learning for my employees and myself. I found particularly instructive how personal tragedies that often bury people were turned into a great strength by this man."

—Len Siegal, President and CEO, Siegal Steel Company

"Interesting and easy to read. *Matsushita Leadership* powerfully demonstrates the benefits of setting long term goals."

—Fabian Baca, General Manager, Casabaca S.A.

"An astounding account of how a man not only overcomes adversity, but uses it as a tool for the improvement of the human spirit. An excellent lesson in life."

—Larry Pitts, President, Plaza Investment Company Inc.

"A great book which captures KM and his background very accurately. In Japan, many admirers of Matsushita have written about his life and strategies. But these accounts are rather 'journalistic.' Until now, we have not had a really good book on KM. This book will contribute much to our understanding of a great business leader."

—Professor Masahiro Shimotani, Faculty of Economics, Kyoto University

"Beyond the lessons which can be learned about management, I very much enjoyed the work as a historical study and as a social statement."

—Paul Hopper, President, Alpha Healthcare Ltd.

"A great book about a great man. We should be proud of both."

—Andrew Bluestone, President, Selective Benefits Group Inc.

"Extremely interesting, useful, and a pleasure to read. The ideas about leadership qualities are easy to understand, with many practical examples. Some illustrations are so lively the reader can almost see them happening. This book will surely remain in people's memories and motivate them to attempt some of Matsushita's powerful practices."

—Sukumar Shah, President and Director, Mukand Ltd.

"Excellent. A great story very well written."

—Robert A. Johnson, President, The Johnson Family's Diamond Cellar

"*Matsushita Leadership* is a wonderful untold story which has powerful implications for businesses and the wider community."

—Trevor Matthews, General Manager for Personal Financial Services,
National Australia Bank

Matsushita Leadership

Lessons from the 20th Century's

Most Remarkable Entrepreneur

OTHER BOOKS BY JOHN P. KOTTER

Leading Change (1996)

The New Rules (1995)

Corporate Culture and Performance
(with James L. Heskett, 1992)

*A Force for Change: How Leadership
Differs from Management* (1990)

The Leadership Factor (1987)

Power and Influence: Beyond Formal Authority (1985)

The General Managers (1982)

Matsushita Leadership

Lessons from the 20th Century's

Most Remarkable Entrepreneur

JOHN P. KOTTER

THE FREE PRESS

New York   London   Toronto   Sydney   Singapore

THE FREE PRESS
A Division of Simon & Schuster Inc.
1230 Avenue of the Americas
New York, NY 10020

Manufactured in the United States of America

10 9 8 7 6 5 4 3 2 1

Library of Congress Cataloging-in-Publication Data

Kotter, John P., 1947–
    Matsushita leadership : lessons from the 20th
  century's most remarkable entrepreneur / John P. Kotter
        p.   cm.
    Includes bibliographical references and index.
    ISBN 0–684–83460–X
    1. Matsushita, Konosuke, 1894–1989.   2. Industrialists—Japan—
Biography.   3. Electronic industries—Japan—History.
4. Matsushita Denk i Sangyo—History.   I. Title.
HC461.5.M34K68   1997
338.7'6213'092—dc20   96–44863
                                                        CIP

CONTENTS

BUSINESS LEADER: 1931–1946

INSTITUTIONAL LEADER: 1946–1970

PHILOSOPHER AND EDUCATOR: 1970–1989

PREFACE

Over six years ago, in the spring of 1990, I decided that I wanted to write an analytical biography of an outstanding business leader. Although I'd been studying organizations and the people who run them for nearly two decades, I had never focused on the life of a single individual and the prospect of doing so seemed like a logical next step in my work. While I was beginning to consider candidates for the project, Harvard Business School Dean John McArthur asked to see me. I knew John fairly well, having first met him before I joined the HBS faculty in 1972, but I had no idea why he wanted a meeting. When I arrived in his office that day I was surprised to learn that Abe Zaleznik was retiring and that the dean wanted me to take his chair. Our conversation, in retrospect a rather absurd exchange, went something like this.

"Thank you very much. This is a great honor. But if you recall a discussion we had a few years ago, I would prefer to wait until Paul Lawrence retires and then be considered for his position. Paul was a special person in my own development. . . ."

"Yes, yes. I understand. But we have a problem here—matching positions with faculty. We have chairs in railroad management and retailing, but no young professors who are much interested in either. We have more chairs in banking than banking faculty. And so on. It's rare that we have a position that is named such that it fits perfectly some faculty member. But that's what we have here. Abe's chair is a 'Professor of Leadership.' And your specialty is leadership."

"Well, yes, but. . . ."

"He's really quite an interesting person."

"Who?"

"Matsushita."

"Mat . . . ?"

"The man the chair is named for. The official title is the Konosuke Matsushita Professor of Leadership."

"Are you sure you couldn't . . . ?"

"Here is some information on Matsushita. He really is a very interesting person."

"Yes, but. . . ."

I left the meeting mad at McArthur for ignoring our previous discussion about chairs, annoyed that my new professorship was named after some relatively unknown Japanese executive, and ashamed that I wasn't feeling more humbly grateful.

The next day, I reluctantly glanced at the materials the dean had given me. The information was hard to believe. Here was a man whose name I didn't recognize, yet who had built a gigantic corporation with innovative management and marketing practices, who had been a key part of the post–World War II economic miracle in Japan, and who had earned billions in the process. Dismissive at first, I eventually overcame my initial grumpiness and began gathering additional information about Matsushita. The more I learned about the man's difficult life yet astonishing accomplishments, the more I found I wanted to learn. Around Thanksgiving of 1990, it finally dawned on me that I had been handed an intriguing subject for my biography—a great business leader whose story was virtually unknown outside of Japan.

I suppose I might have found Matsushita by myself through more conventional means. But then again, who knows? Without a timely retirement and a stubborn dean, this book could have been a biography of Sam Walton or Tom Watson.

Some of the problems with the undertaking were obvious from the beginning. Osaka is a long way from Boston, geographically and culturally. I decided that assistance from people at Matsushita Electric would reduce the difficulties, so I spent six months trying to convince them to help. Executives at the firm were understandably edgy. They didn't know me. They undoubtedly worried that they might have more to lose than gain from an independent biography of their folk hero founder. For a while, I thought they were going to say no. But then I was invited to Japan, and after a series of discussions, they agreed to cooperate—even after I made it clear that they would have no control over the research and no editing rights to any manuscript.

The assistance from the firm proved to be invaluable. Over a five-year period, they helped provide access to: (1) the in-company historical library at Matsushita Electric in Osaka; (2) the library of Matsushita materials at the PHP Institute in Kyoto; (3) corporate records that are in none of the libraries; (4) people who knew KM well (the company set up thirty very important interviews); (5) a wide range of published works on the firm, the man, and Japanese business.

Most of the information gathering was done in 1992 and 1993. This manuscript was written in 1994, '95, and '96. Not until early 1994, no less than forty months after the conversation with McArthur, did I begin to grasp fully the magnitude of my subject. I wanted to write about an interesting business leader. Matsushita certainly fit that bill, more so than I thought at the beginning of the project, and an exploration of his life provided fascinating clues as to the roots of great leadership and to the process by which adaptive organizations are developed. But KM's saga, I found, is far more than a business story. It is about overcoming enormous adversity and drawing strength from trauma. It is about the moral foundations of great accomplishments. It is about the extraordinary growth that is possible even in adulthood.

Hiroyasu "Hiro" Komine served for three years as the primary research associate on the project and helped greatly with all the information gathering. Other research assistance came from Andrew Burtis and Nancy Rothbard. Kiyomu Ennokoshi acted as my liaison to Matsushita Electric. Through him, individuals at the firm's Corporate History Office, the PHP Institute, and the Matsushita Institute of Government and Management donated dozens and dozens of hours to do meticulous fact checking. Another group of people critiqued drafts of this book. They include: By Barnes, David Baskerville, John Beck, Joe Bower, Richard Boyatzis, Michael Cusumano, Nancy Dearman, Barbara Devine, Carol Franco, Alan Frohman, Jack Gabarro, Richard Hackman, Jim Heskett, Monica Higgins, Walter Kiechel, Bob Lambrix, Jay Lorsch, Leonard Lynn, Morgan McCall, Kazuo Noda, Tom Piper, Frederick Roberts, Len Schlesinger, Masahiro Shimotani, Nicolaj Siggelkow, Scott Snook, Howard Stevenson, Renato Tagiuri, Haruo Takagi, Richard Tedlow, David Thomas, Hiroyoshi Umezu, Ezra Vogel, Robert Wallace, Richard Walton, Robert J. J. Wargo, and Mike Yoshino. Still others provided indirect help or inspiration, including John McArthur, Paul Lawrence, Tony Athos, Abe Zaleznik, and Warren Bennis.

Even with all this assistance, the project was more challenging than I expected at the onset. Language and cultural differences created complications, since I am not a Japanologist and don't speak Japanese. The firm's anxiety over whether I would write something unflattering or something that might offend living members of the Matsushita family was most irritating at times. Gaps in the historical record made a complex personality hard to penetrate. The credibility question raised by my holding the Matsushita chair required much explanation (chair money at HBS goes into a general fund and doesn't determine faculty salary levels). Since KM embodied many of the leadership characteristics about which I had been writing for nearly a decade, there was also the ongoing danger that I would project my existing ideas onto the man's life and miss the real story. Perhaps the biggest challenge of all was that the more I learned about Konosuke Matsushita, beyond both the halos and the warts, the more I came to like this man. In a big and time-consuming undertaking where the goal is an honest assessment of someone, admiring the subject is a mixed blessing.

The book that has evolved from this effort was not written as a conventional biography. I am not a historian by training and have little interest in compiling an exhaustive description of Matsushita's life. As a management educator, I have instead tried to find a way to tell the story in a manner which highlights instructive patterns that have interesting implications for the future.

Konosuke Matsushita died in 1989, one year before this project began, so he never learned of how an odd coincidence steered me in his direction. After spending six years studying KM, I think I can say with some authority that he would have approved of this beginning, for he believed in the fate of seemingly random events. Indeed, what else, besides fate, can account for a poor boy's success at creating one of the largest corporations on earth? What else could have vaulted a man with little formal education and no connections into the position of helping lead his country in an economic revolution? What else can explain how someone could start with nothing and end up with both enormous wealth and the admiration of an entire nation?

Indeed, what other explanations are there?

1

THE LEGACY

By many standards, he didn't look like a great leader. Early pictures of Konosuke Matsushita show an unsmiling young man whose ears stick out like airplane wings. He never grew taller than five feet five inches nor weighed more than 135 pounds.[1] Unlike his rival Akio Morita at Sony, he was neither charismatically handsome nor internationally recognized. Unlike most well-known Western politicians, he didn't excel at public speaking, and in his later years his voice grew increasingly frail. He rarely displayed speed-of-light intellectual skills or warmed an audience with hilarious anecdotes. Nevertheless, he did what all great leaders do—motivate large groups of individuals to improve the human condition.

When he died in the spring of 1989, his funeral services were swamped with a crowd of over twenty thousand. In a telegram of condolences to the family, the president of the United States called him "an inspiration to people around the world."*

His legacy is daunting. After World War II, Matsushita was one of the central figures who helped lead the Japanese economic miracle. Through Panasonic and other brands, the firm he founded supplied billions of people with household appliances and consumer electronics. By the time of his death, few organizations on earth had more customers.† Revenues hit a phenomenal $42 billion that year, more than the combined sales of Bethlehem Steel, Colgate-Palmolive, Gillette, Goodrich, Kellogg, Olivetti, Scott Paper, and Whirlpool.‡

On some dimensions, his economic achievements exceed those of much more famous entrepreneurs—including Henry Ford, J. C. Penney, and Ray Kroc (see the exhibit on page 5). Yet because his name is not on the products, like Honda or Ford, because he was not an American in the American century,

---

*"Dear Mr. Masaharu Matsushita: Please accept my heartfelt condolences on the passing of your father, Konosuke Matsushita. Mr. Matsushita was an inspiration to people around the world. With his own hard work and vision, he built Matsushita into one of the great firms of our time, a leader in new technology. At the same time, Mr. Matsushita understood the larger obligations and responsibilities that success brings. He worked hard for international understanding and world peace. He urged Japan to take its place as a full member of world society and to help others achieve the prosperity that the Japanese worked so hard to attain. We will miss him, but his spirit will always be with us. My best wishes to all your family at this time of sadness. Sincerely, George Bush."

†It is difficult to estimate the number of customers major businesses have. Simple rules of thumb lead to this conclusion about Matsushita Electric: (1) large firms tend to have more customers than smaller firms; (2) consumer product companies tend to have more than other types of corporations; (3) multinationals, especially those that genuinely sell around the world, tend to have more than firms embedded in one country or continent. The world's largest, global, consumer products company is Matsushita.

‡As this is written in 1996, Matsushita Electric yearly revenues are about $65 billion.

and because he never aggressively sought media attention outside of Japan, he is still largely unknown beyond his native land.

His incredible successes generated billions of dollars in wealth which were used not for villas in France but for the creation of a Nobel Prize-like organization, the founding of a school of government to reform Japan's political system, and a number of other civic projects. During his later years, he wrote dozens of books, studied human nature with a small group of research associates, and prodded his government to do more for the citizenry.

There are those who accumulated larger personal fortunes. There could be others who built even bigger enterprises or who made equally large contributions to their countries. But overall, it is difficult to find 20th-century entrepreneurs or executives with a longer list of accomplishments. And as an inspirational role model, he is without peer.

The small actions so defied stereotypes of rich and powerful industrialists that they became the subject of folklore. A typical story: in 1975, Morimasa Ogawa and five other division general managers were invited to have lunch with their firm's founder.[2] At this point in Matsushita's life, he had already been on the cover of *Time* magazine and was regularly being reported to pay more income taxes than anyone else in Japan. Because Ogawa had little contact with The Great One, he looked forward to the luncheon with both excitement and some trepidation.

The setting was a restaurant in Osaka. The six men met shortly past noon. After greetings and small talk, everyone ordered steak. Matsushita had two glasses of beer while telling stories about the business and the history of the company. When all six finished the main course, Matsushita leaned over to Ogawa and asked him to find the chef who cooked his steak. He was very clear on this point: "Not the manager, the chef." Ogawa then noticed that Matsushita had only eaten half of his entree.

Preparing himself for what could be an extremely awkward scene, Ogawa found the chef and brought him to the table. The cook arrived looking distressed, for he knew that the customer who had summoned him was an exceptionally important person.

"Is there anything wrong?" asks a nervous chef.

"You've gone to all the trouble of broiling the steak," says Matsushita, "but I could eat only half of it. It's not because it's not good. It's quite delicious. But, you see, I'm eighty years old and my appetite isn't what it once was."

The chef and five other diners exchange confused expressions. It takes everyone a few seconds to realize what is happening.

"I asked to talk to you," Matsushita continues, "because I was afraid you might feel bad if you saw the half-eaten steak back in the kitchen."

Even the most rapacious businessmen occasionally show a kind side, usually as a manipulation. What is remarkable about Matsushita is the sheer volume of theses acts which, in combination with his many accomplishments, the public loved. Surveys showed that he was more admired than movie stars and professional athletes.

In an age when successful business executives throughout the world are sometimes looked upon with suspicion or even contempt, he died a national hero in Japan.

Konosuke Matsushita was born at the very end of the 19th century. During his youth, he experienced much hardship. When he began working for himself in 1917, he had 100 yen, less than four years of formal education, no connections to important people, and a history of family trauma. Yet his small and poorly financed firm flourished under the guiding hand of an increasingly clever merchant entrepreneur.

His counsel from that period was market oriented and very pragmatic. "Treat the people you do business with as if they were a part of your family. Prosperity depends on how much understanding one receives from the people with whom one conducts business. . . . After-sales service is more important than assistance before sales. It is through such service that one gets permanent customers. . . . Don't sell customers goods that they are attracted to, sell them goods that will benefit them. . . . Any waste, even of a sheet of paper, will increase the price of a product by that much. . . . To be out of stock is due to carelessness.

Famous 20th-Century Entrepreneurs*

Name	Company	Revenue Growth (Billions of 1994 Dollars)†
Konosuke Matsushita	Matsushita Electric	$49.5
Soichiro Honda	Honda Motor Co., Ltd.	$35.5
Sam Walton	Wal-Mart Stores, Inc.	$35.0
Akio Morita	Sony Corporation	$33.7
David Packard/William Hewlett	Hewlett-Packard Company	$20.6
James Cash Penney	J.C. Penney Company, Inc.	$17.4
Ken Olsen	Digital Equipment Corporation	$14.5
Henry Ford	Ford Motor Company	$10.3
Andy Grove‡	Intel Corporation	$8.9
Ray Kroc	McDonald's Corporation	$4.7
Bill Gates‡	Microsoft Corporation	$3.8

*Not a complete list of the most successful entrepreneurs.

†Growth while the entrepreneur was associated with the firm in either operating or nonoperating roles. Figures go through mid-1994.

‡Still running their firms.

If this happens, apologize to the customers, ask for their address, and tell them that you will deliver the goods immediately."[3]

As both he and his firm grew, so did the scope and breadth of his ideas. By the early 1930s, pragmatic advice became increasingly intermixed with broad philosophical statements about the purpose of business enterprise, human nature, and more. "The mission of a manufacturer," he told employees in 1932, "is to overcome poverty, to relieve society as a whole from the misery of poverty and bring it wealth. Business and production are not meant to enrich only the shops or the factories of the enterprise concerned, but all the rest of society as well."[4] He never talked narrowly about maximizing shareholder value as the proper goal of an enterprise. He did speak often about generating wealth, but for the benefit of everyone, not just owners, and even that idea was tempered by an emphasis on the psychological and the spiritual.

"Possessing material comforts in no way guarantees happiness. Only spiritual wealth can bring true happiness. If that is correct, should business be concerned only with the material aspect of life and leave the care of the human spirit to religion or ethics? I do not think so. Businessmen too should be able to share in creating a society that is spiritually rich and materially affluent."[5]

The horror of World War II increased greatly his concerns about government. One of his last big ideas was to try to help develop a new generation of Japanese politicians by means of education. The concept was simple and extremely idealistic. Create a small, independent graduate school of government. Stress vision, integrity, the broader view, and rational policy analysis. Encourage alumni to run for elected office with the hope that over a long period of time they would become successful and alter the very culture of politics.

He built the Matsushita Institute of Government and Management (MIGM) on five acres of land in Chigasaki City. The first class entered in April of 1980. As of mid-1993, 130 students had graduated. In the July 1993 national elections, twenty-three MIGM alumni ran for seats for the national Diet, the equivalent of the U.S. Congress. Most were members of new Japanese political parties and almost all were under forty years of age. They ran against incumbents from the LDP, the party that had been in power since shortly after World War II.* In the United States or nearly anywhere else, most of the young challengers would have been defeated easily. But in the summer 1993 elections, fifteen of the twenty-three MIGM graduates won seats in the national legislature.

Masahiro Mukasa worked with Matsushita for nearly twenty-five years. His comments are not unusual among those who knew the man well.

"In Japan there are various orders that are conferred upon individuals by the emperor. KM received some, yet he never developed airs. He always thanked other people in a very natural way. That's what impressed me the most about him. He was always remarkably humble. He behaved as if he held everyone in high esteem. As a result, people who are usually reserved when talking to a powerful individual found it easy to speak with him. KM's demeanor encouraged them to be frank and to tell him what was really on their minds.

"He studied very hard. I think partially because he had little educational background, he listened carefully to what other

---

*Of the twenty-three MIGM candidates, three were associated with the LDP. The other twenty were members of mostly newer parties.

people told him. He was very skilled at using that knowledge to create his own ideas.

"Despite all the money he made, he never seemed to be impressed by riches. He didn't spend his wealth in a luxurious way. He had a strong sense of morality, and seemed to focus on elevating his mind. He wanted to take a gradual step forward every day, little by little, toward greater knowledge.

"He believed that by improving other people, he could improve himself, that helping other people was like helping himself. These ideas were almost religious beliefs. He thought that without the cooperation of other people, he would not be able to achieve his goals. He always gave that impression to everyone he met. Without *you,* we would not be as successful.

"He was a very idealistic person, and I enjoyed working for him very much. He was more than an outstanding executive. He was a great man."[6]

During his youth, few saw Matsushita as above average, much less great. He was a mediocre student. As a young adult in his early twenties, he was nervous and sickly. Yet by the time he was thirty, he was inventing business practices that would be highlighted in the late 1970s by Tom Peters and Bob Waterman.[7] By age forty, he had become the kind of visionary leader that has been championed recently by Warren Bennis, Noel Tichy, and others.[8] After World War II, he created an institution that adapted phenomenally well to rapid growth, increasing technological change, and globalization. In the 1970s and 1980s, he took on additional careers as author, philanthropist, educator, social philosopher, and statesman. Most of all, throughout his life he demonstrated a capacity for growth and renewal that is astonishing, a capability that virtually all experts agree will be more important in a faster-moving 21st century than it has been in a slower-moving past.

Most children learn easily and develop skills at a rapid pace. Many adults learn slowly if at all. On numerous occasions, Matsushita told others that his perspective on all this was well summarized in a poem, the beginning of which reads:

> Youth is not a time of life, it is a state of mind; it is not a matter of rosy cheeks, red lips, and supple knees; it is a matter of the will, a quality of the imagination, a vigor of the emotions; it is the freshness of the deep springs of life.
>
> Youth means the temperamental predominance of courage over timidity, of the appetite for adventure over the love of ease. This often exists in a man of sixty more than a boy of twenty. Nobody grows old merely by a number of years. We grow old by deserting our ideals.*

His ideals powerfully influenced his actions, but in a way that created a more complex personality than surface appearances would indicate.

After watching Matsushita deal with the chef at the Osaka restaurant in 1975, Morimasa Ogawa concluded that his boss was a saint. That initial impression made an episode that occurred five years later all the more confusing.[9] At the time, Ogawa's division was losing money. When the chairman paid

---

*By Samuel Ullman. General Douglas MacArthur is generally credited with introducing the poem to the Japanese after World War II.

him a visit, the conversation, according to Ogawa's written account, became very heated.

"I could understand if sales were zero and the deficit was in personnel costs," Matsushita yelled, "but you've got sales of one hundred billion yen and are nine billion yen in the red. Responsibility for running this mess lies with you and the executives under you. The head office must also take responsibility because they recently lent you that twenty billion yen. Tomorrow, I'm going to talk to them about getting it back."

"But Mr. Matsushita, that would mean disaster for us! It's five days to payday. At the end of the month we will owe money for materials and parts. If you take that twenty billion yen back now, we won't be able to pay for them."

"That's right, but I'm not going to lend you any money if you and your colleagues are going to run an operation like this. I'm pulling your loan tomorrow."

"But then we'll go bankrupt!"

"You've got four thousand superb employees working here. Talk it over with them, get their ideas, and come up with a reconstruction plan that will work. If you can get a plan like that together, I'll write a letter of recommendation to Sumitomo Bank for you. With that letter, they're sure to give you a twenty billion yen loan using the land, buildings, and equipment here as collateral. Now, get to work!"

Although few stories like this one have ever been reported, Matsushita appears to have yelled regularly at key executives, occasionally becoming so angry that his face would turn a deep red.[10] The closer people were to him, the greater the opportunity to be reprimanded. Because of both family and corporate ties, no one was more in the inner circle than his son-in-law and successor as president and chairman, Masaharu

Matsushita,* and no one felt the brunt of KM's anger more. "He could be exceptionally charming to customers and sales agents, but to those of us who knew him best, he was sometimes cold and harsh. Even at home, at the dinner table, we often saw little warmth."[11]

There are other indications that the Matsushita story is more complicated than the usual national hero headline. His emphasis on the greater good and all of humankind is legendary, yet he was a supplier to the Japanese army in World War II and in the late 1960s his firm was accused of participating in an industry cartel which kept prices high in Japan and dumped goods into the United States. For much of his adult life he was surrounded by thousands of admirers, yet in some ways he was a lonely man.[12] He stayed with one woman in a marriage that was successful by most standards for over seventy years, but he also kept at least one mistress for decades and had a second family with her.[13] His demeanor often appeared to have a Zen-like tranquillity and strength, yet during his last forty years he suffered from insomnia and required a sleeping pill every single night.[14]

The Matsushita story resides at least on three levels. The public persona was a great businessman who often behaved like a saint. The private side included screaming, sleeping pills, and a mistress. Deeper than both was a tornado of emotions that came to be directed by a set of beliefs and convictions that are difficult for the skeptic in all of us to comprehend.

Yasuo Okamoto has written what many consider to be the

---

*His name was originally Masaharu Hirata. He adopted his father-in-law's last name. See Chapter 9, page 135.

finest book thus far on KM's company, a best-seller called *Hitachi to Matsushita*. Says Okamoto: "He was a complex man with a lot of self-control."[15]

This book is not meant to be a conventional biography, although it does retain a chronological structure.[16] Instead of establishing an exhaustive historical record, the focus is on Matsushita's long list of accomplishments and what can be learned from his experiences. Any exploration of these issues inevitably leads to a discussion of Japan, but our primary purpose is not yet another study of Japanese management. The main questions explored here are: why is Matsushita's legacy so unusual compared to managers' anywhere, including those in Japan; and how might the lessons of his life inform effective action around the globe in the next century?*

KM was very much a product of a particular time and place. If he were miraculously transported to Chicago or Frankfurt today as he was at age thirty, he would no doubt achieve less than he did during his actual lifetime. Nevertheless, his 20th-century Japanese story offers interesting insights about dealing with difficult circumstances generally and excelling in an environment of rapid change. If the next few decades were going to offer a business climate with much stability, those lessons would be of limited relevance. But no credible evidence points to such a benign future. Just the opposite is true.

If the 21st century evolves as an era of increasingly tur-

---

*Readers who prefer to begin with discussion of the conclusions should go directly to the epilogue.

bulent and rapid change, the Matsushita saga strongly suggests that common business strategies, organizational arrangements, and career paths utilized in the past will not prove
very sucessful. The mission-centered, customer-focused, high-
productivity, employee-involved, and constantly improving
Matsushita Electric from the 1950s and '60s may offer a far
better role model than GM, Philips, Sears, or most other well-
known businesses during that same time period or even today.
An examination of leadership at MEI, which started with the
CEO and was pushed deeply into one of the first truly divisionalized organizations anywhere on earth, shows how firms
can remain adaptive and outmaneuver rivals in a dynamic environment, even when competitors have more resources at
their disposal.

The story of Matsushita Electric Industrial demonstrates
how great business strategies, when implemented well, are not
just the product of rational economic analysis but have a powerful visceral component relating to personal history. The story
of Konosuke Matsushita shows how great leadership is not a
static quality but a crucial element that evolves over decades,
often built on a base of pain, not privilege.

Perhaps the most interesting finding of all from this study is
what does *not* seem to be associated with KM's astonishing
accomplishments: the stereotypical dominating personality of
J. D. Rockefeller, the camera-ready charisma of Walt Disney, the
inventive genius of Thomas Edison, the financial shrewdness of
J. P. Morgan, the privileged background of Akio Morita, the
physical presence of Charles de Gaulle, or the educational credentials of Andy Grove. In some ways KM was quite ordinary.
Certainly no one who knew him during his youth predicted great
achievements. Yet he grew to be anything but ordinary, and the
key to his story lies in his phenomenal drive for growth.

From a sickly, heartbroken, and poverty stricken nine-year-old, he learned to be a competent apprentice in a bicycle shop with a sensitivity to the importance of customers. As a young adult, he developed into an up-and-coming employee in the Osaka Light Company and a successful merchant-oriented entrepreneur who used strategies that were far from the 20th-century norm. Instead of decelerating after gaining some degree of wealth and fame, he grew to be a strong business leader, an even more unusual builder of a huge business institution, and finally a statesman and philosopher who far transcended simple economic interests. While others leveled off in their thirties or forties, a consequence of the pain of failure or the arrogance of success, Matsushita continued to learn and evolve.

Certain habits fostered this growth. KM pushed himself and others out of comfort zones, challenged conventions, took risks, assessed weaknesses and failures, sought new ideas, and listened with an open mind. These habits were supported by vast and humanistic goals, ambitions which also grew over time and which placed all his actual achievements in a humbling perspective. Those goals, in turn, emerged from a series of tragedies, hardships that generated intense feelings, fueled big dreams, and inoculated him against the minor downturns in life. The overall pattern is summarized in the exhibit on page 244.

Hardships sometimes create a fierce need to conquer one's environment, a workaholic personality, a value system that justifies ends over means, and an insatiable drive for money and power. But the Matsushita saga is about how tough times produced increasingly large yet humanistic ambitions, a set of growth-inducing mental habits, decades of continuous learning, and then phenomenal accomplishments that benefited millions of people. It is the tale of a revolutionary, of sorts, who spent most of his life swimming against strong currents. It is a slice of 20th-century history, in some sense a condensed version of the entire Japanese story, that is educational in many ways and on many dimensions.

Perhaps most of all, even in a world with nerve ends deadened by conflict, poverty, and the cold light of scientific rationalism, it is a drama that can both inspire resolve and warm the heart.

STUDENT, APPRENTICE, EMPLOYEE

1894–1917

2

EARLY LOSS AND
ITS CONSEQUENCES

Tokyo is on the east coast of Japan in roughly the center of the country. Two hundred and forty miles to the southwest lies Osaka. Another thirty-seven miles in the same general direction is Wakayama. Konosuke Matsushita was born in the nearby farm village of Wasamura on November 27, 1894 (see map on page 20).

If his large and relatively affluent family had been more fortunate, he might have lived a comfortable existence and be unknown to us today. But the Matsushita clan saw little fortune after Konosuke was born, and the tumultuous times greatly affected the youngest child.

The specific events are unique to KM's youth, but the gen-

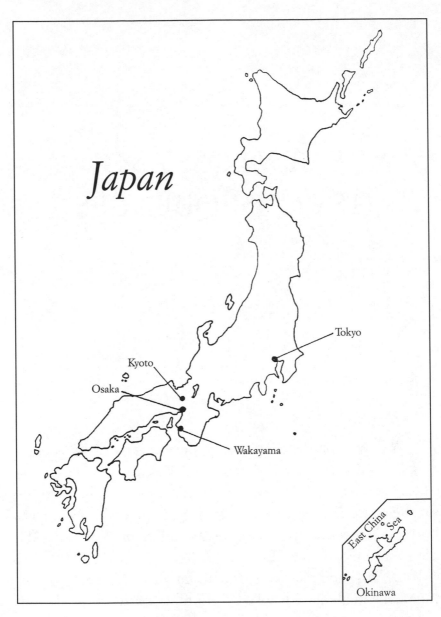

eral pattern is not. Early losses fuel feelings, hopes, and fears which eventually emerge as a basis for entrepreneurship, leadership, or some other form of exemplary activity. In most cases, certainly Matsushita's, one cannot begin to understand extraordinary achievements that occurred during adult years without first appreciating the childhood roots—often difficult, painful roots.

The Death Register of the Matsushita family at Gokuraku Temple in Wasamura lists names that go back into the 17th century, but virtually nothing is known of those who died before 1850. One source has described KM's paternal grandfather as a relatively large man with a long beard who established a good reputation in the village and lived until he was eighty-one.[1] Matsushita's father, Masakusu, was born in 1855, two years after Commodore Matthew C. Perry steamed into Tokyo harbor to awaken a sleeping nation from a self-imposed isolation that had lasted for two and a quarter centuries. KM's mother, Tokue Shimamoto, was born in 1856. She and Masakusu were wed in 1874 when Tokue was eighteen years old. Their first child, a girl they named Iwa, was born in 1874. Isaburo (a boy) arrived next in 1877, followed by Fusae (a girl, 1880), Hachiro (a boy, 1882), and three more girls (Chiyo, 1885, Hana, 1888, and Ai, 1891).[2] The final sibling, Konosuke, was born in 1894, the same year that future Matsushita hero Thomas Edison first demonstrated his moving pictures machine.

The ten-person family lived in a village with only sixty houses.[3] In a country the size of California where sixty million people were squeezed onto a land mass no larger than New Jersey,* the little community was relatively spacious and uncrowded. The center of Wasamura included a temple and little else.[4] Since the economy was based on agriculture and the main crop was rice, most of the land was devoted to rice paddies.[5] Much of the visible activity would have revolved around the labor-intensive yearly cycle of planting and harvesting.[6]

By today's standards, the Matsushita family lived at best a middle-class existence. By turn-of-the-century Japanese standards, they were relatively affluent. In a small and poor village, KM's father owned 150 acres of land worked by seven tenant farmers.[7] On two occasions before Konosuke was born, Masakusu was elected to the village assembly.[8] Because the family had lived in the same area for at least three or four generations, the Matsushita name was known and respected.[9] The youngest sibling must have sensed this even during his earliest years.[10]

Tokue cared for the eight brothers and sisters with assistance from hired help.[11] The historical record suggests no unusual problems in the family.[12] The children appear to have been healthy, happy, and loved. KM had a special place in the group. He was the baby, often pampered by everyone.[13]

In his sparse writing about the early years, Matsushita recalled a "peaceful and carefree" life.[14] Konosuke spent his days in and around the ancestral home, a simple but large wooden structure located less than half a mile from the center of Wasamura. The surrounding area included fields of rice, green forests, and nearby mountains. In a simple farming community, much work needed to be done, but little fell on the baby of the family. KM fished in a nearby stream, played tag, and had fun.[15] As an adult, he said that he faintly remembered being carried home along

---

*Japan itself is much larger than New Jersey, but most of the land is uninhabited mountains and forests.

paddy field parkways to the comforting sound of a country lullaby.[16] After a few years, he undoubtedly came to regard this pleasant routine as normal, as an inevitable part of life. It wasn't.

The family's economic fortunes collapsed in 1899. The ten-person household was forced to move into a small tenement slum apartment in nearby Wakayama. Food was scarce. A terrible situation became catastrophic when children began to die. Konosuke survived, but at age nine he was sent to Osaka to work sixteen hours a day and to live with his employer.

Under any conditions, all the tragedy would have been difficult to endure. But the origins of KM's hardships made the pain all the worse. The Matsushita descent into darkness was not the result of an earthquake or war. Poverty and its consequences were thrust upon the family by the actions of Konosuke's father.

Had Japan not embarked on a journey of rapid change in the last part of the 19th century, Masakusu would never have encountered the commodity markets that led to his downfall. But without all the change, his youngest son would never have had the opportunity to build a great enterprise, sell goods around the world, and help his country emerge as a major global economic force.

Until 1868, Japan was mostly a feudal society of peasants and nobles, socially rigid and lacking much Western technology.[17] Yet when the ruling coalition decided to abandon tradition and seek modernization, change came with great speed. A constitution was adopted in 1889. In first-ever elections held that same year, KM's father won his job as a village council member.[18]

Rapid political change was accompanied by equally rapid

shifts in the economy, in the military, and in education.* Written accounts from late 19th-century Japan suggest that all of this was sometimes bewildering, sometimes breathtakingly exciting, and sometimes terrifying. In an exaggerated version of what we increasingly see today at the end of the 20th century, both the opportunities and the hazards offered by the new environment were significant.[22]

Amid all this turmoil, a rice exchange was established at Wakayama in January of 1894.[23] Like similar mechanisms in the United States and Europe, the exchange allowed people to buy or sell an agricultural product sometime in the future at a fixed price. When a contract became due, if the market price of the commodity was above that established in the deal, the buyer would make a profit and the seller would incur a loss. If the market price was below that set in the contract, the opposite would happen; the seller would win and the buyer would lose. Commodity exchanges were attractive, then as now, because a great deal of money can be made without large upfront investments. The opposite is also true. Much money can be lost.

---

*New silk technology was brought into the country in 1868. A model facility, based on a French factory, was completed in 1873. The first modern spinning mill was built in 1882 and a large-scale copy of an English spinning company was created shortly thereafter.[19] In total, the number of spindles rose from 8,000 in 1877 to 971,000 in 1897. The very first railroad line was finished in 1872, eighteen miles between Yokohama and Tokyo. By 1894, over 2,000 additional miles of track were laid.[20] To build a modern navy, the Japanese looked to the British. For their army, they looked first to the French and then the Germans. A ministry of education was established in 1871. The French system was adapted at first but later modified by incorporating ideas from the United States. To foster higher education, three organizations were merged in 1869 to form what would be later called the University of Tokyo.[21]

A poor harvest in 1897 helped send the price of rice up 36 percent the following year and then back down 33 percent in 1899.[24] KM's father, the gentleman farmer and village council member, made the ten-kilometer trip from his home to the Wakayama exchange during this period. He speculated in rice futures, and not with small bets.

Tokue may not have known that her husband was gambling with commodities. For her and the children, life continued as always. The oldest son was finishing his schooling. Since compulsory education did not exist for girls, and since it stopped for most boys at the fourth grade, the remaining seven siblings were at home.[25] Iwa and Fusae helped raise the younger children. All the girls assisted Tokue with the household chores of cooking, sewing, and cleaning. Hachiro helped maintain the home and watch over the fields.[26] Without electricity or modern plumbing, and with only a straw roof on the house,[27] life was relatively primitive by today's standards. But compared to neighbors, the Matsushitas were fortunate. Their wooden one-story home was large by turn-of-the-century Japanese standards (see diagram on page 26). They undoubtedly had more possessions, more food, and more wealth than almost anyone they knew. They had space and tranquillity rarely found in urban centers. And they had each other—from all known accounts, a big and happy family.

As a novice at a game which experts often find difficult and unpredictable, Masakusu was always tempting fate. We know little about his motives and even less about the positions he took or the size of his bets. We know only the end result of his excursion into the post-feudal economy.

Sometime after KM's fourth birthday, the elder Matsushita gambled away nearly all of the family's possessions.

The Matsushita Home in Wasamura, circa 1895

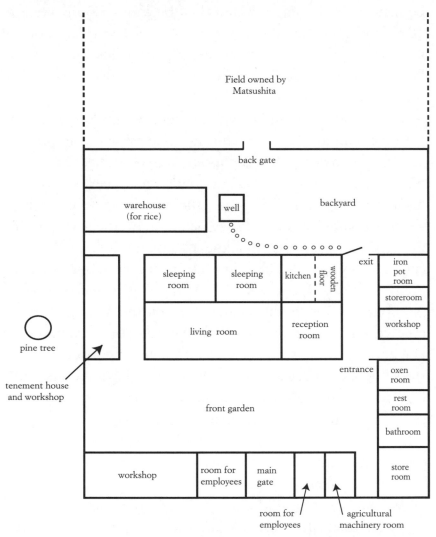

Source: Yutaka Tsujimoto.

The immense shame would have hit Masakusu first. Talking to his wife, tenant farmers, fellow village council members, and neighbors would have been a vastly humiliating experience. To pay his debt at the rice exchange, KM's father was forced to sell all that he had inherited from his ancestors. Kakujiro Tsujimoto, a neighbor and fellow village assembly member, bought the farm lands. Fujikichi Senda, another neighbor, bought the main house, the residential lot, and one attached field. A relative, Shigeshichi Sekimoto, bought the warehouse. Still other neighbors purchased the front and back gates, a tenement house, and household furnishings.[28]

The overall change in the family's position can be difficult for a late 20th-century observer to grasp. Bankruptcy now is a terrible experience, but one that is buffered by laws designed to help people rebound. Although some social cost is associated with relying on those laws, that stigma is small compared to only a few decades ago. Today, a person who loses everything to speculation simply declares bankruptcy, is allowed to keep some assets, and is given a chance to regain his or her economic position. In the feudal culture that still existed in Japan in 1899, modern bankruptcy laws did not exist and even a small decrease in social status could mean fundamentally different treatment by others. Bows, smiles, and great courtesy might be replaced with indifference, aloofness, or rudeness. A demotion in a large firm today from executive vice president to foreman would not be more shameful than Masakusu's fall.

The ten members of the Matsushita household packed up their most personal belongings and moved into a cramped tenement house in a back alley at 1-chome, Honmachi, Wakayama.[29] The city had a population of 64,000, one hundred times that of Wasamura.[30] Instead of more than a dozen rooms, they were crowded into two or three.[31] Narrow urban streets substituted for forests, fields, and mountains. Jarring city noise replaced tranquil country sounds. Deferential treatment from others disappeared. Tension within the family inevitably grew.

For the first time in his life, the head of the household was forced to seek employment.

The move alone meant that the Matsushita youngsters had to give up most of what they had known, including their friends. The home, the familiar stream, the secret hiding place, the playmate next door, the tree for climbing, the path for running—everything was gone. The economic hardships meant less food, lesser quality food, and no new clothing. The cramped tenement meant three to five sleeping in one room and almost total loss of privacy. Poverty in a new city meant that the children were treated as strangers and street urchins instead of a part of a valued family.

The reality for the Matsushita siblings was awkwardly painful. They all suffered greatly, and it was Masakusu's fault. No matter how much they loved their father, and no matter how much they rationalized their bad fate to other people or events, the tension in the small tenement house would have been palpable. The national culture, with its Confucian emphasis on filial loyalties, would have made the situation even worse.

With help from a friend who was a dealer in wooden shoes, Masakusu opened a small retail shop in Wakayama to sell clogs (geta). Twenty-one-year-old Isaburo dropped out of school a year before graduation to help run the store.[32] Despite hard work and a good location,[33] business was slow. Masakusu was not instinctively a good merchant, and no one in the family had any experience in that kind of endeavor.

The daily scene could be depressing. Late in life, Matsushita recalled being hungry during this period and watching his father check coins to make sure they were not counterfeit.[34]

As bad as conditions were at first in Wakayama, they grew

even worse over the next thirty months. In the fall of 1900, eighteen-year-old Hachiro caught an infectious disease. If the collapse of the family's economic and social fortunes had not already made the Mat-sushitas feel powerless, the inability to help Hachiro surely did. No matter what they tried, his condition did not improve. On October 4th, the likable young man died.[35]

The pain of loss was still very bitter when, only six months later, the macabre sequence of events repeated. This time twenty-one-year-old Fusae became sick. In Wakayama, at the turn of the century, the medical care for a poor family would not have been sophisticated. Ultimately, whatever treatment she received did not help much. On April 17, 1901, Fusae died.[36]

To add to all the misery, during that same year, the tiny clog shop failed and was closed. Masakusu tried one job after another without success.[37] Whatever was left of his self-esteem took another battering. The oldest son, Isaburo, did find a position as a clerk in the newly opened Wakayama Spinning Mill.[38] Yet even this small upturn in family prospects did not last long.

Sometime in the summer of 1901, the number-one son caught a cold which eventually turned nasty. With his horrified parents watching, he grew weaker and weaker. Despite all their desperate efforts, the twenty-four-year-old eldest child simply would not recover. On August 22nd, he became the third family casualty within less than a year.[39]

At the beginning of the 20th century, life expectancy in Japan was much lower than it is today. Nevertheless, Isaburo's passing was both unexpected and especially painful after the recent loss of two other children.

The three deaths may well have been related to all the trauma the family was experiencing. But the connections we might make today are different from those that individuals would have seen a century ago in Japan. People in feudal societies are often superstitious. By the end of the summer of 1901, the members of the Matsushita household could have easily believed that someone had placed a curse on them.

Masakusu and Tokue were devastated by the tragedies. "The loss of three children in the family, on top of seemingly insurmountable poverty, caused my parents great psychological as well as financial distress."[40] Powerful images were forever locked into young Konosuke's mind. Late in his life, he wrote: "My mother's anguished face and shoulder drooping in weariness are still a painfully vivid memory."[41]

In the feudalistic culture within Japan, sons were valued much more than daughters and the oldest son was by far the most important child. The first son carried on the family tradition, linking ancestors and the future. When KM became the oldest male child after Isaburo's death, he also became the natural focus of attention. "Despite all the hardships, my parents doted on me, and seemed to put all their hopes on their only remaining son."[42]

When emotionally ravaged people "put all their hopes" on someone, the burden can be heavy. But dreams of achievement can also direct difficult feelings. In Matsushita's case, the channeling of the sadness, anger, anxiety, and depression that accompany loss was influenced by doting parents who spoke often of regaining family wealth and honor.

Amid all the turmoil, in 1901 KM started his formal education. One of his schoolmates has subsequently described young Matsushita as a gentle and shy individual.[43] His academic performance was only average: forty-fifth among a hundred in his class.[44] Later, as an adult, KM readily admitted he was not a good student.

Discussing his early education in his autobiography, Matsushita talks about humiliation and a beloved instructor. The humiliation arose from his economic circumstances.[45] For school ceremonies, students wore pleated trousers (hakama) that were made of cotton. With no money to buy Konosuke the standard uniform, Tokue dressed him in an old pair of Matsushita family hakama made partially of silk. Like children everywhere, and especially in Japan, KM wanted very much to fit in with his peer group. His own sense of vulnerability would have heightened this need. Since the silk hakama clearly differentiated him, he protested vehemently to his mother about having to wear the unusual outfit. One can imagine how all this made Tokue feel.

The teacher was a Mr. Murakami, described by Matsushita as "a good and very kind man who often invited students to his home."[46] At his instructor's house, young KM learned to play a game resembling chess. "My friends and I often played shogi there, and I remember the immense sense of satisfaction at hearing Mr. Murakami's praise when I would win."[47] In a world with few sources of gratification, succeeding at this competition and receiving recognition from a credible male role model were significant events for Konosuke. Later in life, Matsushita spoke of his instructor's home and garden as a rare source of youthful pleasure. "In the autumn we would shinny up the mandarin orange trees and pick our fill of the juicy, golden fruit. It was an ideal place for children and we often played there until dark."[48]

By that time, 1903, Masakusu was no longer living with the family, having left Wakayama for Osaka the year before in search of work.[49] Because of its size, nearly 900,000 people,[50] the larger city offered many more employment opportunities—although tension within the household was probably an additional factor in motivating the move. Once in Osaka, Masakusu found a clerical job in a new school for children with sight and hearing disabilities. His wages were not large, but they did bring some minimum economic security to the family.[51]

Combined with an increasingly satisfying school experience, the greater income made life more tolerable for the youngest Matsushita. He went to school. He played on the stone fences at Wakayama Castle. He scooped shrimps from the Kino River. He visited Murakami's home. His own tenement house was less crowded, with only six occupants. Although far from the comforts of his first four years, life had settled into a more predictable pattern. Under the circumstances, predictability could have been comforting.[52]

Then, once again, everything changed.

In the middle of November 1904, Tokue received a letter from Masakusu telling her about a charcoal room heater dealer from Hachiman-suji who was in need of an apprentice. "Konosuke is already in his fourth year and will soon graduate from primary school. This is an opportunity we can't afford to miss. Send Konosuke to Osaka immediately."[53]

Matsushita has said that he could not remember his first reaction to this letter.[54] One can easily imagine strong feelings, some quite the opposite of others.

On the 23rd of November, Tokue took her nine-year-old boy to Kinokawa Station in Wakayama.[55] After putting him on the train with a small bundle of clothing, she explained to the person in the accompanying seat that her son was traveling to Osaka, where he would be met by his father. The passenger agreed to watch out for the child. In the final minutes before his departure, she tried to offer Konosuke words of both caution and encouragement. And she cried a great deal.[56] When the steam locomotive began moving, Tokue stood on the platform watching the train take away her only living son.

The trip required just a few hours, but it transported young Matsushita into a new world. At the time, Osaka was the fifteenth largest city on earth and a breeding ground for merchants. Moving from Wakayama to this giant urban area was like going from a small midwestern town to Chicago, or from the Russian wilderness to St. Petersburg. KM must have sensed that his life would change significantly, but he could not possibly have understood what lay ahead. Like millions of people who have moved to big cities over the past few centuries, he would face both more opportunities and more hazards, increased sources of pleasure and danger, additional riches and hardships.

In his subsequent writings, Matsushita said he remembered feeling sad and scared as he sat in the train and watched the countryside flash by. He was once again losing all that he had known, a frightening prospect for one so young. But he also felt a great sense of excitement during the journey.[57]

All children develop hopes and fears based on their specific experiences. Given the dramatic nature of his early life, especially all the losses, Konosuke's fantasies and nightmares would have been more intense than average. For this nine-year-old, Osaka was not just a metropolis with thousands of jobs, houses, and stores. The big city represented both another source of uncertainty and pain as well as a potentially better life and a vehicle for making dreams come true.

After the family's economic collapse, the death of three siblings, many disruptions, great humiliations, and increased attention from doting parents, the dreams could have been both large and emotionally powerful.

3

GROWTH THROUGH HARDSHIP

H e began work in Osaka during the same year in which the Wright brothers flew their first plane at Kitty Hawk and Henry Ford organized his car company. Matsushita's master made and sold hibachi. Six people labored and lived in a small shop: the owner, his wife, three other young apprentices, and KM.

The whole arrangement sounds barbarous today: a child working eighty to ninety hours a week and actually living with an employer instead of parents. Yet a century ago in Osaka, an apprentice's job was seen as an excellent opportunity to learn and advance in life.[1]

For Konosuke Matsushita, the years around puberty turned out to be both severe and a source of much growth. Somehow the energy infused in his hopes and fears pushed him to take advantage of his position as a vehicle for personal betterment. In a pattern that would be repeated throughout his life, KM turned hardships that often exhaust people into a source of learning and, ultimately, into a driving force behind his subsequent successes.

For the first few weeks in Osaka, his duties were those of a household servant: baby-sitting the master's children, running errands, cleaning the home and shop. Gradually, Matsushita took on lesser skilled tasks associated with the business, mostly finishing work on the product itself.[2] The job could be physically painful at times. "There were several methods of polishing, depending on the grade of the article in question. The general run of hibachi bases were smoothed with sandpaper and then buffed over with rush stalks. For the finest quality, I might spend an entire day polishing with the rough stalks until my still delicate hands were scratched and swollen all over."[3]

For his labors, he was given housing, food, and five sen twice each month. In purchasing power, ten sen in 1903 is probably equivalent to less than ten U.S. dollars today.* As slave-like as those wages would be now, compared to the poverty he had experienced in Wakayama, Matsushita says that the cash income actually seemed like a lot of money. "I had never received five sen before. At home, . . . my mother would sometimes give me one mon-sen. . . . Five sen is fifty times as much as one mon-sen. I was very surprised that he gave me that much money."[5]

---

*At that time, the starting salary for engineering graduates at Imperial University was 50 yen per month, about 500 times as much as Matsushita's cash income.[4]

Compared to late 20th-century standards in the developed world, his life seems hugely impoverished. He had few friends, no school, few if any toys or possessions, and precious little free time. Perhaps most of all, he had no mother. In his subsequent writings and speeches, the pain Matsushita recalled from those days was less associated with hard work or lack of money than with loneliness.[6] He says he missed his mother a great deal. At night, in bed, he could not help but cry.[7]

He worked at the hibachi shop for only three months. Then the owner decided to eliminate his retail operation, to focus on making the product, and to move to a less expensive location. With these changes, he no longer needed four apprentices. Incredibly, once again Konosuke was uprooted.[8]

His father quickly secured him another job, this time in a newly opened bicycle shop. The owner/master was Otokichi Godai, a former apprentice himself who was the younger brother of the founder of the school at which Masakusu Matsushita was employed.[9]

Bicycles were a relatively new consumer product in Japan at that time. Manufactured in the United States and the United Kingdom and sold with a typical retail price of 100–150 yen,* they were not a source of mass transportation but novelty items purchased mostly for the sons of the wealthy.[10]

The store was located in the Senba section of Osaka. At first, KM's duties were similar to those at the hibachi shop: odd jobs around the house and unskilled labor for the business. The hours continued to be long, with very few days off. He cleaned the floors, took care of displayed products, and cranked a lathe for the master.[11]

---

*Over $10,000 in 1994 currency.

Although not unusual at the time, the general conditions remained primitive by today's standards. "Our meals consisted mainly of rice and vegetables: rice with white radish, or other pickled vegetables for breakfast; rice with some kind of boiled vegetable for lunch; and rice with pickles again for supper. Fish was served at lunchtime twice a month, on the first and fifteenth. . . . There were no luxuries in our lives. . . ."[12]

They labored seven days a week. Work stopped only on New Year's Day and during summer's Bon Festival.*[13] Godai was a tough taskmaster and laziness was not tolerated, but the owner treated his young apprentices more like a stern father than an employer. He watched out for them, taught them, took care of them.

The instability that had marked Matsushita's life from ages four to ten ended at the bicycle shop. He worked and lived with the Godais in Senba for six years. This period was harsh, by nearly any measure, but subsequently events suggest that it was also filled with learning.[14] The education was highly pragmatic, focusing on costs, customers, and merchandising, not history, literature, languages, or the arts. Perhaps even more fundamentally, the lessons were about where and how to apply one's energies in order to satisfy a strong but vague set of hopes and dreams.

During his last thirty years, Matsushita produced enough written material to fill a small library. Virtually none of that mountain of paper refers to his childhood. Dozens of business associates contacted in the writing of this book could not recall

---

*Bon Festival was, and still is, a three- or four-day holiday in which Buddhist rites are held for consoling the souls of ancestors. Family reunions are often held at Bon Festival.

KM ever mentioning his early years. Even his son-in-law says that he rarely talked of that time: "I think the memories were very painful."[15]

The few stories of his apprenticeship years that Matsushita chose to write about are all bittersweet. They involve suffering and sacrifice but also achievement, influence, and recognition. They say something about what KM was learning at the time and provide insight into his adolescent psychology.

The earliest recorded story comes from his brief stay at the hibachi shop.[16] According to Matsushita, he was carrying the master's baby on his back and playing a game of tops with other children when he accidentally dropped the infant. The baby cried loudly and would not stop despite all efforts to soothe him. In a panic, young Konosuke ran to a nearby store, bought a sweet, and gave it to the child. The tactic was successful; the boy stopped crying. But success came at a high price. The shop was expensive and the treat cost one sen, the equivalent of three days' wages.[17]

When he returned home, KM reported the incident in full to his master. The boss was sympathetic and did not reprimand him. Yet sympathy was all he offered his apprentice. Konosuke was never reimbursed for the lost wages.[18]

A second story comes from his early days at the bicycle shop. In 1906, Matsushita decided to compete in the cycling contests that were sponsored by a major newspaper, *The Osaka Shimbun*.[19] He rose before dawn to practice at a track in Sumiyoshi, in the southern part of the city, along with other cyclists. Despite much hard work and a few wins, he never achieved as much as he had hoped. After an accident at a race in Sakai in which he broke his collarbone, Matsushita retired from competitive sports.[20]

Another story from these years involves a fellow apprentice.

The time would have been around 1907. KM was spending his days repairing bicycles and his evenings, from 8:30 P.M. to 10:00 P.M., tending the shop.[21] The fellow apprentice was probably one of five or six employees who were younger than Konosuke. Matsushita says he "was a quick-witted fellow who enjoyed the master's favor and made himself quite useful. . . . For some reason I could not fathom, he stole . . . articles from the shop and sold them privately, using the cash as pocket money. When this transgression happened to be revealed, the master was disturbed, but inclined to forgive the lad this once because he was clever and handy around the shop. [So Godai] decided to give him a good scolding and allow him to continue working."[22]

Matsushita was incensed when he heard that Godai had not fired the thief. "Seething with indignation, I went to the master and said: 'I am very sorry to hear of your decision. I don't want to work with someone dishonest like that. If you allow him to continue working here, I must immediately ask you to let me go.'" His confrontational approach, hardly the norm in Japan, "put the master in a quandary." The details of what happened next are not recorded, but Matsushita has said that Godai "ultimately" dismissed the offending employee.[23]

A fourth apprenticeship story relates how young Konosuke sold his first bicycle.[24] He was either twelve or thirteen years old at the time. As a regular part of his duties, KM had been assisting the head clerk in demonstrating their products to prospective buyers. One day the shop received a telephone call from a nearby mosquito net wholesale house. The owner, a Mr. Tetsukawa, wanted to see a bicycle. Since the head clerk was unavailable and since Mr. Tetsukawa appeared to be in a hurry, Konosuke was sent instead.

At the mosquito net shop, Matsushita made his sales pitch with youthful vigor. Before he was finished, he was interrupted by the master. "Mr. Tetsukawa patted me on the head [and said,] . . . 'All right, I'll buy your bicycle, but you must give me a ten percent discount.'"[25]

With products costing the equivalent of $10,000 to $15,000 in today's currency, a 10 percent discount was a significant figure. KM was well aware that Godai never reduced prices more than 5 percent, yet he told Tetsukawa that he would take the offer to his master. "Back at the shop when I told Mr. Godai that Tetsukawa had agreed to buy the bicycle and wanted a ten percent discount, he said it was out of the question. 'You go back there and tell them our discount will be five percent.' But I was so thrilled to have succeeded in selling a bicycle by myself that I was extremely reluctant to have to go back with such an answer. I begged Godai to agree to a ten percent discount, breaking into tears in my eagerness. This quite surprised him and he said finally, 'Who do you think your master is? Get hold of yourself.' But I kept on crying."[26]

When one of Tetsukawa's employees appeared at the shop to ask what was taking so long, Godai explained. According to Matsushita, the visitor seemed touched by KM's insistence and naivete. After the clerk returned to his master and recounted the scene between Konosuke and Mr. Godai, Tetsukawa softened his negotiating position and accepted the bike at only five percent off. When Matsushita learned of this, he was "ecstatic."[27]

The major themes in the four stories from the apprenticeship years are not surprising in light of KM's stormy history. There is a preoccupation with troublesome father figures who refuse to reimburse wages, fire thieves, or give discounts. There are many losses—of wages, of races, through theft. There is an intense effort to improve his position—through cycling, selling, and eliminating unethical rivals.

Even more telling, as it relates to his future, the stories speak of risk taking that increasingly pays off. In the earliest tale, an innovative action produced mixed results—a happy baby but lost wages. In the final story, the unprecedented offer of a 10 percent discount created a sale which made him feel "ecstatic."

After all the hardships and suffering, a feeling of ecstasy would have been particularly sweet.

In 1905, when Konosuke was eleven years old, his mother and sisters moved from Wakayama to the northern section of Osaka.[28] Even though KM continued to live at the bicycle shop, the change allowed him to see them more often.[29]

After one of his sisters found a job as a counting clerk at the Osaka Postal Savings Bureau, she and Tokue began plotting how they could rescue the youngest member of the family from the difficulties of an apprenticeship. They eventually decided to have KM apply for a job as an office boy at the bureau, live with them, and go to school at night. When they put the idea to Matsushita, he was "overjoyed." With Konosuke enthusiastically behind the plan, Tokue went to her husband. But Masakusu rejected the idea immediately.[30]

His father told him emphatically that he should continue to work as an apprentice so that he could eventually run his own small business. Masakusu argued that the independence enjoyed by an entrepreneur was worth a great deal. True, KM would not be able to return to school, but that loss was minor in the greater scheme of things. A successful businessman could hire people with formal schooling to work for him. By way of contrast, an office boy had a more comfortable life but fewer future opportunities.[31]

We have no record of how much, if at all, young Konosuke tried to argue with his father. If he did attempt to
change Masakusu's mind, he failed. The man who had gambled away the family fortune and pushed his son into
poverty now kept him from school, his mother, and a much
easier job.

At the time, the elder Matsushita continued to be a sad figure. He earned a very modest salary at the school for the dis-
abled. He did not live with his spouse although she was also in
Osaka. He even speculated in commodity markets in a desperate attempt to regain lost wealth that created yet more tension
within the family.[32]

Masakusu's problems finally came to an end in a turbulent 1906.
In April that year, eighteen-year-old Hana passed away. She was the
fourth of the Matsushita children to die. If that were not enough to
send parents and siblings into a deep depression, only one month
later, Chiyo died. She was twenty-one at the time.[33] Within four
months, in September of that year, the fifty-one-year-old father fell
ill at the school where he worked. Like Hana and Chiyo, he then
quickly passed on.[34]

After all the funerals, a combination of economic hardship
and more personal reasons led Tokue and her one unmarried
daughter back to Wakayama.[35] KM did not accompany them.
He continued as an apprentice at the bicycle shop.[36]

Matsushita rarely wrote or spoke about his feelings toward
his father. They must have been complex and conflicted. In his
autobiography he says: "To think of how much he had been respected back in the village . . . and how honored our family had
been in the good old days make his life seem all the more pathetic. [But] for all his mistakes and misjudgment, his advice
and encouragement to me [about running my own business]

had been sound, and whenever I thought of him, I felt even more determination to live up to his expectations."[37]

For KM, Masakusu was both beloved father and the devil who destroyed the family, a source of inspiration for the future and pain in the present, a figure that was powerful and yet pathetic. For a child, all this must have been very confusing at times.

He continued to work in the bicycle shop until he was fifteen, at which point Matsushita decided to break out of a relationship that had spanned nearly half his life.

The high population density in Japan helped create a society that was enormously sensitive to relationships among people and obligations to others. The feudal attitudes that were still very much alive at the turn of the century also created stability in relationships. As a result, voluntary turnover at work was lower in Japan than in most parts of the world. Although this is changing today, Japanese employees are still reluctant to switch companies. Young men have been known to turn down 30 percent salary increases because of perceived obligations to their employers and the shame they might bring upon themselves.[38] In 1909 there was less employee loyalty than we have witnessed since World War II. Still, most of those in Matsushita's position would have finished their apprenticeship, hoping to eventually become a master themselves. KM chose a different course.*

---

*So did Akio Morita, although under different circumstances. Morita was the eldest son in a family business. In Japan at that time, almost all those in his position upheld their obligation and joined the ancestral company. Morita declined, with his father's acceptance, and went on to help found Sony.[39]

Population Density Around 1900

	People Per Square Kilometer of Inhabitable Land
Japan	545
Germany	239
France	113
United States	17

Sources: See note 40.

The shop had done well as a business. The product had become popular, especially as prices dropped. Because Godai was a very customer-oriented merchant,[41] his store had grown from a small-scale retail operation into something much larger. During that same period, Osaka had been building a trolley network throughout the city. After the line was completed between the central railway station at Umeda and Osaka harbor, Matsushita began to wonder about the future of bicycles. He also became fascinated with the potential of electricity.[42]

At that time, Europe was marching mindlessly toward the big war. In the United States, William Howard Taft was president and two explorers, Robert Peary and Matthew Henson, were being lionized for having reached the North Pole. In Japan, the economy continued to move rapidly from feudal to modern. Trolley cars were but one visible sign of massive change.

Sometime in 1909, KM approached a brother-in-law and asked for help in obtaining a job with an electric light company. When he was told that a such a position should be relatively easy to secure, he decided to abandon life as an apprentice and pursue the new opportunity.[43]

According to Matsushita, he started to explain his plans to Godai on a number of occasions, but always backed away from the encounter. His master had been like a father and teacher for nearly seven years. Under those circumstances, even outside a relationship-oriented culture, most people would find such a conversation difficult. KM apparently felt so torn and guilty that he eventually gave up trying to talk directly with Godai. Instead, in a maneuver that would have been scorned in the United States but not in nonconfrontational Japan, he sent himself a fake telegram saying that his mother was ill and that he was needed at home. The ruse succeeded and the master was gracious: "You've worked for us for six long years, and if you want to quit, there's nothing to stand in your way."[44] With that, young Konosuke moved on.

Had he stayed with Godai, he would have continued on a path to become a shop owner himself and to live a better-than-average middle-class life. But such a vision of the future apparently was not satisfying. To achieve more, he was willing to break out of a relationship with a parental figure and embark on a much more uncertain journey.

In the lives of many highly successful men and women, one common theme is related to hardship and its use as a vehicle for growth.[45] This idea is clearly seen in the case of Konosuke Matsushita. Although people of his generation in Japan often suffered, the family tragedies he faced starting in 1899 were not typical of that era. He was thrown into poverty at age four, lost one sibling at age five, two more at age six, and was forced to leave his mother at age nine. These events would have unleashed powerful emotions: sadness, anger, humiliation. As his parents helped direct those feelings, he undoubtedly began to dream of a far better future. Those ambitions then helped him to take advantage of the harsh apprenticeship years. With encouragement and support coming from a master and absentee parents, KM learned about business, merchandising, influencing others, making a profit, selling, and more. At a very young age, he also developed a sense of independence and a willingness to take risks. Perhaps most of all, he learned something about coping with difficult times and benefiting from them.

Nietzsche has written: "Was mich nicht umbringt, macht mich stärker"; that which does not kill me, makes me stronger. Matsushita would surely have agreed that this rather severe idea applied well to his life, especially the years between 1899 and 1910. During that period half his family died. But the youngest son seems only to have grown stronger. Probably, much stronger.

4

RESPONSIBILITY AND EXPOSURE AT AN EARLY AGE

An acquaintance led him to believe that he would be accepted for employment by the Osaka Electric Light Company as soon as he left Godai's. But when Matsushita applied for a job, he was told that there were no positions immediately available. With little money to support himself, he found temporary work at the Sakura Cement Company, a young enterprise that employed Konosuke's brother-in-law in a supervisory position.[1]

The job at Sakura involved shoveling dry cement into a receptacle that resembled a small railroad car and then pushing the container along a track to different parts of the plant. The work was physically demanding in a way that Matsushita had never before experienced. After three months, when he learned that Osaka Light had a vacancy in the interior wiring section of the company's Saiwaicho office, he quickly submitted his application and was accepted.[2]

His job in what he called "the electric business" began on October 21, 1910. Like many famous entrepreneurs, he broke out of a more conventional career and entered an industry when it was growing and constantly changing. The risks of such a move were not then, nor today, insignificant. In young industries, many firms fail. But the opportunities can also be large—for money, advancement, and the kind of challenge that encourages personal growth.

Hundreds of scientists in the 18th and 19th centuries set the stage for the emergence of an electrical industry.* More than anyone else, the person who actually launched the business was Thomas Edison. In 1879 he invented the incandescent lamp and in 1881 he constructed in New York City the world's first central power station and distribution system.

When Matsushita started work at Osaka Light in 1910, the infant industry was a source of wonder and fear. "Electricity was popularly known only in the form of lights, and most people held electric power in considerable dread, believing that one could be killed by the slightest contact. It was something to be handled by experts, and even a lowly repairman from the electric company was treated with great respect as a technician conversant with mysterious powers."[3]

In his first assignment, he assisted a more senior employee in the wiring of businesses and homes for lighting. On a typical day they would begin early, go to five or six sites, and then re-

---

*Individuals like William Gilbert, Joseph Priestley, Henry Cavendish, Charles-Augustin de Coulomb, Count Alessandro Volta, Sir Humphry Davy, Hans Christian Orsted, Michael Faraday, and James Clerk Maxwell.

turn to the office late in the afternoon. Konosuke's job was to pull a two-wheeled cart loaded with tools and fixtures, provide help when asked, and generally be a good personal servant. After a few weeks of training, he began wiring simple jobs himself.[4] His initial salary was one yen per month.[5]

Because Osaka Light was a growing entrepreneurial entity at the time, advancement came quickly for capable and motivated employees. After only three months, Matsushita was transferred to a newly opened branch office, promoted from assistant to installation technician, and given a significant raise.[6]

Compared to the life of a manager or clerk, his job involved considerably more physical labor. After bringing wires into homes through the roofs, installers would put sockets in the ceilings and then attach electric lights.[7] Depending upon the weather, the work could be very uncomfortable. "We would have to climb up electric poles even when the cold wind blew. We would have to work on a hot roof under a burning sun."[8]

The job could be intellectually challenging because the industry was young and because the assignments were diverse. Much that is taken for granted today by electricians was not yet known. Techniques and equipment that make wiring work routine now had yet to be invented. The dangers were also very real; without caution, an installer could be killed.

His assignments exposed him to the diversity of life in a big city. He worked in factories, large and small. He wired shops. He went to houses throughout the metropolitan area. In the process, Matsushita met thousands of people.

In 1912, KM and fourteen other technicians were sent out of the city on an assignment that required that they live for a time at an inn.[9] Unlike today, where professional and managerial personnel stay at hotels routinely, this kind of business travel was not the norm, especially for teenagers.

Matsushita helped rewire theaters so they could show motion pictures. He worked on the Tsutenkaku Tower, a model of the Eiffel Tower built in 1912 in the Shinsekai district of Osaka. He wired mansions built by successful businessmen.[10]

Overall, the early years at the light company were useful but often tedious or unpleasant. "Sometimes the jobs were particularly challenging because the building design was totally new or the fixtures especially difficult. In such work, my skills improved perceptibly, and I felt rewarded by the appreciation of the clients. But there was a great deal of very humdrum work as well, some for clients who were hard to please or downright insulting."[11]

He found housing at the home of fellow Osaka Light employee Ichiro Kanayama. For room and board, KM paid half his salary,[12] but the arrangement worked well, particularly because of Ichiro's mother. Matsushita later said: "I felt very at home with the Kanayamas, not only because it was the family of a workmate, but because my landlady was very kind and solicitous."[13]

Hiroyuki Ashida, another Osaka Light employee who boarded with the Kanayamas, attended night classes at the Kansai Commercial and Industrial School. Urged on by Hiroyuki's example and hoping to receive the education he had been twice denied, KM enrolled at Kansai in 1912 when he was seventeen. Yet after less than two years and a standing of 175th in a group of 380, he quit.[14]

Matsushita blamed his failure at school on his inability to write well. In his description of the episode, recorded years later, bitterness lurks between the lines: "The preparatory course had given me some fundamental knowledge of algebra, physics, and chemistry, so I advanced to the regular course majoring in electrical science. I was delighted with the prospects of what I could learn, but my joy was short-lived. In most of my classes, the instructors used no textbooks and the students had to take copious notes recording the lectures. Since my writing ability was so poor, I found I could not keep up. I might be just as good as my fellows on the job, I might have years of practical training, but I could not write well enough to take sufficient notes in class. I struggled, using the simple phonetic characters and avoiding difficult ideograms, but soon floundered and began to fall behind. I finally gave up and dropped out before completing the regular course."[15]

In his Osaka Light years, Matsushita learned about a technology that would help create four industries* and that would eventually employ tens of millions of people around the globe. But only a fraction of that education came from books or lectures. The company was his classroom and fellow employees were his instructors.

B y the time he was sixteen, Matsushita was managing and directing other people, usually individuals who were older by three or four years. Few in his generation had an equivalent experience. By age nineteen, he was handling projects of substantial size and complexity. In some cases, dozens of employees were under his supervision.

In wiring the Ashibe Theater in Sennichimae, he acted as foreman in charge of three teams of technicians. Since the playhouse was being remodeled into a Western-style motion picture theater, the electrical work had to be coordinated with other construction crews and subcontractors. To meet a difficult

---

*(1) The generation of electricity, (2) the transmission and distribution of electricity, (3) consumer electronics, and (4) industrial electronics.

deadline, Matsushita had to convince his people to labor around the clock for three consecutive days. When the job was successfully completed, he found that his self-confidence "increased tremendously."[16]

During his middle years at the electric company, KM began to see firsthand more and more economically successful individuals and the luxuries they commanded. While wiring one mansion, he met Yosaburo Yagi, a cotton yarn wholesaler who was among the largest dealers in Osaka. Matsushita also worked on a building for Soichiro Asano, one of Japan's leading businessmen in the early part of the century.[17]

After wiring a theater in the amusement area in the south of the city, KM was sent to work temporarily as a spotlight man for the geisha performances held there. At the theater, he met the famous Yachiyo, of the Tomitaya geisha house. When Matsushita learned that her patron was the president of a sugar manufacturing company, he became "even more fascinated" with the beautiful and talented performer.[18]

During this period, vague notions of accumulating an economic buffer against tragedy, or rebuilding his family's reputation, could easily have begun to focus on the idea of running a substantial business. Godai the shop master may have once been the role model, but now the presidents of companies captured his attention. He saw their mansions and mistresses. He heard tales about great wealth and witnessed the deferential way in which successful entrepreneurs were treated. To a teenage boy who had experienced much tragedy, these men must have seemed nearly invulnerable.

I n 1913, three years after KM joined the electric light company, Tokue died.[19] She was fifty-seven at the time. The ten-person family from Wasamura was down to three: KM and two sisters. The average age of the seven who had passed away was only thirty years.

After his mother's death, Matsushita says that he began to entertain for the first time the possibility of marriage. With no parents to select a bride for him, as was the custom of the day, he turned to his sister who was living in Osaka. She agreed to search for a suitable wife and, in May of 1915, she told KM that she had found one.[20]

The young woman was Mumeno Iue. Born on Awaji Island, a 954-square-mile enclave located about one hundred miles southwest of Osaka, Iue was raised in a farming and trading family along with three brothers and four sisters.[21] Mumeno had eight years of schooling, nearly twice as much as Konosuke. When his sister discovered her, she was in the domestic service of a merchant family in Kyomachibori.[22]

As was the custom then, Matsushita agreed to a ritualistic encounter with his potential bride, a meeting in which they barely saw each other and spoke not a word. With sister and brother-in-law urging him to wed, KM agreed. The ceremony was held on September 4, 1915.[23] Konosuke was twenty years old. His new wife, a young woman he did not know, was nineteen.[24]

They moved into a two-room tenement in the eastern part of Osaka. His salary was twenty yen a month. Their expenses included three yen for rent, three yen for rice, four yen for other food, one yen for newspapers and magazines, two yen for using the public bathhouse, one yen for electricity, coal, and firewood, two yen for pocket money, and two yen for savings.[25]

Pictures of Mumeno from this period show a pleasant looking woman with a determined expression. As a "strong minded" and "competitive" person,[26] she certainly did not dampen her husband's growing ambitions. If anything, she fanned the flames.

Two years later, Matsushita was promoted. Hard work along with a business savvy learned at the bicycle shop helped him perform well. In his new role, he visited fifteen to twenty wiring sites a day to check on the quality of the installation done by others. As one of the youngest people at the inspector level within Osaka Light, his future looked very promising.[27] Yet within six months, he left the company.

Matsushita has offered a number of different explanations as to why he severed relations with his employer of seven years. To some degree, the problem was the new job. The position was unfulfilling, he told others, since it literally required only three or four hours a day of serious work. The challenge that he had grown to know and expect was missing. "I was left with a great deal of idle time to be whiled away chatting with co-workers in the office or window-shopping on the way back from inspection jobs. It was dispiriting and empty. Finally, I began to hate the work and became thoroughly disillusioned about the post I had dreamed so much of holding while still a wiring technician."[28]

During that period, his health deteriorated. He already had one previous medical problem while working at the light company. Coming home from an installation at a bathing place in Hamadera, Osaka, he coughed up blood. A doctor diagnosed the illness as "catarrh of the pulmonary apex," which KM assumed was an early stage of tuberculosis, a disease that killed many people back then. The condition did not get worse, although he did have intermittent medical problems over the next few years.[29]

After his promotion to inspector, health problems reemerged. He developed a chronic cough, broke out into sweats at night, and lost weight. After seeing a doctor, he was once again diagnosed as having a slight case of catarrh of the lungs and advised to rest. The fear that he might have a terrible malady, perhaps like the one that had killed his brothers and sisters, was haunting. "I became convinced I had caught tuberculosis from a workmate . . . who had the dread disease. A photo around that time shows me even more gaunt and pale than before."[30]

Prolonged rest was not possible. No work meant no income. With his meager savings and little government assistance, no salary quickly translated to no food. As a result, he continued in the inspector's job. But instead of resting after the regular four-to-five-hour workday, he began trying to design a light socket that was superior to the one used by the company. When after considerable effort he was satisfied that he had a promising approach, he spoke with his boss. According to Matsushita, the man was totally unimpressed by his proposal and refused to show the idea to others. The apparently unjust treatment from an authority figure provoked an emotional reaction. "I was so disappointed I could hardly keep back the tears even in front of my supervisor." Much later, Matsushita found that his initial design had some serious flaws. But at the time, he was convinced that his boss was being very unreasonable.[31]

"Regardless of what my supervisor said, I still thought the socket design was good, at least better than the existing fixtures we were using in the company, and the desire to prove I was right welled up inside me. Dissatisfaction with my work and confidence in the socket grew side by side. What good will it do me, I began to think, to stay in a job like this? Finally, I decided to leave the company. I would manufacture my sockets and get the light company to market them. I would prove my supervisor wrong, I declared to myself. As my spirits rose, my physical condition improved."[32]

This same pattern would repeat itself for nearly three decades. With too much success, in this case through a significant promotion for a very young man, he would fall ill. When a difficult challenge or problem emerged, here due to a boss's rejection of his socket design, he would recover.

On June 15, 1917, he wrote a letter of resignation and presented it to his supervisor. The man told him that he was making a mistake, but KM continued on his new path.[33]

He left the company on June 20, 1917.[34] The direction he had chosen was risky. Small and young businesses often fail because, as was the case with Matsushita, the founder has little money and few connections. But entrepreneurial ventures offer more control over one's destiny, allow for challenging the status quo, and permit individuals to work for themselves instead of a father-figure boss. Such ventures have also produced virtually all the new economic fortunes in the past two centuries.

At the time, Matsushita was only twenty-two, but he had lived the last thirteen of those years independent of his family. Although still quite young, he already had thirteen years of experience in business. He had assisted a savvy merchant. He had been given responsibility and exposure at the electric company.

In many ways, the initial phase of KM's life ended on that day in June of 1917. He graduated from a difficult childhood, an apprenticeship, and the journeyman years, and he moved in a new direction. For the first time he was without parents, masters, or bosses. His life would become even harsher, at least for a while. But that possibility did not deter him much.

By this time, Matsushita knew he could handle hardship and grow even stronger as a result. He had been doing just that for nearly two decades.

MERCHANT
ENTREPRENEUR

1917–1931

5

RISK TAKING, PERSEVERANCE, AND THE LAUNCHING OF A BUSINESS

When Japanese entrepreneur Noguchi Jun, founder of Nippon Chisso Hiryo, started his first company in 1906, he had a degree from the Faculty of Engineering at Tokyo Imperial University and a 100,000 yen advance from a banker friend. When he needed additional assistance a few years later, he was able to call on one relative who was a member of the board of directors of Nippon Yusen Kaisha as well as other influential acquaintances.[1] Kiichiro Toyoda launched his car company with even more support. Start-up capital from his family equaled one million yen.*

---

*The Toyoda family, with its business base in textile machines, provided still more financing later on.[2]

Konosuke Matsushita began his business in 1917 with savings of one hundred yen,* the equivalent of fully five months of his Osaka Light salary, and with four assistants. The first was wife Mumeno. The second was Isaburo Hayashi, a former co-worker and friend from Osaka Electric who had been working as an electrician for a small firm. The third was Nobujiro Morita, another former co-worker. The last was Toshio Iue, Mumeno's fourteen-year-old brother.

None of the five had the equivalent of a high school education. None had any experience with a start-up company. None was wealthy or had connections to sources of finance. More basically, not one of them knew how to manufacture an electrical socket.[4]

T he Matsushita "factory" was established inside his two-room tenement house. Total space available for working and living equaled 130 square feet. Alterations were made to accommodate the business needs, leaving a corner of the smaller room for KM and Mumeno to sleep in.[5]

With no revenues and very limited financing, they scrambled to manufacture the new socket design. The insulation required inside the product proved to be a major problem. Although a widely understood process today, the creation of insulation was a technical secret in 1917 in Osaka.[6]

To overcome their lack of technological know-how, they worked long hours, seven days a week. With pitifully small financing, they

---

*Matsushita says that the total included 20 yen in personal savings, 33.2 yen in severance pay, and 42 yen that had been withdrawn from his monthly salary by Osaka Electric and put in a company savings plan. Later, to supplement this small capital base, KM obtained a 100-yen loan from a friend of one of his employees.[3]

were under huge pressures to produce. Their inability to make the insulation material was highly frustrating, especially after many weeks had been invested in the task.

Assistance finally came from a friend. According to Matsushita: "We scrounged fragments of discarded insulation at a local factory where it was manufactured and then tried to analyze them, but to no avail. Finally, we learned that a former co-worker at the electric company knew how to make the compound. Apparently, he had tried to create insulation material not long after leaving Osaka Light, but without success. Determined to find out, he had secured a job at an insulation manufacturing company, learned the method, and then quit. He had begun to produce insulating articles himself, but the business had not gone well and he had given up. When he heard what we were trying to do, he very willingly told us how it should be done, providing key know-how we had lacked, and at last we were ready to move on to the next step."[7]

The other parts of the socket proved to be much less troublesome. In the middle of October 1917, after fully four months of work, they succeeded in creating a few samples of the new design.

Morita was chosen to take the product to wholesalers. Matsushita was uncertain as to how many they would be able to sell, but he assumed that with just a modest response from potential customers the five of them would be consumed with making the socket.

When Morita called on distributors, they received him coolly, if at all. Their concerns were the same as start-ups often hear today. "Come back when you have a track record. I can't afford to take you on if there is a risk that you might be out of business in a few months." "Having only one product is a problem. If I bought each item I handle from a different manufacturer, I would have to deal with thousands of suppliers and that wouldn't work. Come back when you have a broader line of products." After a week and a half, Morita sold only one hundred sockets. The total revenue collected was less than ten yen.[8]

Manufacturing businesses that fail during their first year are often based on a flawed product concept, are underfinanced, or encounter distribution difficulties. All three problems plagued the Matsushita enterprise. The new socket by itself was not innovative enough to overcome typical start-up barriers, especially given their lack of capital.

After the poor reception the samples received, Morita and Hayashi began expressing doubts to KM about the venture. "They asked me what I intended to do. Did I have any idea how I was going to get along? Where was I going to find more money? They were close friends and never once pressed me for salaries, but their pockets were about as empty as they could get. They proposed that we give up the business and each go back to trying to make a living. . . . I tried to persuade them to stick through the crisis, but since I had no concrete strategy for making the business survive, nor any money to finance it, my pleas were hardly convincing."[9]

With no income to support their families, and with growing pessimism about the prospects of the Matsushita enterprise, Morita and Hayashi left to take jobs elsewhere. By the end of October, the little business that started with five people had shrunk to three.[10]

The loss of Hayashi and Morita on top of the poor response from the marketplace was dispiriting, and nothing happened over the next month to ease the gloom. Despite much effort, Matsushita could find no solution to his business problems. He tried to develop relationships with distributors, but achieved few breakthroughs. He considered other new product ideas, but with limited success.

By the end of November, depressing questions loomed everywhere. What evidence did he have that this venture was not pure folly? Lacking experience, expertise, and cash, could he realistically expect to create a viable enterprise? Perhaps he should go back to Osaka Light? He had done so well there. Had he left only because of an emotional confrontation with his boss? Or because his illness had clouded his judgment?

He could become a shopkeeper. Nearly seven years had been invested in learning how to operate a store. Maybe his future lay in owning and running a small business that sold electrical goods?

Fears would have amplified doubts. In his father's case, the first major setback was the beginning of a long downward slide. Could this be his fate too? Was he destined to suffer and die like poor Masakusu?

The surroundings certainly did not help alleviate any doubts and fears. His office, factory, and home were in total smaller than a typical two-car garage in today's suburban United States.

To generate much-needed cash, KM and Mumeno pawned clothes and other personal items.[11] They also worked furiously to build the failing business. Matsushita attempted to improve the design of his attachment plug and to invent additional products. He and Toshio visited more distributors. Mumeno encouraged both to keep trying.[12] All three of them undoubtedly worried a great deal.

But they didn't give up.

A wholesaler who liked the young entrepreneurs learned that one of his suppliers was having a problem. Kawakita Electric was shifting from using porcelain insulation plates as

electric fan bases to less breakable ones made from an as-
bestos-like material. The electrical firm needed the new bases
immediately but did not have a source. In early December,
the wholesaler came to Matsushita and suggested that he set
aside the electric plug project and make one thousand insulator plates. KM agreed to do so without hesitation.[13]

The required mold was produced in a week by a local black-
smith. After creating sample plates, Matsushita showed the
product to the wholesaler and obtained approval. The distributor then told him that if he completed the order quickly, he
might receive additional business for as many as four or five
thousand units.[14]

The job was labor-intensive and, after a while, tedious. The same
relatively simple operations had to be performed again and again.
Because Konosuke, Toshio, and Mumeno worked eighteen hours
a day, seven days a week, they were able to fulfill the order before
the end of December. In payment, they received 160 yen. Supplies
and the mold cost half that, leaving a good profit margin.[15]

The money was notable for two reasons: it provided both desperately needed cash and evidence that the enterprise might be
economically viable. The issue of greater significance was customer
satisfaction. If managers at Kawakita were not completely happy,
Matsushita would probably receive no repeat business or recommendations, and the tiny firm would soon be in trouble again.

The response came relatively quickly. In early January, KM was
told that the managers at Kawakita liked the product. They liked
the quality. They liked the speedy delivery. As a result, a second
order was placed, this time for two thousand insulator plates.[16]

The historical record suggests that Matsushita spent little
time celebrating this first entrepreneurial victory before beginning to search for larger quarters for his company. A few weeks
later, in February, he found an acceptable two-story home near
the Noda railway station on the Hanshin line. Located in a sec-

tion of Osaka called Obiraki-cho, the house had three rooms on the first floor, two rooms on the second, and nearly triple the space of their previous dwelling. KM struck a deal with the owner for a monthly rent of 16.5 yen, the equivalent of about 5 percent of the fee that Kawakita was paying for the two-thousand-unit order.[17]

On March 7, 1918, Konosuke, Mumeno, and Toshio moved into the new facility. They converted the three rooms on the first floor into a workshop. Two hand-operated machines for molding insulation were installed. Although still incredibly modest, the "factory" was a significant improvement over their original quarters.[18]

Throughout February and March, they continued to work long hours making both the insulation plates and a few of the original sockets. For a third product, they chose an electrical attachment plug. Late in the spring of 1918, Matsushita completed the design and they began manufacturing. Because their costs were low, they were able to offer the plug at 30 percent less than competitive products. At that price, and from a start-up with a small but growing reputation among distributors, the device sold well.[19]

When they were unable to keep up with demand for the three products despite twelve-to-sixteen-hour workdays, Matsushita began hiring additional workers. As employment grew to five, then six, then seven, he introduced elementary specialization in order to increase productivity and further reduce costs. KM focused mostly on insulators. Toshio split his time between preparing materials for production and manufacturing parts. New employees assisted Toshio and assembled plugs. Mumeno took charge of packaging.[20]*

The fourth MEI offering was a two-way socket with a special

---

*The name MEI (Matsushita Electric Industrial) officially dates back only to 1935 when the firm was first incorporated.

attachment plug. Since houses usually had only a single outlet in each room, two-way sockets were popular. KM designed what he thought was an improved version of the standard product, obtained a patent on it, and then began manufacturing. Within a relatively short period of time, the new item was selling better than their first three offerings.[21]

By the summer of 1918, Matsushita Electric had grown to eight employees and four products. Compared to some well-known entrepreneurial success stories,* the company was still minuscule and vulnerable, more tortoise than hare despite KM's aggressive attempt at growth. But the little firm had survived a difficult initial period and was beginning to establish some momentum.

Hares tend to attract attention, tortoises do not, and young MEI went virtually unnoticed by all but a small community in Osaka. Yet like so many of the other great corporations founded in the last century and a half, the slow, quiet, resource-poor start did not prove to be an obstacle in the long run.[23] Quite possibly, just the opposite is true.

A wholesaler named Yoshida approached Matsushita and asked for exclusive rights to market the successful two-way socket. After negotiation, KM granted those rights in exchange for a 3,000-yen loan to finance increased production capacity.[24]

As employment grew, the facility at Obiraki-cho became increasingly crowded. Instead of moving again to gain space, they

---

*Before the end of its first year in operation, Noguchi Jun's enterprise (see reference at beginning of this chapter) built a hydroelectric plant. By the end of year two, the firm was Japan's largest producer of calcium carbide.[22] More recently in the United States, People Express airlines had over a hundred employees shortly after its first year in business, as did Perot Systems and a few of the biotech start-ups.

built a half story in the main workshop room. The arrangement was aesthetically odd, but the frugality impressed visitors. Matsushita says he often heard others say: "No wonder your costs are so low."[25]

At approximately the same time, KM began hiring live-in apprentices. The arrangement was much like the one he had experienced at the bicycle shop. Early reports suggest that Matsushita treated these young people sternly but with a fatherly warmth. Mumeno fed them and became their substitute mother.[26]

With an increasing number of new products and rising sales from existing items, the enterprise kept growing throughout 1918. By the fall of that year, the Matsushita firm employed over twenty people and was continuing to expand, although it was still tiny compared to the major electronic companies in the world (see exhibit below).

Moreover, the basic pattern that would describe MEI in its first decade was already being established after its initial year of operation. Products would be improved versions of competitive offerings sold at prices below current market rates. Costs would be kept low through minimum overhead, long hours, and general penny-pinching. The firm would be financed

Revenues for Electrical Equipment Manufacturers in 1918

	Revenues (In Millions of Dollars)
General Electric	216.8
Westinghouse	95.7
Toshiba	14.8
Matsushita	.2

Source: Company records. For Toshiba, the figure is for its predecessor company, Tokyo Electric.

in creative ways that gave away no equity. Employees would be treated as if they were a part of the family. An emphasis would be placed on flexibility, speed, and constant new-product introductions.

During these years, Konosuke Matsushita learned the business from the ground up. At one time or another, he did every job, even the most menial. As is often the case with entrepreneurs, he saw everything in detail, up close. The experience was no doubt monotonous at times, but it helped give him an intuitive sense of products, production, customers, and employees, a perspective that would prove to be most useful in the long run.

I n attempting to explain his success in launching a business, writers and commentators have described all sorts of abilities with which, they say, Matsushita was born. These traits include great commercial judgment, an instinct for dealing with people, keen intelligence, a charismatic personality, and more. The one man who knew KM best back then saw it differently. Later in life, brother-in-law Toshio Iue told an interviewer: "I don't think young Matsushita was a brilliant person or a man of great talent. But his zeal for work was exceptionally high."[27] Iue used to joke that over meals, KM talked so much about business that he rarely knew what he was eating.[28]

Successfully starting a new enterprise tends to be more difficult than most people imagine. Many factors can help reduce the burdens: generous financing, a key patent, influential friends, a technological breakthrough. In MEI's case, one searches hard to find any trace of these benefits. In reading early materials about the company, one does sense a customer or merchant orientation coming from KM that certainly helped the firm. The same can be said about frugality, which, like customer orientation, he probably learned during his apprenticeship years.[29] But more than either, one notices the hard work, the competitive drive, and the steely determination to make dreams come true.

A man with little motivation would never have begun the business, given the lack of financing and his own questionable health. An individual with modest determination would have had trouble attracting others, especially since there was no money available for salaries. A less optimistic person may have given up when the first product did not sell and two employees quit. After the business began to grow, many people would have been satisfied with a good living and a dozen subordinates.

At this point in Matsushita's life, he was running probably both from his fears and toward hard-to-articulate dreams. Like so many successful entrepreneurs, past experiences had left him more independent than the average person. He was also more open to risk taking, at least partially because he had faced and conquered difficult times. Most of all, he was hardworking, competitive, and highly motivated.[30] His aspirations, fueled by some mix of hopes and fears, were substantial. As a result, he did not quit easily, but instead kept trying and learning.

Early success, instead of satisfying Matsushita and reducing his ambition, seems to have only increased his desires. The wins were viewed as evidence that he was on the right track. The losses were seen as the inevitable burdens that one must suffer in life.

And suffer he did. Again, according to Iue: "His body was very weak. He often became ill. Thinking too much led to insomnia. His blood pressure was also very high."[31] In contrasting himself to his brother-in-law, KM has said: "Iue was very bright and energetic whereas I was often nervous and anxious. . . ."[32] With no medical records from this period, we know little about Matsushita's physical ailments. Certainly he faced many difficult business challenges that could have stressed his small physique. But powerful internal pressures undoubtedly added to the strain, pressures related to anger, fears, and dreams.

Frailness can seem pathetic and make others uncomfortable. Yet there was something modestly inspiring about the man from Wasamura, perhaps because he never asked anyone to work harder than himself, because he lived in conditions that were not much better than his poorest worker's, and since he appeared so dedicated to making the enterprise prosper. During those years, Matsushita also seems to have been inspired with the growing belief that fate was on his side. In his autobiography, he talks about accidents that could have killed him. The escapes from death include being hit by an automobile and then almost run over by a street car,* as well as an episode when he was knocked off a ferry and nearly drowned.† Anyone with a psychoanalytical bent will wonder if the "accidents" were a sign of a deep depression. But in all of his subsequent writing, that is not the way KM chose to interpret the episodes.

Perhaps the strongest evidence that some force was working on his behalf came from his own family. When he started his company, both parents and five of his siblings were already dead. Then in 1919, twenty-eight-year-old sister Ai passed on. Two years later, Iwa died. She was forty-seven at the time.[35]

At Iwa's passing, KM was twenty-seven years old. The family of ten had been reduced to one. He was the only survivor.

---

*At the end of his first or second year as an entrepreneur.[33]

†When he was working for the cement company.[34]

6

UNCONVENTIONAL
STRATEGIES

The Japanese government, financial system, and business environment did little to encourage rapid entrepreneurial growth. The economy was capitalist, but its structure benefited large corporations that were well connected with politicians and Tokyo bureaucrats.[1] In that context, a small firm with large ambitions had to be inventive. Copying strategies used by the business establishment, but without similar connections or resources, led to stagnation at best. For Konosuke Matsushita, this reality interplayed with a temperament disinclined to replicate the status quo and with a simmering anger easily directed toward conquering larger rivals.

As MEI expanded in 1919, '20, and '21, it faced increasing competition from new entrants into the electrical products industry. Without secret technology, deep pockets, or powerful connections, the tiny firm struggled to grow. Even finding employees could be a challenge. Given a choice, people were not inclined to join a new, small, family-owned company with limited financing.

Matsushita put advertisements for jobs on telephone and electric poles. When the well-educated or highly experienced did not respond, he accepted others and tried to turn their youthful enthusiasm and lack of preconceptions into an asset.[2]

During the early years, he learned that products only slightly better or cheaper than those on the market rarely attracted much attention. His original socket was a prime example. Through trial and error, KM found that the ideal offering had to be 30 percent better yet 30 percent cheaper than the standard fare. Such an item had the potential to grab significant market share and all the associated economies of scale.

Creating new products that were significantly better or cheaper demanded creativity, starting with design. At first, Matsushita himself did most of the invention. As the firm grew, he relied on others, usually a few dedicated people who worked to satisfy perceived customer needs under stringent time constraints. He avoided large development staffs, long product development cycles, and any form of basic research—partially because of limited resources, but also because he found that speed and low costs could be formidable competitive weapons, especially against more bureaucratic rivals.

A search for new markets led to a geographic expansion which came early in the enterprise's history. In 1919, Matsushita began visiting Tokyo, selling to wholesalers and retailers. Encouraged by the potential of Japan's capital city, he sent brother-in-law Toshio to open an office in March of 1920. Iue had already become KM's number-one assistant, even though he was only seventeen years old. In Tokyo, the young man found a room at a student lodging house near Waseda University and spent his days visiting customers.[3]

With increasing business from new products and new markets, once again the factory reached the production limit. When a house next door became vacant in 1920, Matsushita rented the structure and expanded the workshop, even though the economy was in a severe recession. The new building was not ideal, but the larger facility remained very inexpensive.[4]

By mid 1921, piecemeal growth in manufacturing was no longer sufficient or feasible; a bigger and better equipped plant was needed. As soon as an acceptable tract of land became available nearby, Matsushita drew a rough floor plan and contacted a builder. When estimated costs were higher than KM was willing to pay, negotiations broke down until the contractor offered to help finance the work.[5]

Construction began in August 1921 and was completed in January 1922.[6] "It is hard to describe how great my expectations were for the new factory," Matsushita later said. "In a way, it was a fulfillment of the dream toward which I had worked for eighteen years, since beginning my apprenticeship at the age of nine. . . . The new factory would be the foundation upon which I would become a full-fledged businessman, and as it neared fruition, my confidence grew. The construction of the plant . . . was a turning point in my early career."[7]

The building was four times as large as its predecessor. It had modern equipment and over thirty employees.[8] During the year which saw Mussolini form a government in Rome and southern

Ireland become a separate state, Matsushita Electric began to gain visibility as a small but thriving business within the Japanese electrical industry.

By 1922, the firm was introducing one or two new products nearly every month. "Better but cheaper" was the usual strategy, never an easy concept to implement well. The company also continued to expand geographically. It extended distribution into Nagoya and as far away as Kyushu.[9] Although constantly growing, Matsushita Electric was still only a fraction of the size of Toshiba,* the largest Japanese manufacturer of electrical goods.

From the spring of 1918 onward, MEI offerings generally sold well, but none were eye-popping successes in the marketplace.[10] With his new factory to support him, KM began looking for bigger possibilities. In early 1922, he found one with roots in his own personal history.

Demand for bicycle lamps was big and growing, yet all existing models had severe drawbacks. The flame in candle-lit models was often blown out by the wind. Acetylene products were expensive and required constant refueling. Battery-powered units worked for only two or three hours before the power source ran out and needed replacement.

Matsushita was convinced that the battery-powered concept was promising if only his company could manufacture a much improved version. He wanted the lamp to be simple in structure, so that it would not break down easily, and economical,

---

*Then called Tokyo Electric.

meaning that the battery would have to last more than ten hours. At first he thought he had to preserve the linear arrangement of batteries typical of flashlights, and this proved to be a major stumbling block in developing an improved product. After three or four months of effort, he realized that he could re-arrange the power sources, thus permitting fundamentally new structural designs. In six months, after more than one hundred test models of various shapes and sizes, he devised a bullet-shaped lamp that seemed to be especially attractive. Development efforts were further propelled forward when a miniature bulb requiring only 120 to 130 milliamperes appeared on the market. "This was an enormous improvement over the old bulbs that required 400 to 500 milliamperes. With the new bulb and a battery which I had specially reconstructed, I found that the lamp would burn for thirty to fifty hours."[11]

He tested a prototype over and over, using it on his own bicycle. He sent MEI workers out at night to ride over bumpy roads to check for durability.[12] The new product, they all agreed, was excellent. "It was manifestly better than any model on the market, was simply structured, and would run on one set of batteries, at a cost of thirty sen, for forty to fifty hours. This was even cheaper than candles."[13]

Finding a supplier to make the bullet-shaped wooden case at an acceptable price proved to be difficult until Matsushita promised to buy two thousand units a month, a huge commitment for the small firm. After researching alternatives, he picked Kodera to produce the batteries. Genjiro Miyamoto was put in charge of manufacturing the lamp, and assembly started in mid June of 1922.[14]

With samples in hand, Matsushita himself went to a store that had been selling his other electrical products. "I described the merits of the new lamp and expected to hear exclamations of surprise and delight and an immediate offer to buy."[15] Instead, the proprietor showed little interest in the offering. He expressed concern that battery lamps had a poor reputation and that the special batteries required would be difficult for customers to find when replacements were needed.

Surprised but not discouraged, Matsushita visited other electric dealers. To his dismay, he received the same response everywhere. "All of them declared the lamp would not sell." After the great effort that had been invested in the development of the product and given its obvious superiority over existing models, the reaction from distributors was maddening. "I was so disappointed and angry," KM told others, "that I could hardly see straight."[16]

Deciding that Osaka might be too conservative for such an innovative item, he approached electric dealers in more cosmopolitan Tokyo. They received him, listened, and responded exactly as did their Osaka counterparts. Nothing that Matsushita could say would change their minds.[17]

With increasing frustration and full recognition that a financial crisis could be looming, he tried a different distribution system altogether: bicycle dealers. The underlying logic was simple. Bicycle stores should be in a better position to appreciate the value of the new product. But when Matsushita approached a shop owner and described his invention, the dealer talked only of his concerns. A second retailer reacted similarly. Even bicycle shops were reluctant to handle a type of product that generally had a bad reputation in the marketplace.[18]

Because Matsushita had so much faith in the new device, and because the company was committed to buying at least two thousand wooden cases a month, manufacturing had gone ahead despite the lack of orders. The warehouse filled quickly—one

KM's birthplace in Wakayama Prefecture (1967 photo)

View of a typical street in Osaka at the turn of
the century with a newly opened electric street
trolley (1903)

General style of an apprentice
shop in the early 20th century

KM at age ten with Mrs.
Godai, the bicycle shop
owner's wife (1905)

Matsushita in 1910, the first year of his employment with
Osaka Electric Light Company

Matsushita at age seventeen (1912)

KM shortly before his
wedding (1916)

Outside view of a reproduction of the house that served as both factory and home during the early years of Matsushita Electric

With Osaka Electric Light Company colleagues in front of the company's sales office—KM is in the middle of the back row (1916)

Back row, l-r: KM, his brother-in-law Toshio Iue, Mumeno (KM's wife); front row: Iue's three other sisters (1918)

KM in the year he founded Matsushita Electric (1918)

職工ヲ命ス
但日給金四拾参銭支給
明治四十三年十二月廿一日
大阪電燈株式會社

松下幸之助

KM's notice of employment
with Osaka Electric Light
Company—daily salary of
¥0.43 was considered quite
good at the time (1910)

Matsushita Electric's first product,
an attachment plug (1918)

The bullet-shaped bicycle lamp (1923)

Matsushita's company factory circa 1924

Matsushita employees at the Tokyo sales office in 1924

KM with two business associates (1926)

KM at age thirty (1925)

KM with a close friend who was also in the electric business (1925)

Matsushita with his daughter Sachiko (1927)

Borrowing mass production concepts from Ford Motor Company, Matsushita created a huge market for the rugged, inexpensive "Super Iron" (1927)

Sign advertising National-brand bicycle lamp (1927)

Mumeno and Sachiko
(1930)

二重安全装置付温度調節自在

ナショナル電氣コタツ

松下電器製作所

Poster for the National-brand electric foot warmer—Japan's first thermostatically controlled consumer product (1931)

Matsushita's first radio, developed in only three months (1931)

A Matsushita factory in 1933

KM relaxing at the beach with his employees (1933)

KM explaining the division system (1933)

Matsushita with his daughter at the spring employee athletic meet (1933)

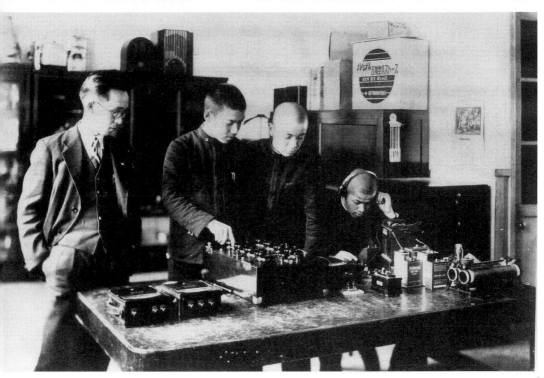

A three-year program at the Matsushita Employee Training Institute covered standard junior high school curriculum in addition to preparing graduates for jobs at the company (1934)

A Matsushita distributor circa 1935

KM talking to employees (1935)

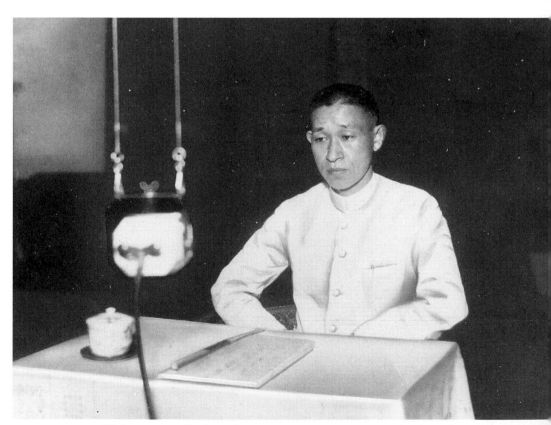

KM giving a talk about business strategy on NHK radio (1936)

thousand, two thousand, four thousand units in finished goods inventory.[19]

We don't know what alternatives Matsushita and his managers considered at that point, but the choice they eventually made is a matter of record. The idea was novel at the time and not without risk. Instead of cutting back to minimize the financial downside, they decided to invest even more funds in a new merchandising strategy.

KM hired three salesmen in the middle of July and put them on the road visiting every bicycle store in Osaka. At each shop, the sales reps left a few samples, put one lit lamp on display, and asked for no money. They told retailers that MEI would accept payment only if the products were sold and the stores were convinced that their customers were satisfied. Curious retailers, having never seen anything quite like that and being asked to assume no personal risk, agreed to the scheme.[20]

KM debriefed his salesmen at the end of their first day on the job and again at the end of day two. The initial news was promising but inconclusive. The display samples attracted attention, which was good. But the key issue was sales, and more time was needed for even a preliminary reading. Matsushita knew that if the plan failed, the firm would suffer a major defeat. The investment was not so large as to send the company into bankruptcy, but the money at risk was significant enough to stop forward momentum and possibly force a layoff.[21]

After four or five days, it became clear that most retailers were impressed when they saw for themselves that the demonstration lamps lasted fifty or more hours. As a result, they showed the new product to their customers. After the samples were purchased and retailers received initial reports that their clients were happy, they began to place orders. Within weeks, as word traveled about the quality of the new lamp, sales skyrocketed, actually passing two thousand units per month.[22] As in the winter of 1917/18, the pendulum swung from near disaster to prosperity in a very short period of time.

With orders booming, KM knew he was onto something good and he stuck to it. The formula used to create the lamp success was employed again and again in the 1920s, '30s, and beyond. The strategy was driven by a keen sensitivity to customer needs and the use of emerging technological capabilities to satisfy those needs. The focus was on items that might be mass produced and mass marketed. MEI was never first to come out with an entirely new product category, but its offerings were almost always better and/or cheaper than the industry norm. The key to product development was perspiration, not PhDs or big R&D budgets. Manufacturing was organized to keep costs as low as possible, but not by treating employees poorly. Relationships with suppliers were often close, not formal and arm's length. Marketing was innovative, especially in the use of promotions and advertising. And the entire process was built on a willingness to take risks, to experiment, and to learn.

The formula worked exceptionally well for bicycle lamps. By September 1924, the Matsushita factory was making an incredible ten thousand units a month.[23]

As lamp sales grew faster and faster, financial, human, and managerial resources were pushed to the limit. To cope, KM chose to focus on design, manufacturing, and marketing, while turning over distribution to various agents. That policy, in turn, created its own set of typical problems, including conflicts among the agents and conflicts between the agents and the company.

In May of 1925, after a new factory was completed and all lamp products were moved to that facility, Matsushita signed a contract with the Yamamoto Trading Company giving it exclusive rights to sell the bicycle lamp nationwide in exchange for a guaranteed purchase of ten thousand units a month. When Yamamoto undertook a major advertising campaign, sales of the popular product grew even more.[24]

Further success in 1925 brought Matsushita health problems, a nearly miraculous recovery, and a first taste of politics. The sickness was the same one that had been plaguing him for a decade, a difficult-to-diagnose malady, probably lung related, requiring rest. The politics was associated with a local election campaign.

As a result of KM's increasing visibility, a group of businessmen from Obiraki-cho suggested that he enter the race for the local district council. Initially, he resisted the idea for pragmatic reasons—his health was not good and the firm absorbed all of his time. When they continued to press and flatter him, he relented. Even when illness forced Matsushita to retire to Kyoto to rest, he stayed in the race with his backers managing the campaign in his absence.[25]

Twenty-eight candidates were running for twenty seats in the Nishinoda district. As the election became increasingly competitive, KM's supporters urged him to return to Osaka to direct his own campaign. His response, as reported in his autobiography, again says much about his psychology. "Hearing about all this in Kyoto, I decided that I could not stay and rest in leisure any longer. Oddly enough, as soon as I decided that, I began to feel better."[26]

Back in Osaka, with only twenty days remaining before the election, KM focused relentlessly on the race.[27] All available evidence says that he was not a good public speaker, but he had an infectious energy level, a sincerity that attracted people, and the credibility of a successful small businessman. What the campaign lacked in political sophistication was made up for by enthusiasm and a certain marketing savvy.[28]

His backers worked long hours, much like MEI employees, spurred on by the strong example of their boss. KM was developing a knack for getting others caught up in his dreams, and he undoubtedly did so in the election campaign. The kind of clever marketing used for products in the firm was also employed to sell the candidate to voters.

In the last twenty-four hours, his volunteers engaged in a great deal of activity and then waited for the results. In a field of twenty-eight, Matsushita needed only to finish twentieth to gain a seat on the council. When the ballots were counted, they found he had done much better than that. He finished second.[29]

With no records of who the other candidates were, how well their campaigns were financed, or how many times they had already been elected to office, we cannot judge how impressive was this victory. But the available evidence does suggest that the assets KM employed in the campaign—a high energy level, clever marketing methods, great enthusiasm, and a capacity to motivate others— were all very effective.

He was only thirty years old at the time. The poor boy from Wasamura had grown to become both the president of a business and an elected official in the Nishinoda district of Osaka. He was still far from rich and famous, but he had come a long way from being a lowly unskilled apprentice with fewer than four years of formal education. The success had not come overnight. Twenty-one years of hard work separated the election victory and his start at Godai's shop.

His early political career lasted a short time. He chose not to run for reelection or for other offices. We don't know how effective he was as a councilor, but it seems relatively clear that he did not much like the job.* The biggest issue may simply have been that the elected position took him away from a growing business that already demanded one hundred percent of his time and attention. At least at this point in his life, given the choice between politics and his own firm, Matsushita Electric won easily.

As the United States jumped to the beat of the roaring twenties, MEI continued to expand. In 1926, the range of electrical equipment offered by the firm grew and the company began to manufacture radio parts.[31]

Success of this sort can create rigidity and egotism instead of self-examination and the search for still more improvements. In Matsushita's case, the latter prevailed. "I had gained a fair amount of confidence as a businessman and plant manager," he later wrote about this period in his career. "My ideals and overall outlook as an entrepreneur were taking shape, and I began to subject my own methods of management to careful scrutiny, finding that there were many ways in which they could be improved. I also realized that I should take still greater care in training my workers as well as in providing leadership in the development of new products, in the negotiation of terms with our customers, and in setting product prices."[32]

Reexamination of policies brought Matsushita into increased

---

*Tomomi Doi worked as a secretary for KM between 1963 and 1967. In an interview, he said: "When I asked Seiichi Goto the reason why KM left the ward assembly, he told me that there was too wide a gap between Matsushita's ideals and the practical political process. KM concluded that he was not suitable to be a politician." Goto, who rose to be a plant manager at MEI and an executive vice president at Sanyo, reported in another interview: "Matsushita said to me, after a meal at his house, that he was going to quit politics. 'I am not fit to be a politician.'"[30]

conflict with Yamamoto, the sales agent for the bicycle lamp. When they had started their collaboration, both men thought the lamp would have a life of only a few years. By 1926, KM had revised his opinion. The product's enthusiastic reception in the marketplace suggested that it might sell profitably for a long time, perhaps ten to twenty years. The key to longevity would be continuous improvement—strategic investments to enhance the product, reduce its price, and maintain volume. But Yamamoto disagreed.

In protracted negotiations, Matsushita finally offered to pay the distributor 10,000 yen to cancel their contract as it would apply to all future lamps. Yamamoto would continue to sell the original bicycle product, but all new lamps would be completely under MEI's control.[33] With this single decision, Matsushita Electric began the development of its own distribution system, an action that would have profound long-term consequences and that was highly unusual at the time in Japanese consumer product industries.*

The design staff already had a plan for the next lamp. MEI bicycle products were so portable and cheap that people were using them instead of traditional kerosene lighting. Knowing this, the designers created a new battery-operated model not intended for use on a bicycle. The product was square, easy to carry, light, and inexpensive. Introduced in April of 1927, they called it the "National" lamp, a brand name that would eventually become as

---

*Twenty years later, Sony did something similar. In his autobiography, Morita says: "In the traditional Japanese system for distributing consumer products, the manufacturers are kept at arm's length from the consumer. There are primary, secondary, and even tertiary wholesalers dealing with some goods before they reach a retailer. . . . Third or fourth parties simply could not have the same interest in or enthusiasm for our products and our ideas that we had . . . so we had to set up our own outlets and establish our own ways of getting goods into the market."[34]

well known in parts of the world as GE or Coke. Matsushita launched the new offering by distributing 10,000 free samples to wholesalers and retailers. To reduce the initial cost of the sales promotion, a deal was struck with Teizo Okada to provide the batteries in those samples for free as long as MEI sold an additional 200,000 Okada dry cells within twelve months.[35]

The strategy was unusual at the time. In general, firms did not distribute large numbers of free samples. Companies did not work with their suppliers on major promotional campaigns. Brand names were rare, and those in existence were seldom supported with aggressive advertising. Corporations did not jump into mass production if the existing market was small. MEI went against the grain in all of these areas, especially in advertising. In *The Matsushita Phenomenon*, Rowland Gould put it this way: "Matsushita promoted the brand name 'National' into a household word through splashy advertising when brand names as marketing tools were considered superfluous by conventional management often coddled with monopoly privileges."[36]

The strategy worked exceptionally well for lamps. To Okada's great surprise, within a year MEI sold not 200,000 but 470,000 of his batteries. By the end of 1928, Matsushita Electric was selling 100,000 dry cells and 30,000 lamps each month.[37]

Also in late 1926 and early 1927, at the same time the National lamp was being developed and launched, the firm began exploring the market for electric irons. Nearly one hundred companies were producing small quantities of these electrical appliances,[38] the best of which retailed at prices that were well beyond the means of an average household. Back then the yearly salary of a teacher with a degree from a teacher's college was 324 yen. Irons cost four or five yen.[39] For an educator making $35,000 a year today, the equivalent would be a product costing over $450.

KM put Tetsujiro Nakao, a former apprentice to a rice dealer, in charge of the iron project. Nakao created a design which sandwiched the heating element between two metal plates. At a volume of ten thousand units per month, he felt the new offering could be sold for 30 to 50 percent less than existing models.[40] Since fewer than ten thousand irons were being purchased each month in all of Japan, the project was viewed by conventional business wisdom as unacceptably risky, if not simply ridiculous. Nevertheless, MEI went ahead with manufacturing the new design. "I was convinced that consumption of irons was deadlocked," Matsushita later said, "because other companies refused to take the crucial step into mass production by which the price could be lowered."[41]

The risk paid off, but not immediately. The new product sold well, but the business initially failed to make money.[42] At MEI, losses were rarely tolerated. As a result, in November 1927 KM stepped in, released Nakao and Itsuro Takehisa from their managerial duties, and took over running the iron business. Nakao was asked to invent a less labor-intensive manufacturing process which, when implemented, helped stop the losses.[43]

By way of contrast, in a typical large 20th-century corporation, within Japan or elsewhere, Nakao would never have been put in charge of developing a new iron. Someone with better credentials would have been chosen. Mass production would never have been started, even with a superior product, as long as the existing market was so small. The risk would have been deemed too large. Having succeeded in expanding the market and capturing a large share, the management would seldom have been replaced because of initial profitability problems. Sheer momentum and a reluctance to confront difficult personnel issues would have carried the day.

Even small businesses back then often copied the practices used by their larger rivals. But that kind of mimicry, which did not approach work with an open mind, a willingness to experiment so as to learn, and a propensity to take risks, rarely if ever created the kind of growth that lamps and irons provided Matsushita Electric.

From a perspective at the end of the 20th century, it is striking how many of MEI's nontraditional early practices are now being advocated by respected management thinkers. In an increasingly fast-moving and competitive world economy, the standard big-business philosophies that dominated managerial thinking in the middle of the century seem more and more out of date, while the strategies employed in the 1920s by the scrappy entrepreneur in Osaka seem ahead of their time.

At MEI, those strategies helped a small and resource-poor firm grow in a business environment dominated by large and well-connected corporations. In 1922, fifty people worked for Matsushita Electric. By the end of 1928, the firm had over three hundred employees.[44]

Mumeno had their first child, a girl named Sachiko, in 1920. Although the couple appear to have wanted more children, a second did not arrive until 1926—a boy they called Koichi. For a man born in 19th-century Japan, sons were very important and KM was clearly delighted to have a male heir. "I felt myself to be the most fortunate of men."[45]

Koichi was not yet one year old on January 20, 1927. Matsushita had been in Tokyo and was returning to Osaka on the night train. The firm was doing well and KM had no reason to expect any sudden problems. Sleeping peacefully, he was awakened by a steward, who handed him a telegram. The communication said only: "Koichi ill."[46]

Aware that no normal illness would require a telegram, Matsushita spent the rest of the trip pondering the dreadful possibilities. When the train arrived at Osaka station, he found brother-in-law Iue waiting on the platform. The child, KM was told, was being treated at a clinic by a Dr. Koba. When the father asked what was wrong, an obviously worried Iue told him they did not know.[47]

The two men went directly to the clinic where they found a distraught Mumeno. Koichi was in a coma. The doctor was trying a number of treatments, but no one was entirely sure what the underlying problem was.

The following two weeks were hellish. The child did not get better. The medical care did not seem to help. And then on February 4th, the unthinkable happened. Koichi died.[48]

The little boy's death was the tenth in a series for Konosuke Matsushita. The first was brother Hachiro in 1900. The second was sister Fusae in 1901. The third was brother Isaburo also in 1901. Then in 1906, two sisters and his father passed away. In 1913, his mother died. In 1919, another sister passed on, as did his final sibling in 1921. And then in 1927, there was Koichi, a baby boy who was KM's only son.

At no time did Matsushita talk at any length about all this tragedy. But the deaths surely influenced him greatly, especially the last. The loss of a son and the subsequent failure to have another affected his relationship with Mumeno. Even more, after ten years of success in business, he could easily have convinced himself that he was no longer vulnerable to the kind of lightning strike that had ruined his whole world in 1899. That was the advantage of becoming rich and famous, having a protective moat around the castle. With a wide and deep moat, one should be safe from nearly any catastrophe.

Comforting thoughts about the invulnerability of wealthy businessmen took a beating on that day in February 1927. Suddenly issues that had wandered through his mind many times once again became salient and troublesome.

What was the point of it all? If power and wealth were not the answer, then what was?

7

COPING WITH
ECONOMIC HARD TIMES

With revenues continuing to climb, the Matsushita enterprise once again needed larger facilities. In 1928, plans were drawn for a main office and factory totaling 15,000 square feet. Land was purchased for 55,000 yen. Another 150,000 yen was required for construction, equipment, and furnishings. To help finance the project, a loan was secured from Sumitomo Bank.[1]

Japanese GNP had been growing at only one or two percent per year. A more cautious businessperson would have delayed expansion until economic uncertainties were reduced. Once again, KM chose to plunge ahead.

Construction began in November 1928 and was completed in May 1929.[2] The timing turned out to be terrible. In July of

1929, the Osachi Hamaguchi cabinet was formed, austerity policies were enforced, and the country descended into a depression.

In the United States, the stock market crashed on October 29, 1929. As the economy slid inexorably downward, General Motors laid off 92,829 employees, nearly 50 percent of its work force.[3] Other firms, both large and small, put millions of people on the roles of the unemployed. Thousands of companies went bankrupt.

The Japanese economy had already been weak in the late 1920s. In the ensuing panic in world financial markets after October 29, the business environment collapsed quickly (see table). Demand dropped along with prices and employment. Factories slowed down, stopped production temporarily, or were closed.

Japanese GNP, 1926–1935
In Current Prices (Millions of Yen)

1926	15,975
1927	16,293
1928	16,506
1929	16,286
1930	14,698/13,850*
1931	12,520
1932	13,043
1933	14,334
1934	15,672
1935	16,737

*New system of measurement employed in 1930. Numbers shown are calculated using both old and new systems.

Source: See note 5.

The depression hit electrical supply manufacturers fast and hard. Frightened by the economic situation, consumers drastically reduced their spending on nonessential items. When electrical distributors saw their trade falling, they responded by cutting or eliminating new purchases. The net effect on Matsushita Electric was staggering. By December 1, 1929, its sales were down by more than half.[4] Warehouses began to overflow with unsold products. A financial disaster was suddenly a real possibility.

KM was once again convalescing from poor health, this time in Nishinomiya, a western suburb of Osaka. On December 20, Toshio Iue and Itsuro Takehisa came to talk to him about the crisis. When Matsushita was ill, Iue and others would visit him regularly, giving reports, discussing issues, and receiving advice. Iue was usually the number-one person in charge of implementing decisions while his boss was absent.[6]

Among the management at MEI, many had concluded that the only possible course of action would require a significant layoff, perhaps half the employees.[7] Iue and Takehisa thought sizable staff reductions would save the company, but also decimate it. Twelve years of momentum would be halted. Excellent labor relations would be shattered. Plans for further expansion would have to be shelved. Furthermore, because the Japanese economy was still deteriorating, the chances of laid-off employees finding work elsewhere were slight. Large numbers of MEI staff would be thrown into poverty. Frightened and depressed, Iue and Takehisa asked KM what they should do.[8]

With his back against the wall, Matsushita says he once again found himself feeling better, not worse. "The news that they felt forced to take the last resort had a strangely invigorating effect on me."[9] It was as if his success somehow made him feel guilty, a sort of survivor's guilt after the death of his siblings, parents, and son, while bad times gave him a chance to redeem himself.

The orders he gave Iue and Takehisa that day were as unusual as the economic depression itself: "Cut production by half starting now, but don't dismiss any employees. We'll reduce output not by laying off workers, but by having them only work [in the factory for] half-days. We will continue to pay the same wages they are getting now, but we will eliminate all holidays. We'll ask all the workers to do their best to try to *sell* the stock backlog."[10]

Both a Confucian and feudal tradition had emphasized a certain paternalistic concern in Japanese labor relations, but this specific idea was novel. A no-layoff policy was adopted by major businesses in Japan only after World War II[11] and has never been the norm among minor businesses. In 1929, there was no tradition of dealing with downturns by shifting manufacturing employees into sales.

Iue and Takehisa supported the idea without argument. They returned to the company and called a meeting of employees to announce the policy. The proclamation was greeted with cheers.[12]

Asking hundreds of manufacturing workers to assume sales jobs will sound odd even today to those accustomed to rigid specialization. Yet the idea apparently did not seem strange at MEI. With everyone spending many hours each week trying to sell the inventory, and with production at only half the old rate, the excess stock disappeared quickly. Employees went back to their regular shifts in February.[13]

As the economy lagged in the early 1930s, thousands of Japanese enterprises cut back, brought out few additional products, and laid off employees. MEI management did the opposite. They built a radio business. They grew their lamp and battery operation. They tried to upgrade the organization by increasing hiring standards, beginning an annual recruitment drive at middle and higher schools, and placing more emphasis on training, usually with an apprentice-type model.[14]*

Had the firm been only an average competitor, none of this would have been remotely possible. But the organization created during the 1920s with unconventional strategies was far from average. No other electrical firm in Japan had a greater customer focus, lower costs, better labor relations, or more clever marketing. Rivals were not weak. Japanese firms were already at this time beginning to develop the capabilities for which they would become famous in the second half of the 20th century. Yet none of Matsushita's competitors were as willing to take calculated risks, to experiment, to jump into mass production so as to lower costs and expand markets, and to learn from all these experiences.

The effort to build a radio business says much about the founder and his company.

Broadcasting in Japan had begun in 1925. Within half a decade, many firms were making radios, producing about 200,000 units per annum.[16] In May 1929, Matsushita learned that a parts supplier to those companies, Hashimoto Electric, was having financial difficulties. Someone asked whether KM would be interested in investing in that organization or in buying it. After studying the situation, he entered negotiations which eventually created a joint stock company, capitalized at 100,000 yen and owned mostly by MEI.[17]

---

*Young assistants lived in a dormitory on company grounds. Mumeno supervised the preparation of meals and, according to a number of sources, treated them as if they were her children.[15] The arrangement was similar, although much larger in scale, to that which KM experienced as an apprentice.

During this time, sales agents were increasingly urging Matsushita to manufacture entire radios, not just parts. After researching the idea, MEI management decided that the then novelty item could evolve into a popular line if certain problems could be overcome. As is common among products in the early stages of their life cycles, radios were delicate and unreliable. They were often damaged during delivery. Even more annoying, they would mysteriously fail while being used. KM himself complained that his radio often malfunctioned in the middle of a favorite broadcast.[18]

A report written by MEI staff at that time says that wholesalers did not see radios as a particularly good business because of breakdowns, customer complaints, high service costs, the rapid obsolescence of inventory due to many new product introductions, and the technical know-how needed to service the merchandise. Nevertheless, "wholesalers see radios as a product of the times and believe they have potential for the future, but this potential will not be realized until they become safer and less likely to break down."[19] More conservative companies stayed away from this innovative consumer offering, despite long-term potential, because of all the problems. KM decided to enter the business anyway, even though the economy was weak. The strategy was fourfold: to learn how to design and manufacture radios, to produce a much more reliable product, to gain a significant market share, and thus to be well positioned for when the business would begin to grow rapidly.

With little or no in-house expertise in the field, Matsushita bought for 50,000 yen a factory that was already producing radios and that had a good reputation.[20] Distribution of the new product was turned over to his sales network and a major promotional campaign was initiated. No one at MEI expected the first radio to be an important source of revenue, but they did assume the product would sell adequately while the firm gained experience.

MEI sold its first radio in August 1930.[21] Almost immediately, serious problems surfaced. Complaints poured in from customers and dealers. Merchandise was returned in a volume that was unprecedented at the firm. Some people were so upset that they refused to pay their bills. Sales agents were caught off guard, and once they assessed the damage to their relations with customers, they grew angry. Matsushita was flabbergasted.

"I was practically bowled over by what had happened. Of course, I knew we did not have the ideal radio set, but since it was a product of a company that had a very low rate of defects, I had figured that even if there were problems, they would be fewer than for competitors' products. . . . When I laid eyes on the pile of defective sets, I was utterly stunned. . . . Worst of all was that I had recommended the product to the agents with great assurance, and they had felt confident and put a lot of work into selling it."[22] The crisis would have been difficult to handle even during good times. The still-deteriorating economy made everything worse.

Caught by surprise, Matsushita decided that they needed to develop quickly a thorough understanding of the problems. "We immediately set out to find what the causes were, re-examining everything inside and out."[23]

He talked to sales agents. He talked to customers. He spoke with his own staff. In retrospect, it was easy to see that the MEI distribution system was unprepared to handle the product. Without even an elementary understanding of radios, the retailers simply did not know how to help their customers. They often returned merchandise to the factory with only a loose tube or screw, creating significant and unnecessary expenses.[24]

Two options were considered for resolving the crisis, and neither involved exiting the business. In the first alternative, they would sell the radio through specialized stores that had the required expertise to deal with the existing product. In the second, they would immediately try to produce a more reliable radio that could be sold through the MEI distribution system. After much discussion and thought, KM chose the latter. When he communicated his decision to the radio factory manager, an executive who was also the former plant owner, the man expressed strong disagreement. He told Matsushita that radios could not be made without defects and that the firm should return to the practice he had previously employed: selling through specialized stores. When KM insisted that a superior product could be designed and manufactured, the other man was dismissive.[25]

The plant manager's argument was not without merit. At the early stages in any product's history, whether automobiles or computers, devices tend to be delicate and finicky. Matsushita was aware of that fact, but he also felt that people used such truths as a defense against change.

The impasse was resolved through negotiations. In the final agreement, the previous owner and his technical staff were allowed to leave and form their own business. MEI kept the factory and all the financial losses. KM then asked his own research department to design a better radio.[26]

"I hear amateurs build radio sets all the time that work perfectly well. Compared to these amateurs, you have all these facilities and equipment at your disposal. There are already a number of good sets on the market. Take a look at these and make up your minds to come up with a better one in as short a time as you can manage. . . . I'm sure success or failure will hang on whether you have confidence and determination. . . . That's why I want you to give it everything you've got."[27]

The research department created a new design in a remarkably short period of time: only three months. Prototypes were built and tested. Everyone at MEI agreed that the sets were a significant improvement over the original model.[28]

During this same time, the Japanese Broadcasting Corporation was supervising a contest to select the best radios in Japan. Someone at MEI entered one of the prototypes. They obviously thought their new model was good enough not to risk embarrassment for the firm. Yet no one seems to have expected a company that had just entered the business to do well against the best of the established competition.

When the winners were announced, to everyone's astonishment the MEI entry took first place.[29] Other radio makers were incredulous. The Matsushita product development staff was overjoyed.

In trying to explain this unlikely outcome, KM later said: "At first I thought it quite strange that we should have beat out all the manufacturers who had been building radios for years. But after all, I guessed it wasn't really that odd, considering the kind of mentality we cultivated at Matsushita Electric. Any person in a position of responsibility should always pay close attention to the problems that are crucial in bringing a certain task . . . to completion. Examining them in a free or creative frame of mind, he will be able to find a workable answer. At the same time, it is also necessary to approach a project with the conviction that it *can* be done, and not to waste energy worrying about its difficulty. Truly able people do not let the difficulties get the better of them. This is one of the things that a person in a position of leadership should keep in mind."[30]

If there were any remaining doubts about whether the Matsushita organization was becoming something special, the radio contest erased them. Here once again, the winning ingredient was not the most sophisticated technical expertise or a re-search staff with a huge budget. In a preview of a strategy adopted by a number of other Japanese corporations after World War II, conviction, customer focus, an openness to new ideas, and hard work produced results that eluded larger or more experienced firms. But just as American corporations had difficulty understanding Japanese successes in the 1950s, '60s, and '70s, electrical manufacturers in Japan in the 1920s and '30s seem to have had a hard time comprehending Matsushita Electric.

KM priced the new radio higher than competing models be-cause the design was more costly to manufacture.[31] But despite the price, it was popular and sold well. As a result, production grew rapidly. Units shipped doubled, then doubled again (see table). Facilities were built to manufacture a broader product line. As costs were reduced through economies of scale and im-proved production methods, prices were lowered, making ra-dios affordable to more and more people.

Production of National Radios: 1931–1938

1931	1,000
1932	28,000
1933	45,000
1934	61,000
1935	135,000
1936	174,000
1937	206,000
1938	237,000

Source: See note 32.

By 1942, ten years after entering the business, Matsushita Electric was the largest radio manufacturer in Japan, with 30 percent market share and a monthly volume of 30,000 units.[33]

The strategy of reducing costs so as to build volume worked well in other product lines too. When the National lamp was first introduced, sales agents paid 1.25 yen per unit. After shipments passed 10,000 a month, the price was reduced to 1.00 yen. Further decreases continued thereafter, and within just a few years the lamp was sold at less than one half the original price.[34] In fiscal 1930, despite the depression, monthly volume grew to 200,000 lamps and one million dry batteries.[35]

Other competitors adopted this strategy, but they also engaged in periodic price wars or extracted monopoly-like profits from high market shares. MEI rarely strayed from KM's formula.

With battery sales at nearly 1.5 million units a month in 1931, Matsushita approached his two suppliers with a request to improve efficiency and reduce prices once again. His longer-term subcontractor, the Okada organization, readily agreed. His newer supplier, the Komori Dry Battery Works, did not. Run by a man whom KM derisively described as more of an "investor" than a "manufacturer," the management balked at reducing short-term profits. The proposal was called "risky." Komori then made a counteroffer: buy us and you can manage the business any way you like.[36]

On September 20, 1931, plans were completed for purchasing the Komori factory. To assist the plant superintendent and his sales manager, KM spent two hours a day for a period of months at their facility. The goal, he told others, was to help his new employees learn "the principles of Matsushita-style management."[37]

The dry battery business grew rapidly during the 1930s and became a very important product area for the company. In August of 1932, MEI purchased Okada. In September of that same year, the firm opened a new battery plant in Kadoma. In March of 1936, it added more capacity by buying the Asahi Dry Battery Company. In 1938, it built a facility in Tienchin, China. Still another plant was completed in Suzaki in March of 1942. By 1943, no other corporation in Japan was selling as many batteries.[38]

By the end of 1931, Matsushita Electric was no longer a small enterprise. It manufactured more than two hundred different kinds of products in four categories: wiring fixtures, radios, lamps and dry batteries, and electrothermal devices (such as irons).[39] Its record in the great depression was most unusual. In 1929, MEI employment stood at 477. Production was running at 200,000 yen per month and the firm had 140 patents. Two years later, despite the desolate economy, an energized organization generated more patents, developed more products, and took market share away from competitors. As a result, employment nearly doubled, growing to 886.[40]

In his subsequent speeches and books, Matsushita said repeatedly that he thought the economic hard times were good for the company. He clearly believed, from his own experiences earlier in life, that adversity could make one stronger. "Workers must submit to many tests and difficult discipline before they can be considered mature and trustworthy," he wrote in his autobiography. "One of the most effective tests of workers' dedication and resourcefulness is imposed when their company encounters financial difficulties and must pull itself out of a crisis."[41]

During its first fourteen years in business, the Matsushita enterprise had seen many tough times. It was a small and resource-poor company operating in competitive markets. MEI succeeded only because it was able to discover and adopt a variety of practices that made it a strong rival. The firm was innovative in product design, marketing, manufacturing, and personnel policies.* It aimed at constantly improving products so that they were good values, better and cheaper than competing models. It was willing to take risks so as to expand markets and gain significant market share. It vigorously worked to keep costs low and productivity high. It had begun building a strong and loyal retail distribution system. It always operated with an eye on its customers, both distributors and ultimate consumers. It expected much from employees and in turn treated them with dignity and concern. It valued flexibility and speed, discouraged long lead times or big R&D budgets, and demanded that all its products and businesses make money.

Success in really competitive environments generally requires a similar approach. Most of these policies seem to have worked equally well for Bill Hewlett and Dave Packard in the 1930s and 1940s, as well as for dozens of Japanese businesses that adopted much of this formula after World War II.

How Matsushita and his managers discovered these policies says much about them and the firm. They couldn't rely on books or consultants because management literature and advisors hardly existed back then. KM did draw heavily on his experiences as an

---

*But not in research. As a result, the firm didn't invent new categories of products. MEI allowed others to invent, then they produced better or cheaper or more cleverly merchandised products of their own.

apprentice and at Osaka Light. Collectively, MEI management paid close attention to what was happening around them and in the electronics industry. Yet they rarely just replicated conventional wisdom. For the most part, Konosuke Matsushita and his staff developed their own methods to cope with a challenging economic environment and the founder's restless ambitions. Approaching work with an open mind and a willingness to take risks, they created powerful new practices and kept growing as entrepreneurs, managers, and executives.

If the economic environment today were moving in a direction where hard times were rare and where industries were becoming less competitive, the Matsushita story might be of marginal relevance. But just the opposite is true. The easy growth and good times that followed World War II are over. Globalization of the economy does offer more opportunities, but the hazards are huge.[42] As the competitiveness in most industries goes up and up, the fundamental approach to business used by so many large companies during good times is no longer working particularly well.

Today's winners do not look like U.S. Steel, Ford, or Chase Manhattan in 1960. Increasingly, they look more like MEI in 1930.

BUSINESS LEADER

1931–1946

8

A MISSION FOR
THE CORPORATION

It happened a thousand times in the 20th century, maybe ten thousand. People created or bought small businesses. They developed entrepreneurial skills. They succeeded. As a result, their enterprises expanded to become medium-sized organizations. Then the nature of the challenge changed. Instead of growing to meet the new demands, those on top continued to operate as they had in the past, often becoming self-absorbed and arrogant. Eventually, the businesses encountered many difficulties, and employees, stockholders, and customers all suffered.

For Matsushita Electric, the transition from a small to a medium-sized company occurred in the late 1920s and early 1930s, with 1932 being a key year. This was a time when more than clever entrepreneurship was needed from Konosuke Matsushita, when a larger organization was in danger of losing its sense of direction. This was a year in which the MEI founder struggled to respond to new requirements—a voyage which took him to a religious cult and to a meeting in which he announced a new mission for Matsushita Electric.

A mong those seeking an audience in the early weeks of 1932 was an MEI customer who requested only a few minutes of Matsushita's time.[1] KM agreed, and then found himself subjected to a proselytizing speech.

The visitor said he had once been downhearted, that one misfortune seemed to follow another until a friend urged him to embrace a religious sect. He said he was not interested at first, but after visiting temples and attending services he gradually began to appreciate the value of religion.

"I realized how mistaken my thinking and way of approaching [life] had been," he told KM, "and saw clearly why my affairs had not been going favorably. As my faith grew stronger, I realized that things I had once found profoundly irritating no longer bothered me. I became more open-minded and less prone to worry. I began to work cheerfully every day. I went to pray at the temple frequently and discovered the joy of religious faith. It was not long before my business and everything else all started going well. For the first time I felt my life worthwhile. I became a firm believer of the teachings of the sect and have subsequently received training in its doctrines. I am very eager to share this joy with other people."[2]

Matsushita did not follow any specific religion and was not looking for a sect to join. He says in his autobiography that he was impressed by the man's enthusiasm and earnestness, but nevertheless declined the invitation. With a busy schedule, the meeting should have faded quickly from memory. It did not. He kept thinking about the man's dedicated manner and "apparent happiness."[3]

After ten days, the customer returned. A few weeks later, he visited KM yet again. Matsushita easily could have found excuses to avoid seeing this individual, but he did not. Instead, he continued to talk with the man and eventually accepted his invitation to visit the religious headquarters.[4]

They left Osaka early one morning in March 1932, arriving an hour later at the head temple of the Tenrikyo sect in what is now called Tenri City. They went to the main hall of the religion first, then to the municipal hall of the founder of the sect, which was still under construction, and on to the mausoleum of the founder. After lunch, they visited a school which had an enrollment of over five thousand students. They also saw a library which KM believed had a collection matching any in Tokyo or Osaka. In the late afternoon they visited a lumber mill which was operated by the sect to facilitate additional construction. Throughout the day, Matsushita was surprised by the number of buildings that were a part of the community, the size of those buildings, the quality of architecture, and the cleanliness of the grounds.[5]

A traveler more than half a century later will find almost all that KM saw, since little has been destroyed or torn down.[6] The facility is impressive. The halls are huge, more on the scale of Western cathedrals than Eastern shrines. The total acreage for the halls, schools, libraries, offices, and dormitories rivals the emperor's former quarters in nearby Kyoto.

But more than the buildings, what caught Matsushita's attention were the people: the quiet reverence of the worshipers, the large number of visitors, the obvious diligence of the stu-

dents, and the energy level of those constructing the temples. The laborers were all donating their time. Although they received no salary, they worked with obvious enthusiasm.[7]

He returned to Osaka that night by himself. The images stayed with him: happy people, hardworking people, yet people without apparent economic incentives. When asked, he continued to decline invitations to join the sect, but subsequent events show that KM became nearly obsessed with what he saw that day. The experience clearly impressed him as a pragmatic businessman. It also touched something much deeper inside.[8]

The pragmatic response is easier to understand. He had witnessed a sizable organization where people worked with the kind of dedication seldom found outside small entrepreneurial settings. "There was something to be learned from what I had seen," he later wrote, "from the way it was apparently thriving, from the mountains of donated logs, from the energetic and dedicated way the members of the sect threw themselves into the construction work . . . , from the pious mien of every worshiper, from the diligent students at the school who would later guide others toward an understanding of the teachings of the sect, and from the way everything worked with clockwork-like smoothness."[9] The implication was clear. If a corporation could somehow be made meaningful like a religion, people would be both more satisfied and more productive.

The implication applied equally well to both employer and employee. By early 1932, the MEI enterprise was a rarity, an organization that was thriving despite very poor economic conditions. Under the circumstances, one might have expected the founder to be an extremely happy man. He was not. Thirty-seven-year-old Konosuke Matsushita was restless, sometimes moody, and still suffering from mysterious physical ailments which forced him to bed. Friends and coworkers have subsequently speculated that he had learned that money did not soothe his soul,[10] that he was feeling guilty about his successes,[11] and that he was searching for greater meaning in life.[12] Whatever the case, the visit to Tenri City unleashed a great deal of reflection.[13] We do not know how much he discussed his feelings with others or sought their counsel, but we do know that two months later he chose to share his emerging ideas with a large group of employees in an unusual and very emotional meeting.

One hundred sixty-eight MEI office workers and executives gathered at the Osaka Central Electric Club Auditorium on May 5, 1932. At ten o'clock in the morning, Matsushita rose to talk.[14]

He began by reminding them of their collective achievements:[15] in only fifteen years, they had progressed from start-up to eleven hundred employees, sales of three million yen per year, 280 registered patents, and factories at ten locations. He told them about his recent experience at the Tenrikyo sect, and how that had inspired him to reexamine his vision of MEI. He built up to a bold proposition: "The mission of a manufacturer should be to overcome poverty, to relieve society as a whole from misery, and bring it wealth."[16]

He used tap water as an example. Here, he said, is a vital product that is produced and distributed so cheaply that virtually anyone can afford it. "This is what the entrepreneur and the manufacturer should aim at: to make all products as inexhaustible and as cheap as tap water. When this is realized, poverty will vanish from the earth."[17]

Achieving the mission, he told them, would obviously require many years, perhaps two or three centuries. But the long time involved should not deter them from embracing the vision. All worthy ideals are difficult to accomplish. Life becomes better only because farsighted people are willing to tackle ambitious projects.

"Beginning today, this far reaching dream, this sacred calling, will be our ideal and our mission, and its fulfillment the responsibility of each one of us. Inasmuch as fate has brought you to work at Matsushita Electric, I trust you will share the joy and responsibilities of pursuing the mission that lies before us. . . . I am determined to lead and guide all of you in this endeavor with fresh energy and enthusiasm. . . . The most important thing is that we enjoy happiness to the fullest in our own lives and at the same time strive for the benefit of the generations that are to follow."[18]

His delivery and eloquence did little to inspire employees, but observers that day say the words came with passion and the sentiments were appealingly idealistic.[19] After concluding his remarks, Matsushita asked if others in the audience would care to speak. Dozens did, with some employees becoming very emotional.[20]

Had he been conducting himself for fifteen years in ways that suggested a lack of concern for others, his speech would have had little if any credibility. But the message was not inconsistent with the manner in which the organization had been run. His words simply articulated a vision for the firm on a much broader and higher plain. The new mission also connected the goals of the company to very basic human values.

Some in the audience received his comments with considerable skepticism. Eliminate poverty? Two or three hundred years? Such concerns only grew when they later learned that MEI was not to become a socialistic or a Confucian enterprise, serving society while ignoring profits.* Instead, the mission was to benefit humankind by producing more and more necessary goods and services at lower and lower costs, all of which required profits to finance new technology and additional factories.

Over time, his ideas would expand and become more explicit. The purpose of the enterprise, he would tell others, was not to maximize shareholder wealth or short-term profits. The main goal was not market share, number of patents, or return on equity. The mission was not to create high-paying and secure jobs for managers. The point was not to maximize exports or ensure Japan's national defense. The main objective was not to become a "socially responsible" enterprise that made no profits or gave them all away to charities.

Although Matsushita's ideas would have been highly controversial in the West, in Japan, at least on the surface, they did not sound very different from what a number of other businessmen were saying.[22] Back then one often heard: "for the good of the country," or "for the good of society." But a closer examination of the specifics shows three important differences. Matsushita talked mostly about serving society by making goods that people could afford, not about developing the econ-

---

*In the developing Matsushita philosophy, social contribution and profits rarely conflicted, at least in a competitive marketplace. The logic was simple. Customers are more than willing to pay a manufacturer a profit as long as the overall price/quality/service is a good value for them. The bigger the value, the more customers will be willing to pay and thus the higher the profit. As such, a product's profitability is one measure of how well it serves society.[21] With this logic, the energy-draining conflict between doing well and doing good disappears, at least in a market with considerable amounts of competition. As economists have convincingly shown, in a noncompetitive market the conflict remains, while in markets with "excessive" capacity and competition, no one will make much profit regardless of the value of products.

omy and technology to protect Japan from Western powers.[23] He talked explicitly about the important role of profit, a highly unusual statement in Japan at the time.[24] He also went far beyond an occasional statement of lofty corporate goals. He put his principles into writing, and he asked that his employees repeat those ideals, out loud, at the start of each and every workday.

In the 1980s, hundreds of corporations around the world adopted statements of ideals or values to guide employee action.[25] A few firms probably did so because these proclamations had become faddish. Others created value documents because they believed that a limited number of sensible principles were more helpful in an increasingly changing world than books full of deadly dull rules, procedures, and policies.

The grandfather of all these corporate value statements in the United States was written by Robert Wood Johnson in the 1940s.[26] General Johnson's "credo," slightly altered, can be found in the offices of most Johnson and Johnson managers even today. The document can sound pretentious at first reading, but J&J executives have regularly claimed that it helps guide management behavior at the firm.

A full decade before General Johnson wrote his credo, Konosuke Matsushita spelled out his own set of business principles.* These were communicated to employees in a President's Message on July 27, 1933. KM urged that they all commit themselves to certain ideals:[27]

---

*A few of the first large Japanese businesses, like Mitsui, wrote statements of precepts or principles as early as 1700. KM was no doubt aware of this. But Matsushita may be the first major firm, in or out of Japan, to create a modern-looking statement of guiding values.

Service to the Public: To provide high-quality goods and services at reasonable prices, thereby contributing to the well-being and happiness of people throughout the world.

Fairness and Honesty: To be fair and honest in all business dealings and personal conduct, always making balanced judgments free of preconceptions.

Teamwork for the Common Cause: To pool abilities and strength of resolution to accomplish shared objectives, in mutual trust and full recognition of individual autonomy.

Untiring Effort for Improvement: To strive constantly for improvement of corporate and personal performances, even in the worst of adversity, so as to fulfill the firm's mission to realize lasting peace and prosperity.

Courtesy and Humility: To always be cordial and modest and respect the rights and needs of others, thereby helping enrich the environment and maintain social order.

Two more items were added in 1937:

Accord with Natural Laws: To abide by the laws of nature and adjust thought and behavior to ever-changing conditions, so as to bring about gradual but steady progress and successes in all endeavors.

Gratitude for Blessings: To forever be grateful for all the blessings and kindness received, so as to live with peace, joy and strength and overcome any obstacles encountered in the pursuit of true happiness.*

---

*Several English language wordings of the principles have existed over the years. Here I am quoting the version in Matsushita's English language autobiography. The currently authorized version, established in 1993, is slightly different.

Sentiments like these are often greeted with skepticism, especially in the West. We quite reasonably worry that they are either meaningless "motherhood and apple pie" statements or that they have a manipulative intent. Although Asians with a Confucian heritage seem to be more receptive to these sorts of ideals, even the Japanese can be cynical, and some were at Matsushita Electric.

When KM asked that his business principles be spoken aloud each morning by every employee in group assemblies, some balked at the formality, others at the pretentiousness of the ceremony. Nevertheless, Matsushita refused to acquiesce. "Human beings are sometimes slaves to the ugly and weak sides of human nature," he told employees. "However, if you set high goals for yourselves and every day continue to reflect on them, step by step you will be more focused and make yourself a better human being, becoming a happier person for it."[28]

The initial resistance to the morning meetings and the principles waned but never totally disappeared. "When I joined Matsushita in 1937," says Toshihiko Yamashita, "I hated the daily ritual of morning assemblies where everyone recited the company creed and pledge and we sang the company song." But in time, Yamashita changed his mind about both the principles and the daily ceremonies. With public repetition, he concluded, "laudable ideas about service, honesty, and teamwork [are] gradually take[n] to heart."[29]

For those who have not experienced a values-driven organization, Yamashita's words can be difficult to believe. Nevertheless, the evidence in this case is clear. To many MEI employees, the seven principles eventually became more than a Japanese version of motherhood and apple pie. For them, these seemingly trite and mawkishly sentimental ideals became inspirational guidelines for living. Together with the entrepreneurial business practices developed in the early years, the corporate mission, and KM's insistence that they stay within the boundaries of the electric home appliance industry,[30] the new guidelines helped shape and motivate behavior at the firm.

Even before Matsushita's 1932 speech and the 1933 principles, MEI had a dedicated and energetic work force, partially because of paternalistic personnel practices (an employee organization created in 1920 had sponsored hundreds of cultural, recreational, and sporting events[31]), partially because of an unusual amount of communication (an in-house magazine was launched in 1927[32]), and partially due to KM's own credibility and role modeling. Yet in the years after 1933, the aligned and inspired work force became a larger source of competitive advantage,* despite ever-increasing size and the general tendency for organizations to lose employee commitment over time. Many of those at MEI came to believe that they were associated with a noble and just cause. Like the people in Tenri City, they engaged in their jobs with energy and enthusiasm. They did not always have the technical resources or the finances of their rivals, but they won again and again nevertheless.

The specific content of the mission and principles, not just their existence, helped produce the inspired response. Had employees been asked to pledge each morning to work for a 15 percent yearly earnings-per-share growth instead of sentiments that tapped into widely held human values, it is hard to imagine that they would have responded as they did. With a narrow financial

---

*In his book on Honda, Tetsuo Sakiya says, "before the end of World War II . . . almost all major Japanese corporations were under the control of [large conglomerates called] Zaibatsu. Although the elite members of these corporations had a strong sense of loyalty, ordinary workers were paid low wages and felt little sense of unity with the company."[33]

goal imposed from above, the boss would have been seen as autocratic, in the most negative sense of the word, and greedy.

Subsequent events also strongly suggest that the appealing principles by themselves would have been insufficient to overcome natural human skepticism. Many organizations in the United States in the 1980s adopted similar value statements but failed to unify and energize their employees. Instead, people rejected the ideas as corny, not credible, or not appropriate.

In MEI's case, the capacity to turn rhetoric into reality was not based on conventional speaking skills. No one has ever claimed that Matsushita was a great orator. Instead, the key was leadership by example. KM came to behave as if he believed deeply in the mission and principles. His visible actions grew to be in concert with those goals and values. He also created structures and systems that were consistent with the guiding ideas. The net effect was powerful: an aligned set of forces that beamed a message at all employees, a communication that grew in credibility over time and that pierced a great deal of self-protective cynical armor.

Of course, not everyone was swept away by the inspirational ideals. The political left saw capitalistic exploitation. The right worried that there was far too little nationalistic rhetoric. Western eyes viewed the resulting behavior at Matsushita Electric as uncomfortably cult-like. Nevertheless, there is little doubt that the mission and principles helped MEI grow.

As the United States and most of Europe sank deeper into an economic black hole, an energized Matsushita organization continued to expand. A trade division was established in 1932, exporting wire instruments and dry batteries. In 1935, liaison offices were opened outside of Japan. The expanded sales network grew to include Korea and Taiwan. Six more offices were opened in 1936.[34]

The firm finally incorporated on December 25, 1935. When stock was issued, Matsushita created a number of plans to encourage employee ownership.[35] To further promote psychological ownership among those in his distribution system, he developed a pamphlet which described the firm's mission/principles for all MEI sales agents.[36] The growing network of shops, in KM's view, was becoming a key source of competitive advantage, so he worked very closely with them.[37]

That pamphlet said, in part: "If you think of the manufacturer as being the factory of a sales agent, and the sales agent as being a branch office of a manufacturer, you will understand why it is necessary for both to exert great efforts to help each other. We will offer advice to you in the management of your offices to the extent that our knowledge permits us. We would like to encourage a close relationship in which we help one another develop spiritually, and both clear and construct the road to truth in business which is in line with the times. I have gradually come to believe that we must cooperate with each other in order to attain mutual prosperity and to create lives filled with welfare. I realize, however, that enlarging the scale of a business easily invites looseness in management, and readily breeds arrogance among personnel. We must take the utmost care to stop this from happening."[38]

As early as the mid 1930s, Matsushita saw that one of the greatest dangers for a successful enterprise was its own arrogance. More importantly, he found a possible solution to the problem—a very far-reaching and humanitarian goal. When your mission is to alleviate poverty on earth, it is difficult to look at your actual achievements and become arrogant.

The MEI vision came to serve a number of important purposes. It inspired employees. It fostered hard work. It helped people from becoming too captivated by their successes. Perhaps most of all, it provided the boss with a potential answer to the question about his fate.

The goal could be a lifelong endeavor: to build an organization that would, over time, help the world eliminate poverty and the related problems he had experienced in his youth. This was a mission that could give meaning to his life and his past suffering. This was a fate that might help relieve any feelings of guilt associated with his success, a fate to which he could relate emotionally in a positive way.[39] This was a calling that might inspire him as a person, a manager, and a leader.

In the decade that followed the 1932 mission speech, both the firm and its founder made transitions, going beyond a small entrepreneurial entity and a merchant-oriented entrepreneur. In the process, Matsushita became less and less like the average Japanese businessman. In a society that focuses on "the group," individuals are not supposed to stand out. Most executives, even company presidents, make themselves an invisible part of the overall enterprise. Taro Nawa, an author who met Matsushita on many occasions, makes the point this way: "There is a traditional understanding in Japan that 'the nail that sticks up will be hammered down.' It is not normal for even the president of a company to express his character or individuality too much. It goes against Japanese culture."[40]

KM did express his individuality and beliefs. As a result, he became a highly visible personality within MEI. Some employees found him to be an odd character, hard to comprehend. But most were impressed by his track record, hard work, and ideals—so impressed, that they were willing to follow his lead with an unusual degree of enthusiasm and commitment.

9

CREATING
"THE DIVISION SYSTEM"

In the beginning, there was no formal organization. Kono-suke, Mumeno, and the others did whatever seemed necessary. Specialized roles were introduced later, and by the early 1920s a conventional structure was in place with employees grouped into departments for manufacturing, accounting, sales, engineering, and so on.[1]

In May of 1933, Matsushita reorganized the firm by product. Division One manufactured radios. Division Two focused on lamps and batteries. Division Three produced wiring implements and synthetic resins. Division Four handled electric heating appliances—irons, foot warmers, heaters.* Each of the four

---

*Division Four was created in 1934.

groups became responsible for a number of factories and branch sales offices. Each grew to be a relatively autonomous entity in charge of everything from product development to manufacturing to sales.[2]

Managers in the new divisions concentrated more narrowly than before in terms of products, but more broadly in terms of business functions and business results. An executive in Division One was no longer involved with lamps, batteries, wiring devices, heaters, or synthetic resins. He focused exclusively on radios and was asked to think about them as a business, not just something to be made, sold, or designed.

The arrangement was unusual at the time. From the birth of the modern corporation in the 19th century until the 1920s, industrial firms took the same initial path as had MEI—from no specialization to a functional organization where all employees with similar jobs were put into one large department. The first company known to evolve beyond a functional structure was General Motors. In 1921, Alfred P. Sloan Jr. split the auto firm into "divisions," each with its own manufacturing, sales, accounting, and personnel departments. The divisions were distinct because each made a different product—Buicks, Chevrolets, Oldsmobiles, or Cadillacs—and each had somewhat different customers.[3]

This new form of organization became popular only after World War II. Widely considered an early adopter of divisionalization, GE switched structures in 1952.[4] In the 1960s, hundreds of other major industrial corporations did likewise, often with the help of the management consulting firm McKinsey. But even then, few went as far as did Matsushita in the 1930s in breaking apart a large organization and pushing down authority.

Although the historical record is not entirely clear, MEI appears to be one of the first firms in the world to adopt a divisional structure.[5] KM's leadership in this area is all the more remarkable because he does not appear to have been copying General Motors or anyone else. He was simply creating what seemed at the time to be a sensible way to implement his new mission and business principles.[6]

The idea of divisionalization within Matsushita Electric dated back to 1927 when the firm began making electric heaters. KM appointed one person to be in charge of the entire heater operation. Although the arrangement created a few problems, such as the loss of some economies of scale, it also demonstrated many virtues. The broader responsibility helped the division manager to grow as a businessman and entrepreneur. Independence from the rest of the organization fostered creativity and eagerness on the part of the staff. The small size and clear focus encouraged everyone involved to think in terms of the business instead of a narrow task.[7]

In 1927, the rest of the company was still organized in functional departments. As these units grew larger, employees were given more and more specialized jobs. At some point in the early 1930s, KM noticed that people were losing sight of the bigger picture: satisfying customers, making a profit. Instead, they focused increasingly on their narrow roles—putting insulation in a product, keeping records of cash received, screening applicants for employment. Only Matsushita, Iue, and a few others felt responsible for the overall health of the various businesses. By pushing responsibility for products lower in the organization and by calculating revenues, market share, and profits for each new division, KM hoped to reverse this trend.

As the company grew, Matsushita and his lieutenants also became concerned that future revenue increases would be limited not by the market but by a lack of managerial talent. Their hope was that divisionalization would "cultivate capable managerial personnel" by giving more people greater authority and thus more opportunity to grow in their jobs.[8]

When Matsushita announced the division system in 1933, he stressed two goals. The first was to increase the number of people responsible for business results. The second was to train managers.[9] The overarching objective was to retain some of the advantages that small businesses have over larger ones. The vision was of a big enterprise made up of many smaller firms.

"Since the division system limited the fields of manufacture and directly linked production and sales," KM wrote, "it was possible through careful management to achieve the kind of mobile production activity that can respond immediately to market trends, one of the greatest strengths of a small business."[10] Instead of one firm with fourteen hundred employees, divisionalization created four companies, each with fewer than four hundred people.

Early in 1934, Matsushita explained the new form of organization to employees by saying: "It's not enough to work conscientiously. No matter what kind of job [you have], you should think of yourself as being completely in charge of and responsible for your work, like being the president of your own company. By doing so, not only can appropriate devices be made [and] new discoveries be born, [you will] also greatly assist your own self-development."[11]

To help make each division feel like an independent business, in the beginning no funds could be transferred from one group to another. Each had to pay its own bills with no assistance from corporate headquarters.[12] The arrangement created a degree of internal competition which was novel, controversial, and powerful.

We have no early detailed descriptions of a typical Matsushita division. A report from the 1970s on two of the older and smaller groups probably says much about what KM had in mind in the mid 1930s.

In the electric iron division, production workers were divided into twelve units, one for each stage in the manufacturing process. Group size varied from five to fifteen. Each team took some other unit's output, added value, and then passed on the in-process goods. Each had someone responsible for group performance. These individuals monitored the price of parts, demand for their output, wage rates, and other factors. They were given accounting information every month on their unit's results and they were expected to make adjustments in their operations in order to help the business grow and earn money.*[13]

The battery division had two small factories, each with only one production line and thirty employees. Despite low economies of scale and a lack of sophisticated equipment, both had very low costs. At the Kyushu plant, the work force had decreased from forty to thirty-two while output had increased 30 percent. At the Nagoya plant, the workers increased productivity with a curved assembly line that allowed people to work on two different tasks. Production targets were set and monitored for the plant, for work groups, and for individuals.[14]

In both the iron and battery divisions, downward delegation of responsibility did not stop at the division head or the plant manager. Initiative was expected from everyone. A significant amount of authority and independence was given to small groups at the bottom of the organization in order to tap their

---

*MEI appears to be one of the first firms anywhere, other than very small companies, to make a practice of giving monthly financial information to employees outside of senior management.

energy and "collective wisdom." At the same time, the division system demanded responsibility and accountability from those same people. Employees knew that if their costs were too high and profits too low, no one would be fired, but a poor record would not be tolerated. Managers and workers at the Nagoya plant were aware that if they didn't perform well, the facility would be shut down and their jobs would be shifted to another factory, perhaps hundreds of miles away.[15]

Matsushita himself monitored all divisions. He queried, listened, and counseled division general managers. "How are you doing? Are there any problems? You might consider this idea." He pored over detailed financial data, looking for weaknesses. When shortcomings were found, he tried to help his executives make necessary improvements. If the problems were large, or if managers were reluctant to confront issues quickly, he was known to scream at people. If it became clear that a division manager was failing, KM would move the executive to another position, usually with a significant effort to minimize damage to his pride. The CEO's style mixed toughness with gentleness.[16]

Because Matsushita did not develop a large corporate staff, the division system at MEI gave the operating units more autonomy than was the case at General Motors and many other subsequent adopters of this structure. Some observers believe that divisionalization at MEI was far from the Western norm, especially in regard to a basic issue of trust. According to Professor Tsunehiko Yui: "KM's version of the division system was premised upon a belief in other people. So you didn't need to watch them constantly. This was very different from the typical American version of divisionalization."[17]

On the surface, the autonomy given MEI divisions looks much like that seen in mid-20th-century conglomerates, but the resemblance is an illusion. In most conglomerates, headquarters provided the operating units with little except funds and financial controls. In the Matsushita organization, corporate gave a mission and operating principles. In addition, since all the divisions were making electrical products, those at the center usually knew enough about the individual businesses to monitor more than just the financials, to ask appropriate questions, and to intervene knowledgeably when necessary.

This organizational arrangement was unusual in Japan. In the early 1930s, Japanese businesses were functionally structured and often had sizable corporate staffs. Furthermore, with the explicit emphasis on the group, specific individuals were not held responsible for much of anything. The whole group was responsible. At MEI, teams were important, but the division general manager for irons was delegated authority and then held accountable for the iron business. The same would have been true for the head of production unit 4 in battery factory 2. Hiding behind "the group" was not acceptable.[18]

This delegation of authority and responsibility probably saved MEI from developing a problem often associated with highly successful entrepreneurs. With KM's growth as an inspirational figure, and with the mission and business principles coming from the top, the Matsushita enterprise could easily have evolved into an organization with one strong leader and fanatical but weak followers. The division system helped work against that tendency. Responsibility was forced onto others. KM was put in a new role, where he had to adapt and learn. Iue is perhaps the best example of the resulting executive development.* Number twos in cult-like firms rarely leave. If they do,

---

*Arataro Takahashi also grew to be a very strong executive, eventually becoming chairman of MEI.[19]

they never reproduce the original charismatic's achievements. Yet after World War II, Iue founded the Sanyo Corporation.

Divisionalization and associated tenets became hallmarks of the Matsushita organization. All available evidence suggests that those ideas proved to be very successful. Expansion tends to slow after a firm has more than a thousand employees, but a mission-driven and divisionalized MEI continued to grow rapidly throughout the 1930s.

In February 1932, an export department was established— probably the first of its kind for an electrical manufacturer in Japan. By 1933, the firm was producing over three hundred products. In December 1935, Matsushita was formally incorporated as nine subsidiary divisions and four associated companies. In 1936, new production was initiated for electric lamps, fans, gramophones, public address systems, lamp stands, and clocks. In 1937, new capacity was added for storage batteries, record players, amplifiers, microphones, trumpet speakers, and electric hair dryers. During this period, employment increased from 1,102 in 1932 to 1,579 (1933), 2,183 (1934), 2,874 (1935), 4,007 (1937), 6,672 (1939), and 9,346 (1941).[20]

Despite the success of divisionalization at GM and MEI, few other firms adopted this organizational innovation until the late 1950s or early 1960s. For some companies, a reliance on a single undifferentiated product made it impossible to switch to a divisional form. But in many other situations, large departments fought the change, since a shift would diminish the power of functional heads. In still other cases, a lack of trust in middle management, missing managerial talent, or insufficient mechanisms to hold the divisions together stopped senior executives from adopting the new form.

The specific conditions at Matsushita Electric made most of these barriers to change less severe. The firm had multiple product lines that could be separated and assigned to different divisions. It did not have huge functional departments run by powerful and parochial individuals. It had a CEO whose tendency was to trust others. And it had a relatively strong culture that helped pull all the groups in the same direction.

Divisionalized organizations almost always, of necessity, give more independence to their parts than do functional structures. But for the overall corporation to succeed in the long term, the relatively independent units need to be operating for the common good, not just in their own parochial interests. Such integration can be very difficult to achieve. Matsushita Electric was able to overcome this problem through a strong corporate culture that stressed the greater good. Without that cultural glue, it is hard to imagine how the post-1933 system at MEI could have been so effective.[21]

But the lack of strong barriers to divisionalization does not explain why Matsushita was one of the first organizations in Japan, possibly the world, to adopt that form of organization.* When asked why KM embraced this structure long before other firms, people who knew him tend to give the same answer: because of his poor health.[22]

The physical problems that first appeared around 1913 continued intermittently throughout the 1920s and early 1930s. In his writings, Matsushita was generally vague about his illnesses, sometimes mentioning tuberculosis or lung problems, often just saying he was sick. Because he periodically took to bed, he relied

---

*Some people believe that MEI was the first corporation of any size in Japan to adopt divisionalization. I have not been able to confirm or refute this assertion.

on others out of necessity. The division system, many say, was a natural extension of this.

Other factors were also important. The boss's openness to new ideas and his strong sense of independence made him less likely than many to copy what other similar firms did. His twenty years of experience in a small business meant that he understood the virtues of small size. His dedication to a broader mission left him less interested in the authority that a functional structure gives a CEO and more interested in the results that could be obtained by the division system.* Perhaps most of all, his enormously ambitious goals spurred him to search for more powerful organizational forms.

Hundreds of well-known companies around the world retained functional structures after World War II because those arrangements were able to produce results that were acceptable to their executives. Especially in slow moving and oligopolistic environments, a centralized and bureaucratic approach to business produced often good, if not excellent, performance. Even after switching to a divisionalized form in the 1960s or '70s, some firms were able to continue operating in a centralized and bureaucratic manner because of low external competition and low internal standards.

In 1917, when he began the business, Konosuke Matsushita demonstrated high performance standards. By 1933, they were even bigger, broader, and more emotionally charged.

---

*The shift to divisionalization pushes power down in an organization. CEOs and department heads who thrive on the authority of their roles will resist such a move. That so many firms resisted divisionalization for so long says little that is flattering about a significant number of 20th-century top managers.

T he rapid growth fostered by divisionalization constantly strained resources, especially personnel. To help develop quality employees, MEI opened a sales training institute in April 1934 and a factory workers training facility in May 1936.[23]

KM called these projects his long-cherished dream. "I envisioned the training center as a place to educate and prepare young people as core employees of the company. I hoped to recruit outstanding primary school graduates throughout the country and offer them a three-year course made up of middle-school-level classes on electrical engineering and subjects from commercial school curriculums chosen as suitable for factory employees. The students would spend four hours in study, and four hours in practical training—altogether eight hours—and Sundays would be the only holidays. This would mean that within three years the students would acquire roughly the equivalent of a five-year middle-school education under the regular system, and be ready to become full-fledged employees two years earlier than the ordinary middle-school student."[24]

The sales training institute taught not only skills, but attitudes. A key lesson was: "You are not working for Matsushita. You are working for yourself and the public. Never forget that every single person you meet is your customer." Another lesson: "Sales is an important and noble profession." In a business culture that did not much value selling, MEI gave unusual status to the lowly salesman.[25]

The lessons KM and his lieutenants hoped to teach with both of the training institutes were only partially associated with business knowledge or technical skill. They also wanted to help people absorb the company's mission, its principles, its organizing methods, and its culture. Early employees had learned from Matsushita himself on a daily basis. By 1935, managers still had some exposure to KM in large monthly and yearly meetings,* but new employees saw little of the founder. The training institutes were designed to help pass on his most basic ideas.[27]

In 1935, Matsushita published a set of directives for employees that were carefully studied at the new company schools. One of those articles, number 15, probably captures much of what KM hoped to achieve with divisionalization. It reads: "No matter how large Matsushita Electric might become in the future, never forget to maintain the modest attitude of a merchant. Think of yourselves as being employed in a small store, and carry out your work with simplicity, frugality, and humility."[28]

As with the mission and principles, the ideas of "simplicity, frugality, and humility" can sound like meaningless bromides. Yet in a competitive environment, the complex, extravagant, and arrogant firm almost always loses.

By 1938, Mumeno no longer was playing any role in the business.[29] Her importance in Matsushita's private life was also diminishing.

The marriage lasted a long time, over seventy years, and whatever problems they had were certainly not very visible. In

---

*As a culture-building exercise, when the firm grew, so did the size of these meetings. By the late 1960s, the monthly conferences were for two hundred while the yearly management gatherings had an attendance of seven thousand.[26]

public Mumeno was the loyal wife, KM the conventional husband. When expected to be together, they were. In his autobiography, Matsushita has nothing but pleasant comments about his wife and their marriage. But at some point, the man with so many strong feelings appears to have stopped investing much of that emotion in his bride. In his later years, KM was seldom seen with Mumeno.[30] His autobiography has forty-four pictures in it, yet his wife is in only two of them. No picture is of her alone.

His spontaneous descriptions of Mumeno, given in interviews during his latter years, tell us something both about her and how their relationship evolved over time. Matsushita said his bride was strong minded, competitive, and seldom defeated. But in moments of unusual candor, probably aided by sake, he also noted that she had a quick temper, often talked too much, was manly rather than womanly, and was uninterested in history, literature, and the theater. On at least one occasion, he also suggested that he and Mumeno quarreled a lot, especially during the early years when they both lived and worked together.[31]

Their wedding, Matsushita reminded one interviewer, was "an arranged marriage. At that time, there was no marriage for love."[32] For a while, they seem to have been close. But we have little evidence that the relationship sustained itself in a romantic way. To some degree, he was just following in the footsteps of his father, Masakusu, who spent his last few decades away from his wife. Even more so, KM mimicked many successful Meiji-era Japanese men. Instead of considering a divorce, he eventually found romance, an ongoing relationship, and intimacy with someone else. As long as this arrangement was handled discreetly, it was seen as acceptable, indeed quite normal, especially among the upper strata of society.*

During the first decade of their marriage, Mumeno probably played an important role in his life. She had two children. She was often by his side. Her strong mind and competitive spirit were assets in the business. Later, she seems to have become a less and less central figure in the Matsushita drama.

By the end of the 1930s, the firm was in the middle of that drama, and by any standard it was highly successful. The business employed over 6,500 people.[34] It sold hundreds of products to millions of customers, and did so quite profitably.

One ring out from the center was his daughter Sachiko, whose engagement helped the decade end on a high note. The husband-to-be was Masaharu Hirata, a graduate of the Law Department of Tokyo Imperial University (now the University of Tokyo) and the son of a distinguished Japanese family. Masaharu's father was the equivalent of a European count. The wedding was held in April 1940. Receptions were given in both Tokyo and Osaka. Matsushita was a very happy father-of-the-bride.[35]

Masaharu had been working at Mitsui Bank. In May of 1940 he quit and began employment at MEI—not an unusual move under those circumstances in Japan.† Also in accordance with

---

*In a recent biography of Japanese entrepreneur Yasujiro Tsutsumi and his sons, Lesley Downer says, "In the classic Japanese way, it was [Yasujiro's wife's] job to run the house and rear the children while her husband's infidelities went unremarked. . . . In Japan until extremely recently, few wives would dream of expecting or demanding sexual fidelity from their husbands. In exchange for turning a blind eye to endless escapades and sexual peccadilloes, they could be assured of a home and financial support throughout their lives."[33]

†Morikawa Hidemasa says, "Companies [like] Morimura, Okura, Fujita, Yasuda, Asano, Furukawa, [and] Mitsubishi . . . made university graduates into top managers by . . . marrying them to the founder's daughters."[36]

Japanese tradition, because Hirata was not an eldest son and because KM had no sons, the new in-law changed his last name to Matsushita.[37]

KM must have marveled at how far he had come in twenty years. He not only restored family honor but vastly exceeded any past Matsushita glory, in both economic and social terms. His wealth dwarfed anything his father or grandfather had known. His new social position, as a relative by marriage of a historically important family, was beyond anything his ancestors could have imagined. He also had a happily married daughter, the possibility of grandchildren, and even a son, of sorts, to succeed him at the firm he founded.

His life may have felt like a fairy tale come true. It was in fact a roller-coaster car at the top of its run and about to descend rapidly.

10

WORLD WAR II

At the time of Matsushita's birth, Western nations were playing a significant role in Asia, and that presence did not diminish over the next quarter century. In the early 1930s, India, Malaysia, Australia, and parts of China had a British influence. Vietnam, Cambodia, and Laos were under French domination. The United States had control of the Philippines. All of the far north was a part of a Western-oriented Soviet Union. In total, much less than half of the land mass was under indigenous control.

The argument had been made for decades in Japan that the Western colonization of Asia should be stopped and reversed. After World War I, a growing coalition supported this idea, although with a variety of different motives and proposed strategies. By the early 1930s, the army and navy were at the center of this alliance and their natural methodology was war.[1]

Throughout the '30s, the military became a stronger and stronger force in Japanese politics and a more aggressive threat beyond the country's borders. In 1931, the army invaded Manchuria and stayed despite U.S. protests. War with China was started in 1937 and by July of that year the army occupied Peking. Back home, the seven cabinets between 1937 and 1941 became increasingly militaristic. Overseas, expansion continued with no formal declarations of war. The Japanese came to control most of China and in late 1940 moved into Indochina.[2]

The armed conflict with the United States began on December 7, 1941 with a surprise attack on Pearl Harbor. For a short time, Japanese victories came swiftly and efficiently. On February 15, 1942, they captured Singapore from the British. On April 9, they conquered U.S. forces at the Bataan peninsula in the Philippines. On May 6, U.S. and Filipino troops surrendered on Corregidor Island in Manila Bay.[3]

The huge momentum was blunted in June of 1942 when the Japanese navy lost the Battle of Midway. After that defeat, the Allies slowly came to dominate the struggle. The final blow came in the form of two atomic bombs, one devastating Hiroshima on August 6, 1945, the other Nagasaki on August 9th. Hostilities ceased shortly thereafter, with Japan in economic chaos.[4]

At the end of the war, Matsushita Electric was twenty-eight years old. For four decades, founder Konosuke Matsushita had been climbing out of the economic disaster into which he was plunged by family tragedies. At age fifty, at a time in life when people enjoy the fruits of their successes, he found himself in an impoverished country with a decimated corporation.

The militarization of the Japanese economy officially began in 1938 with the passing of the National General Mobilization Law. In March 1939, an employment ceiling was set for all nonmilitary industries. In October, price controls were introduced. Throughout this period, an increasing number of firms began producing goods for the army and navy.

Leading the list of war producers were the Zaibatsu, huge conglomerates that maintained close ties with the government and the military and that dominated many industries.* The big four were Mitsui, Mitsubishi, Sumitomo, and Yasuda. Others included Furukawa, Okura, Asano, and newly formed combinations like Nissan and Nakajima.

As early as 1938, Matsushita Electric manufactured a few products for the military. But as the war progressed, MEI and hundreds of other firms increasingly became the instruments of army, navy, and air force policy. Honda was asked to furnish parts to the navy and the Nakajima Aircraft Company. It also invented machine tools for making aircraft propellers.[6] In addition to electrical goods, MEI supplied the armed forces with bayonets, wooden propellers, wooden ships, and planes. In order to preserve resources to meet military needs, the firm had to stop producing room heaters and fans and to cut back on the manufacturing of radios, batteries, and light bulbs for civilian use.[7]

Matsushita Shipbuilding, Ltd., a company started in April

---

*In 1937, the three largest Japanese firms in many industries controlled production: 91.1 percent of the petroleum output, 97.8 percent of the iron, 91.8 percent of the primary aluminum, 67.5 percent of shipbuilding, 100 percent of automobiles, 100 percent of ball bearings, 60.7 percent of sulfuric acid, 100 percent of sheet glass, 83.1 percent of paper, 71.7 percent of flour, 99.4 percent of tar, and 77.7 percent of celluloid.[5]

1943 with capitalization of 10 million yen, was a part of a desperate attempt to reverse the momentum of the war. As KM himself noted on many occasions, the firm had no history or expertise in that field. "It was not as if we already had shipbuilding facilities at our disposal. We did not have the land, the workers, the technology, or the capital required for such a venture. We had been asked to perform a feat of magic, to make wooden ships out of thin air."[8]

Toshio Iue acted as president of the shipbuilding division. KM was chairman. They established factories at Sakai, Osaka and at Noshiro, Akita.[9] The problems encountered were massive. Adequate roads to the plant sites did not exist. Water had to be trucked in. The work force was too small and knew nothing about shipbuilding. Equipment was hard to find.[10]

They launched their first ship on December 18, 1943. With experience, lengthy workdays, and no holidays, output increased to one ship every six days. Under the circumstances, that rate of production was a major accomplishment.[11]

The wooden airplane venture was even more bizarre. Matsushita borrowed 30 million yen from a bank and bought 400,000 square meters of land in Suminodo, Osaka. The factory produced only three planes, but even that was remarkable in light of their total lack of expertise.[12]

As the war unfolded, the company both grew and changed. The division system gave way to a form of organization that emphasized factories and production.[13] Much of the expansion was overseas, following in the wake of military victories. In 1941, lamp and battery facilities were opened in Seoul. In 1942, a trading company was established in Peking, a wireless company in Seoul, another wireless unit in Taiwan, and a dry battery company in Jakarta. In 1943, the year that the airplane venture was launched, a lamp plant opened in Manila, a lumber company was purchased, and an industrial research laboratory was started. Additional plants in Seta, Shijo, Imaichi, and Hojo were established in 1944.[14]

Employment grew and grew. Although the 35 percent per year revenue increases from the 1930s dropped to 25 percent per year, the overall expansion was still staggering. By the end of the war, Matsushita had over 26,000 employees.[15] If the Japanese military had been victorious, MEI would have been well positioned to become a major corporation throughout Asia.

Everyone labored under increasingly difficult conditions during these years. People were asked to mass produce planes and boats without the supplies, the expertise, the money, or the required time. Near the end of the war, employees had to live with few consumer goods, food shortages, and the constant threat of bombing.

When Japan surrendered in August 1945, Matsushita Electric was a different organization than before the war. With sixty-seven plants, it was much bigger. Even more important, it no longer could be called an entrepreneurial consumer electronics company. Parts of the firm acted as a manufacturing branch of the armed forces. All of MEI was much more centralized than in 1939. Marketing expertise was lost, debt was piled everywhere, and employees were exhausted.

Konosuke Matsushita was neither a war enthusiast nor a military booster. Yet like virtually all his countrymen and women, he did little to resist the course of events in the late 1930s and early 1940s. To some degree, he probably felt that "liberating" Asia from Western colonization was a worthy goal. But even more, he was a product of a national culture which dictated that everyone support the emperor. The descendant of gods, the

Japanese head of state was not to be questioned, just obeyed. If the emperor said the war was just, there was no cultural basis for a moral discussion.

In his autobiography, KM says that "it was a time when Japanese were prepared to do anything, even give up their lives, for their country. This meant that, if ordered by the military, a company had no real choice but to make ships or aircraft or whatever else was called for. Part of my feeling, in accepting assignments, was a sense that I had to demonstrate my loyalty to the country."[16] After the conflict ended he expressed reservations. "Perhaps we should have refused the Navy's orders," he said at one point.[17] But during the early 1940s, he showed little inclination to buck the armed forces.

The war raised many troublesome questions. In the immediate aftermath of Pearl Harbor, every day Matsushita's employees continued to repeat the company's principles. But was the firm serving humankind and helping to alleviate poverty by being a part of a war effort? Reports of army brutality were completely censored in Japan, but everyone knew that the military was killing people. How can violence and death fit into a humanistic philosophy?

Hoping to stop the armed forces was unrealistic, but some form of principled resistance was always an option, at least in theory. From the little he wrote or spoke about the war, one gathers that Matsushita felt that any attempt to resist cooperation would be viewed as treason by the military, the public, his own employees, and maybe even himself.

The early 1940s forced him to think about where were his strongest loyalties. Were they to himself? To his family? The nation? His company? The principles and values he espoused? Because KM, like virtually all Japanese of his generation, had little subsequently to say about the war years, we will never know with certainty how he resolved these issues in his own mind. His actions strongly suggest that he gave the company priority. Throughout the horrible conflict, he took steps to protect the firm and keep it growing. At some point, the ritual of saying the principles out loud was abandoned. In the struggle between those principles and daily pragmatic realities, he subordinated his humanistic corporate mission to a lesser status.

He probably felt he had no realistic alternative. The military certainly could have crushed him in an instant. Or perhaps all the great successes from the 1920s and '30s were affecting his judgment. He was, after all, now a rich, famous, and well-connected citizen. Could not his fate be to grow even richer and more famous? And was that even remotely possible if he fought the military?

Ironically, the choice of pragmatics and fame over principles and humanistic goals would create monumental problems for KM and his firm when the conflict was over.

M atsushita and his managers spent most of the war years dealing with increasingly difficult circumstances. With more and more resources going to support the armed forces, less and less cash was available for consumers to buy electrical goods. KM and his lieutenants coped by trying to obtain a larger share of static or shrinking markets, by growing overseas, and by expanding into new product areas. As in the 1930s, they continued to introduce new products, reduce costs, and build the company. The firm still manufactured lamps and batteries and radios. But material shortages and rationing complicated all tasks, and dealing with government and military bureaucracies, instead of markets, could be immensely frustrating.

While some collapsed under the stress of those years, a crisis again seems to have invigorated Matsushita.[18] Before 1940, he often grew sick. After the war began, he gained weight and stopped retreating to bed.[19]

On some dimensions, he emerged from the war a stronger man. He faced a long series of crises, dilemmas, and conflicts, yet survived. He learned how to run a much larger company. He took on projects far outside the realm of consumer electronics. Although there is no evidence that he had learned any profound moral lessons from the war experience by the time that hostilities ceased in 1945, at least the seeds of those lessons had been firmly planted in a mind that was unusually willing to struggle with difficult questions.

Looking back from the 1990s, the terrible world war seems to have benefited Japan, MEI, and Konosuke Matsushita. All eventually grew stronger because of the disaster and then used that strength to excel in a globalizing economy. But the situation looked very different in the fall of 1945. At that time, only weakness and defeat were visible. As bad as the future looked when Japan surrendered, conditions only grew progressively worse over the next two years.

On September 2, 1945, Matsushita Electric received a communication from the Supreme Commander for the Allied Powers instructing it to cease all production. The company was told to check its inventory of resources and to file a report with Command Headquarters. Any use of those materials, without permission, was strictly forbidden. Shortly thereafter, the occupational forces made clear that they were going to reform all of Japan's institutions and fundamentally reorganize the economy. The changes started almost immediately and nearly destroyed Matsushita Electric.[20]

In November, the Mitsui, Mitsubishi, Yasuda, and Sumitomo holding companies were designated as Zaibatsu, gigantic anti-competition trusts, and told that they would be dissolved. The Mitsui, Iwasaki, Sumitomo, and Yasuda clans were called Zaibatsu families, and were subjected to a variety of new laws and controls. In March 1946, ten more companies were added to the list, including Nissan, Konoike, Riken, Furukawa, and MEI. In June, the Matsushita family was included in the Zaibatsu family grouping along with Furukawa, Kawasaki, Nomura, and others. In November that same year, Occupation Headquarters issued an order saying that all people of executive director rank or higher in Zaibatsu firms would be purged from their corporations.*

The net effect of these and other actions was devastating. KM was forced out of his company, but was left with huge personal debts. The firm itself was ripped apart. Thirty-nine factories outside of Japan were confiscated by other nations. Seventeen domestic subsidiaries were forced by the occupational authorities to become independent companies. Overall employment shrank from nearly 27,000 at the end of the war to 7,926 in 1947.[22]

In that year, 1947, the future of both Matsushita Electric and its founder looked bleak. Only those who knew KM's personal history could have seen the possibilities. Only those who had watched him conquer hardship and grow would ever have dared to predict his comeback.

It turned out to be a phenomenal comeback.

---

*By throwing out an entire generation of Japanese management, over 3,600 key executives, this order allowed younger men who were more open to new ideas to take over in the 1950s and 1960s. Those men eagerly adopted good practices from everywhere and, in the process, helped create an economic powerhouse.[21]

INSTITUTIONAL LEADER
1946–1970

11

UP FROM ASHES

T he war cost Japan millions of lives and a quarter of its national assets. One estimate places the number of buildings destroyed at 2,252,000.[1] People were disoriented, trying to grasp the meaning of defeat in a nation that had never lost a major war to a foreign power. Food was scarce and starvation was not unknown. The aftermath of two nuclear bombings was terrifying almost beyond comprehension. The economy was in a shambles.

Recalling those days in his autobiography, Sony founder Akio Morita said "only ten percent of Tokyo's streetcars were running. There were only sixty buses in operating condition and just a handful of automobiles and trucks. Most had been converted to [use] charcoal and wood when liquid fuels ran out.

Sickness was rampant and the tuberculosis rate was somewhere about twenty-two percent. Hospitals were short of everything, including bandages, cotton, and disinfectants. Department store shelves were empty or held a lot of useless unsold goods like violin bows and unstrung tennis rackets."[2]

Anyone could have seen that the immediate future of the nation and of Matsushita Electric would be difficult. Both the general conditions in the country and the specific circumstances affecting the firm were exceptionally harsh. Yet few people would have guessed the number or the extent of the crises that lay in MEI's path. Compared to the war years, the following half decade was even more hellish for the company, its employees, its management, and its founder.

M ost Japanese had never heard the emperor's voice until the radio broadcast on August 15, 1945 when he announced that the war was over. Since the middle of the prior year, Matsushita had known defeat was possible. Nevertheless, he was still surprised to hear the emperor declare an unconditional surrender.[3]

He slept little if at all that night. On the 16th, while millions of Japanese were immobilized in shock, KM brought his executive staff together to discuss the situation facing the country and the firm. In a meeting only a day after the emperor's announcement, he told his colleagues that he had strong feelings about what they should do. The message was focused, moralistic in tone, and delivered with steely determination.

"We must . . . set ourselves to the task of rebuilding the nation. This is the supreme duty of all citizens. The company, too, in accordance with its corporate mission, must rebuild its factories and strive to increase production of household appliances as quickly as possible. This is not only our mission, but our responsibility."[4]

Because he developed, of necessity, a great deal of self-control and talked rarely about his deeper feelings, it is hard to know what was going through his mind that day. For years, tragedies had been encouraging him to rethink goals and examine the purpose of life. The power of a humanistic vision was clearly demonstrated to him in the 1930s. By 1944, when the war was going badly, he must have considered what he would do if Japan were defeated. The answer for him and his company, he could easily have concluded, was but a slight variation on the mission already articulated in 1932 yet often ignored during the war. Selling such idealistic sentiments in the gloom following August 15, 1945 was no small task. But in a very real sense, Matsushita had been learning for decades the complex skills needed to inspire optimism in others—and in himself.

We have no record of precisely what happened over the next few weeks, except that KM and some of his staff worked exceptionally hard at beginning the reorientation to a peacetime economy. Whatever little momentum they built was stopped shortly thereafter. On September 2nd, the firm received orders from the Occupational Forces to cease production. All factories that had supplied the military were given the same command. Operating without approval from Allied Headquarters was strictly forbidden.[5]

The company submitted an application to manufacture household appliances. As they waited for a response, MEI management attempted to make changes that would shift the firm back toward a civilian consumer focus.[6] Permission from the authorities came in less than six weeks, a relatively short period of time, but a frightening period nevertheless because of all the uncertainties.

On November 3rd, Matsushita tried to rally his employees around the work that lay ahead. "The paucity of goods since the end of the War," he told them, "has been more severe than we ever expected. The only way open to Japan if its economy is to recover is to drastically increase and expand production, yet under present circumstances, this is no easy task. Our own living conditions, which provide the very basis and energy for increasing production, are extremely austere. We cannot survive simply on rationing, and the prices of goods continue to rise. We are rapidly heading for a crisis. If things continue in this direction, the Japanese economy may come to the verge of disaster. Therefore, no matter how difficult the circumstance from which we suffer, we must make one more resolute effort to resume production. I ask you all to grit your teeth and stay on your jobs. I firmly believe your brave perseverance will be rewarded. Let us try not to become defeated and demoralized by our hardships. This is the time when we must reaffirm our mission as manufacturers and do our best to increase production. I beg your cooperation and sincere effort."[7]

When the Occupational Forces passed a law in December 1945 that encouraged labor organizations, Matsushita workers formed a union, as did employees at all major firms.* Most of the time these new associations were being influenced by Socialists and Communists and were distinctly anti-company.[9] When managers attended inaugural union meetings, they were ignored or put on trial.[10] Sensing the mood of employees, corporate presidents kept their distance. The fact that only one major

---

*According to Michael Yoshino, "To the great majority of workers who were desperate to keep their jobs in the face of rampant inflation and to maintain at least a subsistence living standard, the organized labor movement appeared to be the only solution." As a result, "by 1947, more than four million workers, representing nearly half of the total of wage and salary earners, had formed unions."[8]

CEO is known to have acted otherwise says something about the times, the type of "Japanese management" practiced immediately after the war, and the unusual nature of that one CEO.

The Matsushita union held its first meeting in Nakanoshima Central Public Hall at the end of January 1946. In attendance, along with more than four thousand employees, was KM himself. Arriving uninvited, he took a seat on the main floor with thousands of others. At some point during the session, he asked to make a short speech. Those in charge said no at first, but then relented.

It was a bold move which could have backfired, strengthening the hand of radical anti-capitalistic elements. But some combination of luck, skill, compassion, and vision carried the day.

His talk is reported to have lasted only three minutes. He told his employees that he trusted their intentions. He said he believed management and the new union would be able to live together in harmony.[11] The more rabid unionizers hated the speech, but one of those in attendance that day claims that the audience responded with loud applause.[12]

It was a small but important victory during an exceptionally difficult period.

Like all the new labor organizations, the Matsushita employee association made demands on the firm that complicated its recovery. Yet compared to other unions, little militancy developed at MEI. Anti-company rhetoric was ignored by most employees. Communist propaganda gained few converts.

By February 1946, the magnitude of the reconstruction task was already immense. In March it grew even larger as the Occupational Forces designated Matsushita Electric a Zaibatsu company.[13]

Zaibatsu were large conglomerates often controlled by privileged families and actively nurtured by the government. One well-regarded estimate says that over a third of the total paid-in capital in Japan was held by the ten largest of these firms.[14] The Allies saw the huge combines as the core of a pernicious military-industrial complex. Although most policymakers were interested in rehabilitating Japan after the horrible war, others clearly wanted punishment.* A number of decrees issued around this time, including the attack on Zaibatsu, seem punitive in nature.

Once on the Zaibatsu list, MEI was given no relief from its huge wartime debts. The firm was subjected to a variety of controls that slowed decision making and severely limited management's autonomy. By mid-1946, both labor union demands and earlier government restrictions suddenly seemed like relatively minor problems.[15]

Matsushita was stunned by MEI's inclusion on the Zaibatsu list. His company was young and founder-led. In general, the big conglomerates were much older and much better connected with the Japanese government.[16]

While he was struggling to cope with all the proclamations announced in March of 1946, still more restrictions were imposed in June. During that month, the Matsushitas were designated a Zaibatsu family. As a result, all of their assets were frozen. Living expenses were capped at a level to match the salary of a typical public servant. To write even the smallest of checks required permission from Allied Headquarters.[17]

The problems continued to grow in July when five MEI plants were seized as "war reparation factories." Assets disap-

---

*Some people suggested that Japan not be allowed to reindustrialize. Others demanded reparation payments like those required from Germany after World War I.

peared overnight, but debts were left on the company books. In August, the firm was listed as a Special Accounting Company, subject to a variety of financial restrictions that made recovery still more difficult.[18] An increasingly angry Matsushita was prevented from taking actions he knew were necessary to rebuild the firm.

The biggest disaster of all came in November. As a part of the Measure to Purge War Criminals from Public Office, all MEI executives above a certain rank were told that they would no longer be allowed to work for the company. Those principals included KM himself. After founding and running the firm for twenty-nine years, he was being thrown out.[19]

Matsushita told others that the rulings were grotesquely unfair and highly illogical, but he was powerless to change them. At times distraught, he said he could not entirely believe the way events were unfolding. In November 1946, the situation looked so hopeless that his two closest advisors left to find work elsewhere.* Topping off an unforgettable year, in December, seventeen of the firm's subsidiaries were forced to split off and become independent companies.[21]

H e made more than fifty trips between Osaka and Tokyo to plead his cause to Allied Headquarters. Two other Matsushita Electric executives, Arataro Takahashi and Karl Scriba, made more than one hundred trips to the capital.[22] They all argued that the Zaibatsu label should not apply to MEI. They said

---

*Toshio Iue and Takeo Kameyama. Both men were related to KM. Iue was his brother-in-law. Kameyama was a nephew (sister Iwa's son) and was married to Mumeno's younger sister (Yoshino). Iue was a managing director and the number-two person at the firm. Kameyama had been promoted to managing director in 1942.[20]

that the firm was a young consumer electronics company with a good reputation. They maintained that they had been pulled into the war by the military. They pleaded with the Allies to allow them to help reconstruct the firm and the nation.[23]

For Konosuke Matsushita, the entire situation was humiliating, frightening, and enraging. His considerable anger is barely concealed in subsequent reporting of those events. "Far from being able to concentrate on the task of rebuilding the company, we were forced to spend time organizing information about our operations, and the reports and data we compiled at the time—all duly translated into English—came to a massive 5,000 pages."[24]

During the gloomy winter of 1946/47, assistance came from a number of sources. When the MEI labor union heard that the firm's founder was to be purged, it gathered more than fifteen thousand signatures from members and their families asking the Allied Command to allow KM to remain as president.* At the time, the Minister of Commerce and Industry in Tokyo was being petitioned daily by groups that wanted the heads of their businesses *removed* from office. When Minister Jiro Hoshijima received the Matsushita union's request, he was so surprised that some have claimed that he laughed out loud. With additional effort, the MEI labor organization managed to communicate to General MacArthur himself.[26] Sales agents also gathered signatures asking authorities to keep KM in charge. Actions by agents and the union may not have had a decisive influence, but those in Allied Headquarters and the Japanese government certainly took notice because the petitions were so unusual.[27]

The first concrete sign of a turnaround came in February of

---

*According to Okamoto, 93 percent of those union members asked to sign the petition did so.[25]

1947. The company was officially shifted from a "Class A" to a "Class B" list, allowing for an investigation into whether its executives should be allowed to remain in office. The inquiry was conducted in March and April. After looking at the facts, those in positions of authority apparently agreed that the firm had been incorrectly or unfairly classified. In May they announced that KM and all his executives would be allowed to continue working for the company.[28] After a year of continuously descending fortunes, the May proclamation was a godsend.

Other onerous restrictions continued to hinder the firm in late 1947 and into the following year. In February 1948, Matsushita Electric was made subject to the Law of Excessive Concentration. Until twelve months later when it was taken off the target list, the very real possibility existed that the company might be completely broken up.*

The struggle to regain control required in total more than four years. Not until 1950 were both KM and his firm released from various regulations and allowed to operate freely again. It was a long battle, nearly as long as the war itself. But this time, they won.

As the company fought to reestablish control of its operations, it suffered one financial crisis after another.

Inflation was rampant. Between mid 1946 and mid 1948, salaries at MEI grew by a factor of 7.5.[30] Price controls initiated in March of 1946 to help stop inflation created a black market for goods and made it virtually impossible to make money without breaking the law.[31] Under price controls, a Matsushita light bulb officially sold for 4.2 yen. In the illegal market, people paid

---

*According to Arataro Takahashi, the threat was to split the firm into six parts.[29]

100 yen for the same product. Because of the hard times and sensing an opportunity, the MEI labor union requested that workers receive at least part of their salaries in light bulbs. On one occasion, employees were paid with products, but KM stopped the scheme.[32] Supplying salaries in goods rather than money could have eased the firm's financial difficulties, but the practice would have implicitly encouraged workers to deal in the black market, something Matsushita thought was "corrupting."[33] It also could have drawn unfavorable attention from Allied Headquarters.

In mid 1948, Matsushita Electric ran out of funds and was forced virtually to beg for a 200 million yen loan from Sumitomo bank. Even with the infusion of cash, in October, for the first time in its history, the firm had difficulty making its payroll.[34]

During 1949, the Japanese economy grew worse after the government announced the Dodge Plan, an effort to balance the national budget by cutting government spending. As the economy slid into a deflationary spiral, a number of MEI competitors went bankrupt, particularly those in the radio industry.[35]

To survive financially, KM paid his bills slowly, especially debt to the government. In April 1949, the newspapers reported that Matsushita Electric owed an immense sum in taxes with total liabilities exceeding one billion yen.[36] In July, the firm cut back to half days only. Then in March 1950, for the first time in its thirty-two-year history, MEI laid off some of its work force.*

As a financial tactic, KM always maintained that he cut employment only as a last resort. "In all the time since the founding of Matsushita Electric, we had never discharged a single em-

---

*Out of 4,438 employees, 567 were laid off, nearly 13 percent of the work force.[37]

ployee in order to save money. Even during the tumultuous time . . . in 1930, we had laid off no one. But the postwar situation left us powerless. . . ."[38]

Matsushita's own finances were also in disarray. His bills were large because of the money he had personally borrowed near the end of the war to build the facilities needed by the military. In total, the debt was 7 million yen.[39] Because he could not sell assets to pay his bills, and because all of his wealth was tied up in the company, he had to borrow heavily to make ends meet. Friends extended funds that totaled in the hundreds of thousands of yen.[40]

The economic crises did not abate until 1950. The company began to make money that year and employment actually grew in 1951.[41] Details of Matsushita's personal finances have never been made public. He may have finally become solvent when the government unfroze his assets in July of 1950. Or it may have required still more time to settle all his debts.

A s difficult as were the control and financial troubles, the personal crisis loomed even larger.

The questions were haunting. After forty years of hard work, why was he once again suffering so? Could he have somehow avoided collaboration with the military? Did his zealousness to protect the firm and have it grow encourage production for the army? Did mistakes in his judgment nearly destroy the company?

The pressures were enormous, both externally and internally imposed, fueling fears that he could once again be plunged into the kind of horror experienced in his youth. During the postwar years, Matsushita developed serious problems with insomnia. He also started drinking more. Sleep came fitfully, only after alcohol and pills.[42]

The kind of reflection seen in the early 1930s became an obsession. "I began to study human nature and the reasons Japan
had come to such a pass. I asked myself: Why is it that humankind is in such a sorry state? Even though we are seeking
prosperity and peace, we destroy our own prosperity and wreak
havoc with peace. Is it true human nature to do this? Why do
people engage in such wars, bringing down tragedy upon themselves and literally inviting misfortune? Even the flitting sparrows
know how to enjoy life after eating a full meal. But human beings
get embroiled in wars and bring starvation upon themselves. Is
this truly humanity as it was intended to be? Isn't it possible for
us to have a better way?"[43]

His struggle to find the heart of important matters played itself out in daily interactions. When a recent graduate of Kobe
University's management program met Matsushita after World
War II, the first question KM asked was: "Would you please tell
me what you think 'management' is?" The young man rambled
on for a while, but failed to answer the question. Later, he said:
"I realized for the first time that although I had studied management at the University, I had never really understood the
essence of the subject. I had somehow missed the point."[44]

With self-reflection and the questioning of others, Matsushita increasingly did not miss the point. Before the war, he
had already developed into an unusual business executive. The
average company president was a competent manager. Matsushita had grown to be a leader. His inquisitiveness, his willingness to challenge the status quo, his vision, and his ability to
inspire his employees were far from the norm among corporate
heads in the 1930s and '40s. Yet those capacities developed
even more in the tragedies following World War II.

In 1950, the company that emerged from the ashes of war was
in many ways weaker than the same firm in 1940. It was smaller

and held more debt relative to its assets. But the leader who emerged at that time was certainly stronger. Once again tragedy had tested him, forced him to think and rethink, and rewarded a certain kind of courage and boldness.

The man who went into the war a citizen of Japan came out more of an internationalist. The man who wished to serve society as a means to grow his firm became more concerned with the condition of humankind as an end in itself. Company-centered visions gave way to broader social goals. Self-knowledge grew through painful reflection. Arrogance and egoistic pride took a beating. In the process, Matsushita became more than just a successful business leader.

In the 1950s, his focus began to shift toward building an institution with the right values, a company that could prosper in a rapidly changing global economy, an organization without the self-destructive seed that nearly ruined both Japan and his firm.[45]

The task was huge—which is probably just what he wanted, and needed.

12

THE GLOBALIZATION
OF AN ENTERPRISE

The year was 1950. North Korea invaded the South on June 27th, starting the first major war conducted in a nuclear age. Puerto Rican nationalists attempted un-successfully to assassinate U.S. President Harry Truman. Three million dollars was stolen in a daring robbery from a Brinks truck in Boston. European recovery from World War II was still in process, supported by the Marshall Plan and dozens of smaller relief projects.

In Japan, the economy was expanding robustly. Real GNP grew over 12 percent. But in noninflated currency, the gross national product in 1950 was still only three quarters as large as in 1939.[1]

Freed from postwar controls, Konosuke Matsushita and his

management began rebuilding MEI. They reintroduced methods and ideals that worked well in the firm's early years but were lost in the war and its aftermath. They began a search for more advanced technology. In a very big move, they aggressively sought to expand not only in Japan but throughout the world.

T he divisional management system introduced in 1933 was designed to foster growth by keeping product lines very responsive to their specific markets. When those markets became increasingly irrelevant during the war, the system was abandoned in favor of more centralized direction, a factory focus, and economies of scale. In 1950, when Matsushita regained control of the firm, he reinstituted the division system.[2]

Three product groups were created, one run by KM himself, another by son-in-law Masaharu, and the last by Arataro Takahashi. The first division manufactured radios, communication equipment, light bulbs, and vacuum tubes. The second made dry batteries and equipment related to electric heaters. The third sold storage batteries and transformers.[3]

To help direct the new organization and motivate the management, Matsushita brought together his executive staff on July 17, 1950 and gave them one of his optimistic pep talks. "Over the five years since the end of the war, Matsushita Electric has faced one problem after another. But even when confronted with adversity, we threw ourselves into the tasks that had to be done and worked as hard as we could. . . . We have at long last reached the point where we can see light at the end of the tunnel. . . . Now . . . we have a whole new mission to fulfill as a company, and when I think of Japan's reconstruction, I feel a tremendous sense of hope that inspires my work."[4]

Two of the new divisions were operating above break-even.

The one run by Takahashi was not. When he examined productivity, quality, technology, and skill levels among the work force, he found all needed improvement. But for this man who had worked with Konosuke Matsushita for decades, none of those factors seemed to be the central problem. The division was performing poorly, Takahashi eventually concluded, because they had abandoned key policies and strategies that had made MEI successful before the war.[5]

The seven business principles were no longer being read out loud in a morning assembly. When Takahashi asked one of his executives why, he was told that the union objected. But when he talked to representatives of the labor association, they gave a different story. According to the union officers, they had no basic problem with the seven principles or the practice of saying them daily. That ritual, he was told, had simply been discontinued by the previous management.[6]

Takahashi called his work force together, told them that he had studied their lack of profitability from many perspectives, and then delivered a KM-like speech. "The fundamental cause of our problems is that we no longer act according to Matsushita's basic policies. If we follow those principles, if we modestly examine our activities in light of those principles, we will succeed. If quality is bad and a product does not sell well, we have to stop the factory and improve the product. When we make goods of inferior quality, we are not contributing to society, and that is inconsistent with the principles."[7]

Takahashi revived the morning recital of the Matsushita creed and had his management reexamine the business in light of those ideals. As a result, dozens of practices were altered. Scrap iron that was discarded during the war was saved and sold. The factories were inspected every morning, and work would not begin until they were clean and litter free. The quality of products was studied from a customer's perspective and then improved.[8]

We know less about what happened in the other two divisions, but the general pattern seems to have been the same. Managers attempted to reinstitute or reinvigorate the mission, organizational system, and culture from the 1920s and '30s. The speed and difficulty of change varied somewhat from factory to factory, office to office. Overall, the misadventures of the 1940s did not destroy the core of the old company, for the organization was back on track in a relatively short period of time. Quality and productivity improved in all three divisions. A customer focus was renewed. Morale increased.

By early 1951, MEI was once again ready to expand.

As a consequence of World War II, businessmen in Japan became much more aware of the world beyond their national borders. With the military's encouragement, Matsushita had built dozens of facilities throughout Asia and then lost them all in 1945. A more conservative executive might have concluded that the risks of venturing outside Nippon's borders overwhelmed the advantages. KM and other farsighted Japanese drew a different lesson. The war convinced them that the Americans and Europeans were still much more technologically advanced. If Japanese firms were to flourish, they would have to learn from these superior powers. Learning, in turn, would require reaching out, travel, and foreign operations, all of which could be risky. But the alternative—a xenophobic focus inward—would be even more dangerous over the long term.

Konosuke Matsushita was fifty-six years old in early 1951. Despite the general human tendency to be less open to new adventures as one ages, KM decided to journey outside his homeland for the first time in his life in a trip that was ten times as long as anything he had experienced before. "We had to take a plunge into the international world of business," he told others, "and exploit the best traits of the Japanese in expanding our enterprise on a worldwide basis. Realizing that humility was the better part of valor, I decided that what I needed to do first was go abroad and . . . acquaint myself with what were then the world's most advanced management philosophies and practices."[9]

He left for the United States on January 18, 1951. He was scheduled to stay, mostly in New York, for one month. After only a week, Matsushita changed his plans and extended the length of the trip. One month stretched to two and then nearly to three before he returned to Japan.[10]

New York was vastly different from Osaka at the time, with the economic gap as large as or larger than the cultural divide. Back home, a chronic power shortage plagued the nation. In Tokyo electricity was turned off from 7:00 P.M. to 8:00 P.M. every evening. In New York, the lights in Times Square were bright twenty-four hours a day. A radio cost a factory worker in Japan one-and-a-half months' wages. In the United States, a radio could be purchased with only two days' earnings.[11]

He bought equipment for his plants. He talked to managers in at least a half dozen firms. Most of all, nearly every day he walked around New York. He was fascinated by the city, which is why he kept extending the length of the trip. He often went to movies, even though he did not speak English, because they showed him America—north and south, east and west. When he noticed that his hair style was out of fashion, he stopped having it cut short for the first time in his life.[12]

Subsequent events suggest that the three-month experience had a powerful effect on the man.[13] New York provided exciting possibilities that fueled his imagination. Many Japanese who visited the United States at the time became depressed by the vast gulf between living conditions in the United States and Japan. Once again, a huge challenge only energized KM.

When he arrived back home on April 7, 1951, he carried with him a vision of a prosperous and democratic community.

U nlike Sony, MEI was never a bold technological innovator. With its history and culture, the Osaka-based corporation was poorly positioned after the war to establish a basic research laboratory and leapfrog the West. But Matsushita's trip to New York reinforced his belief that the firm needed to move quickly to upgrade its technological capabilities.

In October 1951, he left Japan again for the United States. On this second excursion outside his native country, KM also visited Europe. His primary purpose was to find potential sources of advanced technology.*[14]

Executives at Matsushita Electric considered a number of joint-venture partners before finally choosing to focus on N.V. Philips. The Dutch electronics company was the fifth largest corporation of its kind in the world. MEI had done business with the firm before the war and Philips had reestablished contacts in 1948. KM believed that the two companies—both the

---

*In the following decade and a half, hundreds of others did the same. Between 1950 and 1966, 8,561 technical licensing agreements were made between Japanese firms and foreigners.[15]

product of small and resource poor nations[16]—had compatible corporate cultures.

On July 13, 1952, Arataro Takahashi was sent to Holland to negotiate an agreement with Philips. Because of the extensive homework already completed, Matsushita assumed the terms could be settled quickly and easily.[17] They weren't.

The general idea was to establish a joint-venture company in Japan with Philips providing the technology and owning 30 percent while MEI managed the enterprise and controlled the remaining 70 percent. In the negotiation with Takahashi, Philips asked for an up-front payment of $550,000 and a yearly fee of 7 percent of revenues. Takahashi said he would accept the terms, with a few modifications, if Philips agreed to pay MEI a yearly management fee. When the Dutch balked, the talks stalled.[18]

Major Electronic Companies, circa 1951

	Revenues (in millions)
General Electric	$2,319
Westinghouse	1,241
Western Electric	805
RCA	376
Philips	326
Siemens	235
Motorola	135
Honeywell	135
Zenith	110

Part of the problem was undoubtedly related to subtle yet important differences in philosophy and corporate culture. Philips was run by engineers. MEI had a more eclectic management and was driven by a mission that said almost nothing about technology per se. But Matsushita also saw a David and Goliath drama playing in the background.

"In the early fifties," he later reported, "Japan was still a poor, weak nation, and Europeans were inclined to think they could throw their weight around. The talks dragged on for a while and then the Philips side proposed that the deal be called off since no progress was being made. But Takahashi stuck fast and kept trying to persuade them of the validity of our claims."[19]

When many an American would have gone away howling mad, the MEI executive checked his frustration and stayed in Holland to communicate the merits of his case. With little weight to throw around, he stuck to the issues, repeating again and again the capabilities he felt his firm brought to the venture. Did not a great company like Philips want to work with the best Japanese electronics firm, an enterprise with excellent management that surely was worth a small fee? Did not Philips want better access into the large Japanese market? Did not Philips feel some obligation to help a country which, like the Netherlands, was small and lacked resources?

In the end, Takahashi somehow prevailed. "They had never encountered such stubbornness," Matsushita wrote in his autobiography, "but they seemed impressed with our persistence; perhaps it struck them as a sign of reliability."[20]

The historical record is unclear as to why the Dutch eventually gave in. They may have found no better alternative for increasing their presence in the difficult-to-penetrate, very protected Japanese market. Or they may have come to see that Matsushita Electric was an unusual, special corporation. Whatever the case, in the final accord MEI agreed to pay Philips a technical guidance fee of 4.5 percent per year and Philips agreed to pay Matsushita a 3 percent management fee.[21]*

The new company was established in December 1952. For a firm as big as Philips, the venture was not a major undertaking. For Matsushita, it was a huge commitment. MEI was officially capitalized at that time at 500 million yen. The new venture was capitalized at 660 million yen.[22]

A Philips/Matsushita factory was built in Osaka to produce television picture tubes, vacuum tubes, fluorescent lights, and other electric products and components. The plant opened in 1954, and most of the output was purchased by other MEI divisions to create finished goods for the Japanese market. A customer-focused, high-productivity, and well-led organization was now fused with world-class technology. The combination was powerful, and the products sold very well.[23]

In retrospect, the joint venture with Philips was an enormous success for MEI.[24] It helped the Japanese company gain access to advanced technology. It exposed the firm to a major European competitor. It sent MEI executives and technicians on a regular basis to Holland, giving them more of a global perspective.

When the contract with Philips expired in 1967, it was extended for a decade. The royalties this time were set at 2.5 percent for the technical fee and 2.5 percent for the management fee.[25]

On his first trip to the United States in early 1951, Matsushita purchased state-of-the-art dry cell manufacturing machinery. In the fall of 1952, when touring one of his battery

---

*Philips asked for a 7 percent per year fee but ultimately accepted 1.5 percent (4.5 percent less 3 percent).

plants in Japan, he found that those machines were the oldest type used in the facility. The lesson was obvious: "Machinery available on the market, I realized, was of generally mediocre quality. All the top manufacturers used equipment developed in-house, and they jealously guarded both the machines themselves and the technology by which they were made. . . . This discovery firmly convinced me that there would be no strength in relying on the teachings of others without a basic capacity for self-reliance."[26]

Using technology from abroad was essential in helping the firm catch up to world standards. But long-term dependence on others had many drawbacks, especially in a world of global competition.

In 1953, Matsushita Electric built a Central Research Laboratory in a suburb of Osaka. That facility, and others built over the next four decades, conducted research and assisted divisions in the development of technology that went into TVs, mixers, microwave ovens, recording heads, refrigerators, rice cookers, washing machines, and more. Consistent with the firm's past, the lab did not create whole new product categories, but instead improved offerings already on the market and developed equipment for automated production.[27]

The increasing sophistication of MEI technology both helped the firm grow in Japan and made the company's products more attractive in other countries. As a result, exports that were only .5 billion yen in 1954 grew to 3.2 billion yen in 1958, an increase of over 600 percent in only four years. In 1959, a sales company was established in the United States, where products were sold under the brand name Panasonic. By 1961, overall exports leaped to 13 billion yen.[28]

Foreign expansion required the establishment of overseas sales companies. Growing international demand eventually led to offshore manufacturing. As Matsushita Electric ventured further and further away from Japan, it found that most of its corporate philosophy could be implemented outside the home country, although with difficulty. Human nature was the same everywhere, but in some nations, especially in the West, the mission and principles seemed at first very "foreign" to local management. Trial and error taught the firm that sending its own employees abroad was necessary to transfer the company's culture.[29]

In the 1960s and '70s, MEI products began finding their way into more and more cities around the globe. Under the brand names of National and Panasonic, millions of VCRs, radios, shavers, TVs, and more were purchased by citizens of dozens of countries—hundreds of millions of people who, even today, would not recognize the name Konosuke Matsushita.

MEI's growth in the early 1950s was driven by an expanding world economy, the Korean War, and many new product introductions. In 1949, the firm began making cable broadcasting equipment and auto parts, in 1950 straight fluorescent light bulbs and FM wireless equipment, in 1951 washing machines and intercom systems. The company succeeded with these offerings due to a variety of strengths, including its mission and culture, technology from abroad, and a large domestic retail distribution system.[30]

As the firm once again expanded rapidly, MEI management grew increasingly proud of the company's successes. When self-confidence slipped into arrogance, Matsushita was quick to caution his people. "Some of you think that we have been developing without any serious errors," he told his managers at one meeting. "But we cannot allow ourselves to have that view.

When we look at management in the United States and Holland, when we study the reconstruction in Germany, it is obvious that our ideas and thoughts are far from perfect. If we continue in this way, we will never succeed in reconstructing Japan, developing Matsushita, and providing for the welfare of our workers."[31] To compete on a global basis, more would be needed.

One of the lessons from World War II was about the perils of hubris. As KM reflected on the disastrous 1940s,* he became increasingly convinced that a myopic point of view and a closed mind create great dangers. The best merchants he had known at the beginning of the century were open to new ideas and always humbled themselves before a customer. The military and government leaders he had witnessed at mid-century were often rigid and dogmatic.

The biggest factor that could limit the firm's future, he told others, was not the market. The potential around the globe was enormous. Technology was also not the central issue. They were learning about the best from Philips and would develop even better ideas themselves. No shortage of employees could be foreseen in a world with billions of people. Money could be a problem, but only if they stopped following his policies concerning profits.† The biggest issue was the firm's management, especially their attitudes. The challenge, as he saw it, was to create an increasingly large cadre of people who believed strongly in the company's core precepts, but who otherwise were receptive and flexible.

---

*And perhaps, the tragedy of 1899. He may have linked arrogance and disaster not only with the generals, but also with his father.

†Unlike most Japanese corporations, MEI's higher margins allowed it to fund more of its own expansion and to be less dependent on banks.

Konosuke Matsushita
with his wife Mumeno
at Arashiyama in
Kyoto (1941)

Matsushita with com-
mendations from the
Japanese government for
his firm's contribution to
the war effort (1943)

(Top) Matsushita giving a speech at the opening ceremony of the PHP Institute (1946)

(Middle) Osaka after WWII (1946)

(Bottom) KM at the signing ceremony which founded the Matsushita Electric Labor Union (1946)

KM at the time of Matsushita Electric's
30th anniversary (1948)

The first issue of the *PHP* journal
(1947)

Matsushita leaves Japan for his first U.S. visit (1951)

In New York (1951)

KM speaking to employees at the "Meeting to Swear a Great Leap," the
first anniversary of Matsushita Electric's reconstruction (1951)

KM signing a joint-venture agreement with Philips Electronics (1952)

Matsushita with one of his company's television sets (1954)

Matsushita relaxing at a New Year's party (1958)

Relaxing in 1961

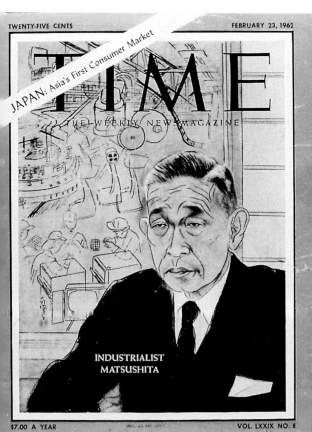

TWENTY-FIVE CENTS

FEBRUARY 23, 1962

JAPAN: Asia's First Consumer Market

TIME

THE WEEKLY NEWSMAGAZINE

INDUSTRIALIST
MATSUSHITA

$7.00 A YEAR

VOL. LXXIX NO. 8

On the cover of *Time* magazine (1962)

Doing a tea-ceremony at
Shinshin-an (1963)

Enjoying a walk in the Japanese garden at Shinshin-an (1964)

Photographed with his company's products when *Life* magazine interviewed him in 1964

Speaking to supporters of the PHP Institute (1965)

Honoring a Shinto shrine at
Shinshin-an (1965)

Doing calligraphy at Shinsin-an
(1967)

KM speaking to employees at Matsushita Electric's 50th anniversary (1968)

Explaining ideas from his book,
Thoughts on Man (1972)

Visiting China in 1979

Guiding Emperor Showa on the grounds of the Asuka Preservation Foundation (1979)

The Matsushita Institute of Government and Management

With students at MIGM (1982)

Chairman Masaharu Matsushita (left) and President Toshihiko Yamashita (right), Hall of Science and Technology (1981)

In 1984, at age eighty-nine

At the second Japan Prize award ceremony (1986)

With MIGM students at the Matsushita Memorial Hospital—this is the final photograph of KM released to the public (1989)

Panasonic Information and Communications Systems Center in Tokyo (1992)

"What is most important," he told one interviewer, "is to have an open mind. A man should not act only upon his own knowledge. There is a saying that 'a man will not become confused if he keeps his eyes open, nor will he be confused if he always listens to what others say.' Regardless of who the other person is, you acquire unexpected knowledge if you listen with a modest attitude, expecting to learn something."[32]

When Matsushita Electric began to internationalize in the early 1950s, it faced competition that was much bigger, better financed, and more technologically advanced. Many factors helped the firm overcome these obstacles. Japanese restrictions on foreign companies and foreign goods gave MEI less competition in its domestic marketplace. A strong customer orientation, low costs, a loyal and hardworking labor force, innovative marketing, a strong retail distribution system, an aggressive product improvement and new product development process, a capacity to adjust quickly to the marketplace, clarity of mission, a divisionalized structure which pushed authority and accountability to lower levels, and good leadership at the top all proved to be competitive weapons domestically and internationally. But subsequent events suggest that nothing may have been more important to MEI's success than open minds and humble attitudes. In the early 1950s, these qualities helped Matsushita and his managers absorb a great deal of new technology. Later, the same attitudes encouraged employees to bring in a myriad of useful ideas and practices from around the world.

In the process, the firm became stronger, renewed itself again and again, and outmaneuvered rivals. Thus, MEI began to position itself as an important competitor in an increasingly globalized marketplace.

Compared to nearly every other company in and out of Japan, Matsushita Electric's growth starting in the 1950s was explosive. Only two other firms saw equal success: Honda and Sony.

The Sony comparison is particularly interesting, because of the overlap in products.[33] There are many similarities between the two firms that may well be related to their phenomenal accomplishments. Both focused on consumer electronics at a time when the industry was booming. Both were run during their early years by remarkable two-person teams: Matsushita and Iue at MEI, Masaru Ibuka and Akio Morita at Sony. Both were much more entrepreneurial than other corporations, especially in Japan. They were willing to take risks, be bold, question convention, and move fast. Both tried to build strong brands—Panasonic, National, and Sony—and used advertising innovatively to do so. Both established their own retail networks to avoid a cumbersome distribution system at home. Both expanded internationally at a much faster rate than most Japanese companies. In all of these ways, the two firms were much more like each other than like the Japanese or world norm.

Both Sony and MEI were run by visionary leaders, but the visions were different in important ways. Tokyo-based Sony has always been a more urbane, educated, and sophisticated firm. Osaka-based MEI is the country cousin. Sony has been a high-technology company, pioneering totally new devices and new product categories. Matsushita took existing products and made improved versions that were less expensive and that could be priced for mass consumption. MEI critics called Sony "cutting edge" and Matsushita Electric "copy cat."

Differences in corporate vision and culture are directly related to differences in the histories of the firms and the key players. Konosuke Matsushita had very limited formal education, grew up in poverty, and began work as an apprentice in a bicycle shop. Both Morita and Ibuka were raised in wealthy settings, received university training in the sciences, and spent World War II developing technology. Ibuka was a gentleman of the old school, a fine scientist, and a man with a strong sense of morality. Morita was more of a wheeler-dealer, a salesman, and a publicist, but in a highly cosmopolitan way. Unlike KM, he learned to speak English fluently and socialized with the world's rich and famous.

In some ways, all four men—Ibuka, Morita, Matsushita, Iue—were alike. They were restless, ambitious, and much more willing than average to challenge conventions. Like most Japanese, they had known hardship. They were visionary, with big ideas and goals. They all developed many new skills during their adult years. But of the four, Matsushita was the extreme case. The other three suffered, but not as much as KM. The others talked of big goals and aspirations, but not on the same scale as Matsushita. The other three grew greatly during their adult years, but only KM took on totally new careers in his sixties, seventies, and eighties.

Of the four, the runt of the litter was Konosuke Matsushita. He was the sickly, nervous one from rural Wasamura. Yet even in this phenomenal group, his accomplishments would eventually stand out. Ibuka, Morita, and Iue were truly outstanding business leaders. KM would grow to be more than that.

Few pictures taken before the early 1950s show Matsushita smiling. During and after his first trip to New York, this changed, partially reflecting new photographic customs and partially reflecting an inner transformation.

When it became clear that the company would survive and

start growing again, KM acted as if he were being given another lease on life. The survivor guilt which turned success into sickness may not have disappeared completely, but it clearly receded into the background. Even with victory after victory, he no longer retreated to bed, as if he thought there was no time for rest. He could barely stop his mind at night, despite sleeping pills, and sometimes called associates at 2:00 A.M. with new ideas.

He wanted to internationalize the company. He wanted to help Japan grow economically. He wanted to guide others in the building of an organization that could prosper with less of his involvement. He wanted to direct the firm and the country toward meaningful goals.

The agenda was huge. In light of his history, it was also exhilarating, psychologically satisfying, and deeply meaningful.

13

FIGHTING ARROGANCE
AND COMPLACENCY

Japanese companies in the 1950s and '60s grew at rates that seemed to defy the laws of gravity. Near the front of the pack, a role model that influenced many others, was MEI.

A Comparison of Matsushita to Four Other
Successful Japanese Companies: 1950–1965

	1950 Revenues (In Millions of Yen)	1965 Revenues (In Millions of Yen)
Matsushita Electric	5,600.00	203,500.00
Kajima Corporation	4,382.24	147,549.40
Bridgestone	5,586.00	73,640.00
Kao Sekken	2,557.00	29,802.00
KDD	4,532.00*	14,075.00

* The figure is for 1953.

Source: Company records.

Revenue increases were associated with the new Philips venture, internal product development, and two major acquisitions: Nakagawa Electric, a refrigerator manufacturer with a value of 300 million yen, and the Victor Company of Japan, a nearly bankrupt record player producer that had been established in 1927 by the Victor Talking Machine Co. of the United States.[1]

The approach to acquisitions says much about MEI. When entrepreneur Yasuharu Nakagawa contacted Konosuke Matsushita with a proposal to sell his refrigerators through Matsushita Electric, the entire deal was done in thirteen minutes.[2] Later, when the refrigerator organization became a division at MEI, Matsushita asked Nakagawa to stay on and run the business. After selling their enterprises, successful entrepreneurs often leave because they find the environment in the buyer's company too stifling and risk adverse. But Nakagawa continued to head his former firm and eventually rose to become an executive vice president in the parent organization.[3]

At Victor, an outsider with no experience at a phonograph company was hired to head the new acquisition because Matsushita respected the man as a leader.* Although MEI was already selling products that competed with Victor, top management made no attempt to consolidate the product lines. The acquisition was allowed to operate as a separate unit. Matsushita told others that any loss in economies of scale or orderly organization would be more than overcome by the innovation and hard work encouraged by interdivisional competition.†[5]

---

*Kichisaburo Nomura, the Japanese foreign minister in the 1930s. Matsushita saw Nomura as "the ambassador to the U.S. who made efforts to prevent the war."[4]

†In the words of one long-time subordinate: "He liked competition and believed that though we may lose a few races, the important thing was that we won the bigger game. He believed competition led to progress."[6]

Fueled by these purchases and much internal development, the firm began to resemble the fast-growing prewar MEI. The sense of mission, reinforced in May 1955 by a gala thirty-fifth anniversary celebration, energized people.* The pain from the 1940s, if not totally forgotten, was no longer ever-present. Revenues increased rapidly. Sales for popular products grew at the rate of 50 percent a year or more. Profits went up and up. The employment office had trouble hiring people fast enough. Of all this, the firm's management was justifiably proud.

The management policy meeting on January 10, 1956 was a time of celebration for MEI executives. Few, if any, seem to have known what Matsushita had planned for the occasion.

Instead of dwelling on their many accomplishments, KM began his talk that day by saying that their current path was not, in his view, acceptable. The nation was still far behind the United States and Europe. Too many Japanese families did not have labor-saving devices like washing machines. MEI's duty was to help people obtain useful home electronic appliances and obtain them sooner rather than later. As such, the management should set an aggressive revenue target for 1961. They would have to decide what the right objective was, but Matsushita offered an opinion. The goal, he said, should be to quadruple sales in five years.[8]

Japanese politeness being what it is, no one stood up and said "The boss has lost his mind," but some of those attending the session in January of 1956 thought just that. Even Matsushita says his staff was "incredulous."[9] Lest anyone misinterpret his

---

*The thirty-fifth anniversary should have been held in 1953 but was postponed because KM felt the company was not yet ready for a big celebration. On May 5, 1955, he gave a speech to employees asking them to renew their vows of achieving the firm's mission. Later that month, sales agents, suppliers, politicians, and some well-known entertainers were invited to factory tours and parties.[7]

objective, he also made clear that "quadrupling sales is a goal set not out of greed for fame or profit, but as a means of fulfilling the duty I believe we as manufacturers have to society."[10]

For those who thought the target was too ambitious, he pointed to what they had accomplished in the past, to technological advancements that were possible in the near future, and to all the resources at their disposal. An honest and unprejudiced examination of the facts, he told others, would show that the 400 percent goal was not unrealistic. An open mind could see many opportunities.

The details of the plan developed by MEI executives and announced later included the following: sales would go from 22 billion yen to 80 billion. Employment would grow from 11,000 to 18,000. The research budget would expand by a factor of ten.[11]

Because of its boldness, the plan caught everyone's attention. Managers talked about it. Employees talked about it. Sales agents and bankers talked about it. As a pronouncement from someone without Matsushita's credibility, the objectives might have been ridiculed. With KM's backing, they had to be taken seriously.

Plan implementation encountered predictable obstacles. In 1957, Junnosuke Shinya attended a meeting in which engineers claimed that the screen portion of a new TV set could not be changed despite complaints from sales and marketing executives. According to Shinya, KM asked the head designer: "Do you know how many people live on this earth?" The man said: "Maybe two or three billion." Matsushita told him: "And they all share the same basic components, like a TV screen. In the case of faces, we have eyes, ears, noses, mouths, and hair. Yet the final design of faces takes two billion or more different forms. You're a professional designer. Given that a person's face is much smaller than a TV screen, you should also be able to create at least two billion different television screens. That's the mission of a professional designer."[12]

He fought relentlessly the idea that "it can't be done." According to Shinya: "We often read statements such as 'people have infinite potential and infinite possibilities available to them.' However, we often doubted the reality of such statements. We didn't really believe them deep in our hearts. But KM helped make us believe. He helped convince us that infinite possibilities really did exist."[13]

As did most of the very best Japanese businessmen from this period, Matsushita stressed "collective wisdom" as a tactic for accomplishing the seemingly impossible. In a division managers meeting during October of 1958, he told his executives: "From now on, we must face price competition. We have to reduce costs by as much as 10 percent. This may seem impossible at first because we will view such challenges with a limited perspective. We must learn to collect wisdom from others, including people from outside the company, in order to expand our perspective. Not only must we collect additional knowledge, we must also ask other corporations for support in helping us to implement new ideas. If we only see problems from our own vantage point, our ability to overcome them will remain extremely limited. Tapping into collective wisdom on the other hand will enable us to achieve our mission."[14]

If he were an arrogant and autocratic executive who rarely listened to others, his words would have carried little weight. But despite his strong individual presence, Matsushita relied on a broad spectrum of people for information, knowledge, and counsel. His example once again gave increased credibility to his words.

To shake others out of comfortable routines and to force them to draw on collective wisdom, he tied big goals to compelling ideals. In 1960, when Toyota told the car radio division at Matsushita Communication Industrial that it wanted a 15 percent reduction in prices over the next six months, the division's management complained loudly. In a meeting on November 24, 1960, Matsushita told them: "We must recognize that the issue here is not just an unreasonable request from Toyota. We are talking about a need for Japan to cope with increasing trade competition in the world, especially with the U.S. Trade is going to be liberalized and cars are our main export. In order to compete against America, Japanese cars must be very affordable. . . . We can't allow ourselves to wait for more demands like Toyota's before we effect significant change. We need to anticipate such requests and then position ourselves to meet them ahead of time."[15]

To fulfill Toyota's price objective, the car radio division implemented two sets of techniques borrowed from the United States: statistical quality control and value engineering. They also began to use product-development teams made up of engineers, purchasing agents, and salespeople. Brainstorming by the teams helped create better products at lower costs.[16]

With innovation, cost reductions, and new product development, the five-year revenue goal was ultimately accomplished, although not in the time frame stated in the original plan. The quadrupling of sales did not come in five years. It came in four.

The complacency-killing hand grenades went off again and again.

In January of 1960, at the annual managers' meeting, KM told his executives that he wanted MEI to become the first well-known Japanese corporation to change to a five-day work week while keeping wages at the same levels as other firms that still worked six days. The goal, he said, should be to adopt the system by 1965.[17]

He offered a number of reasons for the new five-year plan. He talked of the need to increase productivity in the firm and in the country. He talked about catching up with the United States where a five-day week was common. He spoke of giving Japanese workers time to enjoy their economically more prosperous lives. The audience listened politely, but with skepticism.[18]

The immediate concern among executives was that the firm would be giving away a key source of competitive advantage: significantly lower hourly wage rates than found in the United States and Western Europe. Even labor union officials, initially delighted, began to complain in 1963 that the plan was too good to be true. (How could salaries, fringe benefits, and other conditions remain the same if the work week were to shrink by nearly 17 percent?).[19]

Without MEI's mission, principles, culture, track record, and competent management, it is hard to imagine such an ambitious goal achieved in a firm that had grown so large. Even with all these factors pushing for plan accomplishment, because the Japanese economy was in a recession in 1965, a number of individuals advised Matsushita to delay the plan, not an unreasonable suggestion at that point. As usual, he listened to the advice and challenged their assumptions. Since the ambitious objective was ultimately good for the firm, for employees, and for the country, KM asked his management to find a way to make it work, despite the difficulties.[20]

On schedule, in April of 1965 MEI became the first major Japanese company to adopt a five-day schedule.[21] In the process of achieving this goal, productivity was increased significantly, while the shortened week made the Matsushita work force the envy of employees throughout Japan.

Rapid growth required constant hiring which began to affect the culture at MEI. Fewer and fewer people had lengthy exposure to Matsushita's mission and principles. A steadily increasing number of employees had experienced only great success. The net result was corrosive.[22]

To help counteract these trends, Matsushita repeatedly stressed the challenges that would come from a more globalized economy. "Protection has nurtured domestic industry and put foreign products far beyond the reach of most Japanese consumers. But these controls will eventually have to be discarded. When that day comes, American and European products, some clearly better than those made domestically, will be widely available. The consumer will have a broad choice of goods made by both foreign and Japanese manufacturers, and domestic industry will be the loser if it cannot beat the international competition. Up until this point, when we have thought of the 'competition,' it meant only other Japanese electrical appliance makers; now we will have to contend with other manufacturers throughout the world. I am determined that we shall not be easily bested."[23]

When his management achieved major growth goals without corresponding increases in profitability, he lectured them on their careless spending.[24] "If we cannot make a good profit, that means we are committing a sort of crime against society. We take society's capital, we take their people, we take their materials, yet without a good profit, we are using precious resources that could be better used elsewhere. . . . If many people in Japan do not make a profit, the country will grow poor quickly."[25]

Demands for big budgets, especially in R&D, were often met with stern and, some observers would say, old-fashioned sounding speeches. "Do you think Thomas Edison had any money at all to throw away on R&D? He had to support himself when he was young by selling newspapers. And yet without any R&D expenses, he was still able to make numerous contributions to the world." To reinforce the words, KM hung portraits of Edison on office walls and put a statue of the inventor in a garden at corporate headquarters.[26]

To help prevent individual executives or small groups of managers from behaving in parochial ways, he constantly stressed "collective wisdom" and encouraged others to do the same. Expanding on a practice found in virtually all successful Japanese corporations, KM insisted that decisions should be made with input from many employees and should be implemented only after everyone has had a say. The point was not to create a democracy where 51 percent of the vote carried the day. Matsushita was more than willing to be decisive. He wanted well-informed decisions that focused always on the broader mission of the corporation.[27]

Above all, he stressed humility. A humble person will not become reckless or arrogant. A humble person will pay attention to the idealistic mission, listen to others, and do what is right.

If Konosuke Matsushita had followed the practices of many of his U.S. peers, executives with expansive offices, hoards of corporate servants, and gigantic salaries,* his words would have had little influence. But even as he became a public figure, receiving an award from the Dutch government in 1958, flattering press in the *New York Times* that same year, a *Time* cover story in 1962, honors from Los Angeles in 1963, a major story in *Life* magazine in 1964, an honorary doctorate from Waseda University in 1965, and a medal from the Brazilian government in 1968, he rarely if ever seemed to succumb to the pomposity that so often accompanies great success.

Nearly everyone interviewed for this book spoke at length of KM's humility. Toshihiko Yamashita's comments from his own au-

---

*Matsushita's wealth came from his stock, not his salary.

tobiography are typical: "Mr. Matsushita is invariably courteous regardless of the other person's rank or status. At testimonial parties for retailers, for example, he used to bow politely even to junior store clerks and pour them a cup of sake. He lowered his head in a special way when bowing, fairly deeply but not exaggerated. I often stood beside him on such occasions, but I could never bow quite the same way. Either I didn't bend far enough or it was too deep and seemed affected. My bow was just a neck-stretching exercise; Mr. Matsushita's expressed his unassuming personality."[28]

For a man of Matsushita's immense stature to bow humbly to a junior store clerk is nearly unheard of in Japan.* Yet he did so, again and again. At one company anniversary celebration, he gave a speech to a large audience in which he thanked them for all their efforts on behalf of the firm. At the end of his talk, instead of going to his seat, he stepped off the podium, walked in front of the group, and bowed three times. Hundreds of grown men then broke into tears.[29]

If his primary goals in life had been fame and fortune, it is inconceivable that he would not have become insufferably proud of his achievements by 1970 and behaved accordingly. That Matsushita did not become an arrogant corporate chieftain suggests that his most basic objectives had grown to be elsewhere.

There is an irony here. The stereotypical arrogant self-made man wants desperately to obtain more riches and glory, yet his demeanor often undercuts that very objective. In Matsushita's case, as his most important goals became more social and humanistic over time, those values prompted a humility which helped him do precisely what was needed to keep his firm and himself growing richer and richer.

---

*As in Yamashita's example, I'm distinguishing here between mechanical bowing, which occurs as often in Japan as a Western shaking of hands, and humble bowing.

A t the yearly management policy meeting in 1967, at a time when the firm was experiencing incredible success, KM told his people: "Japan has achieved much in the past twenty years, but we are now at a point where we ought to carefully reflect on our assumptions and ways of doing things. Indeed, this is a time when all of us ought to seriously reconsider our fundamental outlook on life. Since the end of the war, we have worked feverishly and single-mindedly to rebuild the country. And today we have virtually accomplished that goal. We now have the leeway to pause and think about the future. What kind of a society, what kind of lives, do we want? I believe that it is time for soul-searching and reflection in preparation for a new beginning. Matsushita Electric should take this opportunity to look long and hard at itself before hammering out specific policies and plans for the future. We should make a genuinely honest appraisal of things, and consider the future of the whole country and the whole world as we do so."[30] He urged them to "free themselves from the force of habit." He urged them to "muster the courage to effect reforms, however drastic they had to be."[31] And then he offered another complacency-breaking scheme: to raise employee wage levels so that they would exceed those in Europe and be compatible with incomes in North America.

Once again, he asked them to look at the facts with an open and unprejudiced mind. Did they seriously think that low wages could always be a source of advantage for Japan? If not, was it better to adjust to future conditions before or after competitors? Would not this new five-year plan force them to increase productivity, benefiting the company, its customers, its stockholders? With the talent at their disposal, surely the collective wisdom of employees could find a way to make this seemingly difficult objective a reality.

Even after lengthy discussions, some people were not convinced that a steep raise in wages was a prudent idea. But with KM's high credibility, with many others eager to cooperate, and with a shrewd productivity-enhancing logic, once again most managers worked hard at trying to implement the boss's latest quest.

As wages rose, both managers and their employees discovered that they had to make significant changes in order to keep their costs competitive. Small and incremental improvements within existing systems were insufficient. They had to invent new and better methods, to adopt labor-saving devices, to cut out traditional practices that were no longer relevant, to further automate the factories, and more. As a result, by 1970 MEI was probably the most efficient large enterprise in all of Japan. More efficient than Sony. More efficient than Honda. More efficient than mighty Toyota.[32]

In 1971, four years after the commencement of the five-year wage plan, MEI salaries rose to approximate those in West Germany, the highest-income country in Europe. In 1972, the fifth year of the plan, employee wages at Matsushita Electric were close to the average in the United States.[33]

Average Yearly Earnings at Matsushita vs.
All Electrical Machinery Manufacturers in Japan,
1967–1971 (in Thousands of Yen)

	1967	1969	1971
Employees in Electrical Machinery Enterprises in Japan*	494	686	874
Matsushita Employees†	731	1,000	1,296

*Source: See note 34.

†Source: See note 35.

S uccession at the top of large Japanese enterprises is very much tied to seniority. The chairman retires or becomes an executive advisor, the president becomes chairman, and one of the two or three executive vice presidents becomes president. Among large Japanese corporations, this pattern has been widely viewed as the only reasonable way to conduct business.

Other alternatives obviously exist. People can be brought in from the outside or more junior executives can be brought up from below. In both these cases, more risk is involved. Yet with that risk can come new ideas, new approaches, and more innovation.

On January 10, 1977, eighty-two-year-old Konosuke Matsushita met with Toshihiko Yamashita, the head of his air conditioner division. At the time, Yamashita was twenty-fifth in the pecking order at the company, the second most junior of the twenty-six director-level executives. He had spent most but not all of his career at MEI and had recently taken a troubled air conditioner division to number one in market share in its industry.[36] With a strategic mind and a tendency to speak his opinion, the youngish executive "was not subservient to KM the way many other board members were."[37]

Yamashita was understandably nervous when he arrived at the chairman's office that day. "I realized something important was in the wind, but I had no idea what." Matsushita wasted no time in pleasantries. According to Yamashita, KM looked at him and said: "Board Chairman Araturo Takahashi is resigning and my son-in-law, Masaharu, will take over his duties. I want you to become president." The junior executive told others that he almost fell off his chair. "I was speechless. For an instant, I wondered if Mr. Matsushita was becoming senile."[38]

Many in the Japanese business community reacted in shock when the firm announced that a lowly division manager would become president of MEI. The press called his promotion the "Yamashita Leap," after the extraordinary jump by gymnast Haruhiro Yamashita that won a gold medal in the 1964 Olympics. Some predicted that the succession decision was a mistake, that the firm would run into difficulties, and that the new president would have to be replaced.

Matsushita's goal was simple, although risky. With incredible success and growth, MEI was beginning to experience the problems of size that have been seen subsequently at IBM, General Motors, and dozens of other companies around the world. His solution—not one employed by the faint of heart— was to shake up the organization.

At the time, an increasingly large number of executives inside the firm rationalized that any problems were due to the maturation of the home appliance market in Japan. "The market is no longer growing fast, competition has intensified, so what do you expect." Yet when Yamashita studied the situation with KM's "open mind" and "collective wisdom," he drew a different conclusion: "We had become sluggish, overweight, and myopic. Worst of all, the patient was so complacent that he didn't recognize his own mid life crisis."[39]

The new president announced that his first goal was "revitalization." He warned his executives that they were losing sight of how they had become a great corporation.[40] He eliminated a management level high up in the hierarchy*[41] and pushed for more candor,[42] more interdivisional personnel moves,[43] and more offshore production.[44] Most of all, he stressed "constant reform."[45]

Yamashita's boldness ran into predictable resistance, especially from some of the old-timers at the firm. They talked, al-

---

*Executive vice presidents.

ways in a very public-spirited way, about potential problems with his ideas. They knew that some face-saving action could be found to move the Young Turk out of the way. When Matsushita listened to these people, he found defensiveness and prejudice in their comments, so he took no action except to quietly praise and encourage his new chief executive.[46]

Yamashita left business decisions to division management with a few important exceptions. He committed the firm to making a four-hour VHS videotape for RCA even before his design staff had created a two-hour version. In a story that has parallels in the company's early experiences with radios, the product-development people then performed a miracle, customers loved the four-hour tape, and Matsushita won the battle against Sony for dominance in video recorders.[47]

Yamashita also put the firm back into computers. In 1964, KM stopped the manufacturing of mainframes, a widely criticized decision that has been seen by some observers as proof that Matsushita was not the "management god" so often adulated by the business press.* Yamashita did not reenter the big computer market, but pushed for the aggressive development of semiconductors.[50]

When he retired in 1986, few of those who questioned his appointment in 1977 had unflattering comments about his tenure as president.

Even innovative entrepreneurs can become conservative in their old age. Boldness gives way to caution, as they try to retain

---

*The move to exit the computer industry is generally believed to be one of KM's worst decisions ever.[48] Huge R&D costs eventually pushed a number of firms out of the industry (GE, RCA). In Japan, the government helped fund R&D through MITI. Some observers say that KM was convinced that MITI would never give his firm sufficient support but would instead favor older, better-connected Tokyo corporations.[49]

power and wealth. Ironically, the switch to risk aversion usually weakens a firm and makes it more difficult to preserve past gains. This did not much happen in Matsushita's case. In some ways, KM may have grown to be a little wilder in his eighties and nineties after Iue, Takahashi, and a few other counterbalancing forces either left or retired.

The Ullman poem he so loved says: "Youth means the temperamental predominance of courage over timidity, of the appetite for adventure over the love of ease. This often exists in a man of sixty more than a boy of twenty. Nobody grows old merely by a number of years. We grow old by deserting our ideals."

Instead of withering in his later years, Matsushita's ideals seem to have grown stronger. And with them, the reach of his influence expanded even more broadly.

PHILOSOPHER AND EDUCATOR

1970–1989

14

THE STUDY OF
HUMAN NATURE

In 1961, at age sixty-six, Konosuke Matsushita became chairman of MEI. Son-in-law Masaharu was appointed president. After stepping back into an operating role briefly in the mid-1960s, Matsushita moved further away from daily involvement in the firm when he became executive advisor in 1973 and Arataro Takahashi was named chairman.[1]

After succeeding brilliantly, no matter what the vocation or when in life, the question that looms is: what next? More of the same? Often a repetition of great accomplishments is not feasible after a certain age, as in athletics, or not in the best interests of the community, as when entrepreneurs refuse to empower the next generation. But if more of the same is not the answer, what is? Basking in past glories? Retirement on a golf course?

During his latter years, Konosuke Matsushita spent little of his time in traditional retirement activities. He did not play golf. He rarely attended the symphony or went on long vacations. Instead, he wrote books, funded a variety of projects, and worked with the PHP Institute.

PHP was officially founded by Matsushita himself in November of 1946 in the depths of postwar gloom. The stated purpose of the organization was to study human nature and help keep Japan from ever again embarking on anything as suicidal as World War II.[2] The basic concept was implied in its name. PHP stood for "peace and happiness through prosperity."

The institute was shut down in 1950 except for the publication of a monthly magazine. Research projects were resumed in 1961 when KM became reinvolved. With the completion of an office building in Kyoto in 1967, the scope of PHP increased considerably.[3]

During his last twenty-seven years, Matsushita spent many thousands of hours working with the little institute. Like any number of his initiatives throughout the 20th century, it was an unusual venture. Nothing quite comparable exists in the United States. On the surface, PHP activities can look naively idealistic, especially to a Western eye, yet those activities accurately reflect KM's priorities during the winter of his life.

He founded PHP in the same month in which he was officially purged from his company by the Occupational Forces. Since the institute stood for peace, and since its name was printed and spoken in English instead of Japanese, a skeptical observer cannot help but wonder if this was some kind of public-relations ploy aimed at the Americans.

At the institute's first official meeting, KM gathered thirty employees from Matsushita Electric.[4] He talked about the misery in Japan and raised questions about how that had come to pass. He spoke about prosperity and happiness and how both might be achieved.[5] He rambled on and on. People listened out of respect. One wonders what they really thought.

When he was unable to work for six months because of the Zaibatsu purge, he labored full time for the PHP "movement." Matsushita passed out handbills in front of Umeda Station in Osaka, leaflets that described PHP and announced the time and place of meetings. He made speeches once a month at Osaka Furitsu Library in Nakanoshima. He organized PHP activities in Tokyo and Nagoya.[6]

The Japanese responded with little enthusiasm. The MEI labor union asked why KM was not spending more time trying to save the company. When he attempted to convince them to join his crusade, they declined. Other groups reacted similarly. Despite considerable effort, PHP meetings rarely gathered an audience of more than one hundred people.[7]

In his autobiography, Matsushita reports vaguely that "at first, PHP activities did not go very smoothly, and there were various complications."[8] He does not say what these complications were, although one suspects a hungry nation was more interested in finding food than in discussing human nature.

In April 1947, the small and struggling institute published its first issue of a monthly magazine. In July 1950, after MEI was freed of all Occupation Forces control, KM suspended PHP activities except for that publication.[9] The timing of the decision again raises the question of his true objective, but there is no evidence that the institute endeared him to the Occupational authorities.

Matsushita himself said that PHP activities immediately after the war did not accomplish much. But he also said that the organization played an important role for him personally. "For those three years . . . PHP really was my emotional mainstay."[10]

The institute may have achieved some public relations goals. Yet Matsushita is right; even more so, the organization helped him personally. The early postwar years were enormously stressful. For a while, the real possibility existed that his firm could be destroyed, that he could be economically ruined, and that he might even be labeled a warmonger. Just as bad, for a time he was almost powerless to deal with these problems. Under those circumstances, and in light of his background, an idealistic activity could have been comforting.

If the institute were only a public relations ploy to impress the American Army, it would have become irrelevant after 1950. Yet when KM decided to cut back his involvement in his firm in the 1960s, he turned immediately to PHP.

I n 1961, Matsushita retired as president of MEI and became chairman. He continued to play an active role in the firm, but not in any operating position. In August of that year, he reactivated PHP's "research" activities and became heavily involved himself.[11]

By this time, he had enough money to buy a palace and a hundred ghostwriters to pen books on the secrets of great management. Yet when *Time* magazine sent reporters to talk to Matsushita in late 1961, they found the famous Japanese entrepreneur spending many hours in a "modest Kyoto town house" with a few employees from PHP. "In the monastic atmosphere of the institute's serene gardens," wrote *Time,* "he sips tea, eats flower-petal cakes, and holds seminars with his three young research fellows, discussing how best to bring prosperity and happiness to all. . . ."

He told the *Time* reporters that he believed that prosperity would be elusive until they could better understand people. "So with a humble heart," he said, "I want to study human nature."[12]

For the following quarter century, Matsushita encouraged PHP activities and personally participated in them. He spent thousands of hours discussing human nature and the implications for management, government, public policy, and everyday living.

With KM's support, PHP began a book publishing division in 1968, an international division in 1969, and an English language edition of its monthly magazine in 1970. In 1975 the institute published Matsushita's *Ningen o Kangaeru Dai Ikkan, Atarashii Ningenkan no Teisho Shin no Ningendo o Motomete* [*Thoughts on Man*] and in 1977 his *Watashi no Yume Nihon no Yume, 21seiki no Nihon* [*A Vision for Japan in the 21st Century*]. PHP began the first of a series of seminars in May 1977, started a magazine called *Voice* in December of that year, opened a branch office in Singapore in 1979, launched the first Asian-Pacific edition of *PHP* the following year, published a Spanish edition of that magazine in 1980, and held the first PHP seminar outside of Japan in 1981.[13]

In May 1983, the institute created the Kyoto Colloquium on Global Changes to generate policy proposals for the Japanese government, business community, and people. In his autobiography, KM says that he envisioned the colloquium "as helping Japan to fulfill a suitable role in international society." A core membership of prominent writers, scholars, and business leaders guided the project. Their objective, a typical Matsushita you've-got-to-be-kidding goal, was to seek, "by gaining a fundamental grasp of the problems shared by Japan and other countries, to provide feasible answers to difficult questions. With what philosophy should the peoples of the world pursue harmonious coexistence? What guiding principles can help bring about the creation of a new global system and order?"[14]

By the time of his death in 1989, the PHP Institute had grown to employ over three hundred people. The majority of these individuals were involved with publishing activities. PHP offered eleven magazines, most of them monthly, with a total circulation of over three million. The institute also published around four hundred books per year, including general interest nonfiction, textbooks, research manuscripts, and fiction for children. Hundreds of titles were also offered on video.[15]

Nonpublishing ventures now include management seminars, friendship clubs, and research activities. The PHP Management Seminars are mostly two- or three-day programs that over 180,000 people have attended. PHP Friendship Clubs are three thousand voluntary associations that engage in a wide range of activities with PHP encouragement and support. Research is guided by three major groups, one of which is the Kyoto Colloquium on Global Changes.[16]

Judging the influence of all these initiatives is very difficult. In many ways, the firm, which employed nearly two hundred thousand people at the time of KM's death, completely dwarfs the institute. Yet its magazine, *PHP,* has for some time had a larger circulation than any other monthly publication in Japan, a fact that is difficult to comprehend within the context of the United States or Europe.

The English version of *PHP* describes itself as "a Forum for a Better World." In one typical issue from the 1980s, a department called "Voices" featured short essays from readers in different countries. Dan Townsend, a camera repairman living in the United States, wrote on disarmament. K. Radhakrishnan Nair, an economist from India, focused on national enmities. Sushila Agarwal, a teacher in India, wrote about education for peace.[17]

The magazines, seminars, and books can all seem naively idealistic or worse to a skeptical observer,* but they accurately reflect most of Matsushita's activities during his latter years. Depending upon the lens one uses, PHP looks bold and visionary or like an expensive toy created by a very rich man.

T he body of thought that he developed in conjunction with PHP can seem as vast and complex as some religions. To a contemporary ear, the ideas often sound old-fashioned. Upon first exposure, people sometimes find the concepts to be simplistic on the surface, yet confusing or contradictory in their details. KM's habit of listening and borrowing pragmatic ideas from anywhere certainly contributed to this.[18]

Although expansive, the core of the PHP philosophy, very much Matsushita's philosophy, can be summarized in just a few points.

1. Human beings are by nature basically good and responsible.

"A noted political scientist once remarked that all realistic political philosophies are premised on the notion that people are inherently evil. Machiavelli's *The Prince,* of course, is the example par excellence, but there are many others. Plato's idea of the 'philosopher-king,' as developed in the *Republic,* and the Confucian ideal of government by the sages, both being expressly elitist, assume at the very least the people's inability to govern themselves. Such thinkers may be brilliant, but

---

*"A minor league religion," sniffed one interviewee who asked that he not be quoted by name.

they are wrong. Man is *not* evil by nature, nor is he foolish.
People are weak at times and fail to follow their conscience,
and too often they are lured by malign temptations, but there
are few whose hearts are not basically good and few who
cannot follow the dictates of reason to control harmful
desires."[19]

In light of his own personal history, especially the tragedies of
the 1890s and the 1940s, one might have assumed that Matsushita would draw more pessimistic conclusions about humankind. But he told others that he saw the vast majority of his
life as a testimony to the inherent goodness of people. Again
and again he gave individuals responsibility and trusted them.
Again and again they performed small miracles for him.

2. The human race has demonstrated a capacity for growing
   and progressing, both materially and spiritually.

"It is true that human history can be read as a chronicle of one
tragedy after another—wars, atrocities, persecution, starvation,
and more. But we have also continued to grow and progress, both
materially and spiritually. Science and technology have produced
security and comfort in our lives, and have given us the leeway to
grow in creativity. And through the ages the great religions have
helped more and more people attain peace of mind. Or think of
how greatly literary and artistic masterpieces enrich our lives, and
how much philosophers and thinkers have done to help us understand ourselves."[20]

He said his own life experiences supplied much evidence to
support this belief. He had watched hundreds of people, often
individuals with little education, grow to assume major responsibilities and to perform their duties exceptionally well. He had

seen his country go from a feudal kingdom to a rich and power-ful modern nation. He had watched his company grow and help make life more comfortable for billions of people. Perhaps most of all, he had witnessed firsthand his own phenomenal de-velopment over a period of eight decades.

3. Human beings have the power of choice.

In traditional societies, the gods or nature were believed to rule the world. Today, modern social science tends to see human behavior as being controlled by powerful genetic, psychological, social, and economic forces. The concept of free will sits uncom-fortably with both views. Yet free will was an important part of the Matsushita philosophy.

"I believe that people are free agents responsible for their own destiny. They have a choice. . . . One [road] leads to peace and happiness, while the other draws us toward chaos and self-destruction."[21]

The idea that we are mostly helpless pawns made no sense, he told others. In his own life, he had faced hundreds of im-portant opportunities to choose, starting when he was young and penniless: to stay with the Godais or leave, to continue working for Osaka Light or start his own business, to give up in November 1917 or to keep trying, to let up in the mid 1920s or set even higher goals. As he and his PHP research assistants reflected on his experiences, he concluded that if he had believed himself to be a powerless pawn, events would have swept him in a different direction, creating a very different life.

The whole idea that one has little choice, he felt, was crip-pling and disempowering.

4. We have the capacity to bring material and intellectual resources to bear on the difficult problems facing the world.

Assuming people are basically good, progress is possible, and the power of choice, axiom number four, follows directly.

"At this critical juncture in the history of our civilization, we need to get back our confidence in the essential rightness of human wisdom. We must reassure ourselves that we have the capacity to bring our material and intellectual resources to bear on finding solutions to the problems confronting our world. It is always easier to rally our forces in the face of a crisis, but we must not let the sense of crisis overwhelm us with unnecessary pessimism, for that leads to despair and immobility. Let us never lose hope for the future. Let us believe that the popular will ultimately governs the course of human affairs, and that because it is essentially good, the will of the people will prevail and lead the world into a new and better era."[22]

5. Solving difficult problems requires, above all, an open mind and the willingness to learn.

"Sunao is a Japanese word that usually denotes weakness or tractability in a person, an openhearted innocence and a willingness to be sincere. One could say that a sunao mind is an untrapped mind, free to adapt itself effectively to new circumstances. A person with this mind looks at things as they are at the moment and colors them with no special bias, emotionalism, or preconception. A biased person sees everything through filters or a distorting lens. To him, white paper might look blue or a straight line crooked. The true quality of the substance remains unseen, and the decision maker will be led astray if his judgments are based on what his biased perceptions tell him rather than what is actually there."[23]

The concept of the sunao mind is at the heart of Matsushita's thinking. Treat reality in a direct, straightforward, and honest way, he would tell people. Do not let neurotic impulses or political intrigue distract you. "When it rains," KM would say, "open your umbrella."[24]

He believed that this kind of mind could be cultivated by nearly anyone with effort. Schools could teach youngsters to think this way. Societies could help their citizens to see this way. The end result would be powerful. With a sunao mind, he reminded others, one can learn from any source, any encounter, anytime, and anyplace.

A well-educated person cannot help but be skeptical about PHP and its philosophy. With the exception of the "sunao mind," the ideas are not new. The overwhelming sense of optimism can seem naive. One logically wonders whether this entire endeavor was designed for some hidden yet instrumental purpose, possibly good public relations for the firm or the founder. When told that Matsushita deeply believed his institute's philosophy, that it was a part of his character, and that it helped him succeed, skeptics often smile knowingly and talk about mistresses, temper, or World War II.

Those who knew him well invariably maintain that he did sincerely embrace the PHP philosophy.[25] Most argue that this optimistic set of beliefs was a central part of his being, at least in the second half of his life. Look at his actions, they say, and imagine what would have happened if he held a different set of assumptions about human nature, progress, or the importance of humility. Without his belief in the inherent goodness of people, they argue, he would never have

developed the 1932 corporate mission nor given his employees great responsibilities in a divisional organization. Without
his belief that progress was possible and that humankind
could direct it, he would never have adopted a long-term
point of view, invested, taken risks, and encouraged others
to do likewise. Without his belief in the power of an open
mind, he would never have been able to keep his organization
as flexible and adaptive in the 1950s, '60s, and '70s.[26]

He also came to believe, they tell us, that humankind could
achieve much more if only people would embrace this kind
of philosophy. Matsushita did not see PHP's most basic ideas
as bound in time and space. He felt that they were as relevant to America as they were to Japan, as potentially powerful
in the 21st century as they had been in the 20th. And so, in his
declining years, he devoted great energy trying to create more
believers.

While others his age stopped to rest, KM sought to educate
and mobilize increasingly large groups of people. He worked
tirelessly to propagate the optimistic PHP philosophy. "Normally when we get older and attain a certain degree of wealth,
reputation, and social honor, we become satisfied," says
Masaaki Arai, a man who first met KM in the 1950s and served
as chairman of the board of the Matsushita Institute of Government and Management at the time of Matsushita's death.
"We think, 'OK, I've done enough. Now I'd like to resign and
enjoy myself.' But KM never thought this way. He continuously
pushed his goals higher and higher, always setting more difficult
objectives. He always believed that there were more things to
be achieved, that society could be improved more."[27]

He never retired, at least in the conventional sense, but he
gave up operating roles in the firm he founded and moved on.

For an action-oriented businessman, sitting in a modest Kyoto townhouse with research assistants and a philosophic agenda seems an unlikely next step. Yet somehow, this was not a discontinuity in Matsushita's life. For decades, he had been learning, growing, and reinventing himself. At age sixty-five, seventy-five, and eighty-five, he continued to do the same.

15

BOOKS AND
PHILANTHROPIES

Matsushita's first book dates to 1953, his last to 1990. In total, forty-six manuscripts bear his name.[1] Although many of these publications are short, the sheer volume of written material is still staggering.

His charitable contributions look more conventional to a Western eye, but in Japan there has been no tradition of wealthy self-made individuals providing large sums to good causes. KM gave away $291 million out of his own pocket and another $99 million from corporate funds.[2]

Both the books and the charities flowed from the work done in conjunction with PHP. He wrote about his philosophies in manuscripts that were widely read and gave large sums of money to support activities that were consistent with those philosophies.

The young research assistants at PHP did most of the actual writing, but the concepts came from Matsushita. The books explored a variety of ideas with one underlying theme— that we should reject the status quo and strive for something much better.

In *Shin Kokudo Sosei Ron,* he talked about Japan's lack of usable land.[3] Because 70 percent of the country's acreage is mountainous, the population density has been exceptionally high compared to most other nations. Crowding has created many problems: traffic congestion, pollution, poor housing conditions. The lack of arable land has also made the country dependent on food imports.

Matsushita urged that the nation embark on a mammoth public works project, an endeavor that would require a few centuries, with the goal of doubling the amount of usable land. This objective would be accomplished by leveling off mountainous regions, then transporting earth and rocks to extend the coast line into the ocean and to create new islands.

Sound planning and preparation would require the rest of the 20th century. The pace of construction thereafter could be adjusted to fit the short-term economic situation. During recessions, the amount of the work would be increased. During boom times, it would be slowed.

For those who thought such an undertaking was unrealistic, he pointed to Port Island, a 430-hectare landfill built near the city of Kobe. The project had been completed in a relatively short time, thirteen years, using material from local hills. If a city government could accomplish this, why could not the nation do much more? Were not the benefits—much less congestion, more farming land, more space for housing—worth the effort?

In another proposal from 1978, Matsushita suggested that Japan be eventually converted into a tax-free state by accumulating surpluses in each annual government budget. The idea was simple, and radical. Instead of budgeting to break even or to run a deficit, the national government would set aside 10 percent of all revenues each year into a savings account. The interest on these funds would be used to reduce the tax rate. After a century or so, the accumulated surplus would be large enough to run the government. To prevent the gap between the rich and the poor from growing, levies on the wealthy would continue. For the average citizen, the Japanese equivalent of the IRS would disappear altogether.[4]

Both the land use and the tax proposals are vintage Matsushita. They are boldly optimistic about humankind's potential. They demand that the government take a long-term point of view. They require sacrifices for the benefit of future generations.*

His proposal to change higher education was also radical, although in a different way. In Japan, elementary and secondary schooling tends to be challenging and rigorous. University education is less so. In a pattern that is often the opposite of that found in the United States, high school graduates sometimes see their college years as a vacation. KM argued that the nation could not afford four-year holidays for young people during what could be enormously productive years. Given the choice between making universities more rigorous and eliminating half the colleges in the country, he chose the latter. More people should get an excellent elementary and secondary education and then go to work. They

---

*Heavy deficit spending makes grandchildren pay for their grandparents' lifestyle. Heavy savings, as in the Matsushita proposal, does the opposite.

could then learn on the job. Quality education did not require a classroom.[5]

Lest his point be misunderstood as an elitist challenge to second-rate colleges, Matsushita wrote: "Now the University of Tokyo is one of the world's great institutions of learning, and even if half of the universities in the country were abolished, it would no doubt be preserved. Still, it is interesting to consider the hypothetical economic effect of shutting it down, for it costs the Japanese government on the order of fifty billion yen a year to operate [$500 million at 1994 exchange rates]. To eliminate this expenditure would be no small saving in itself, but we must also take into consideration that the University of Tokyo has land, facilities, and other properties that by a conservative estimate must be worth something like one trillion yen [$10 billion]. If these possessions were sold off to the public at the price named, and the interest on the proceeds calculated at 10 percent per year, the resulting income on savings to the government per annum would be one hundred billion yen [$1 billion]. Adding to this the previous fifty billion yen in operating costs, we find that closing the University of Tokyo would save the Japanese government about one hundred and fifty billion yen [$1.5 billion] each year."[6]

In a nation where most of the elite have attended the University of Tokyo, the idea was outrageous, even more so than if someone in the United States suggested that we examine the economic implications of closing Harvard, Yale, and Princeton.

When he first began making proposals about education, taxes, and land use, many people counseled that a successful businessman should keep his odd ideas about life to himself. Outrageous recommendations might turn people off, thus hurting his company. He listened to their advice, even agonized over it.* Ultimately, he published the books anyway. The manuscripts would provide him with an audience beyond Matsushita Electric employees. He clearly wanted a bigger audience.

His books on management were no less radical. At times, they ramble on and on, lack organization, or seem superficial. But the basic ideas are powerful and often controversial.

Nowhere does Matsushita talk about maximizing shareholder gain. Instead, he describes "private" enterprises as public trusts with broad responsibilities. "I believe that the mission or principal role of business management is to respond to and fulfill the desire of human beings to improve the quality of their lives."[8] Within Japan, talking about private industry as a public trust was not unusual, but the normal rhetoric emphasized "serving the nation," not "improving the quality of people's lives."

While others wrote about marketing or financial strategies, KM discussed human nature, the role of profit, the customer, the power of belief, and the importance of self-reliance. In the 1960s and '70s, while new conglomerates were being built in the United States and old ones were growing in Japan, he wrote that "it is my belief that a company should always specialize rather than diversify its operations."[9]

Most of all, he wrote about people, the human side of management, and leadership.[10]

People are important, he said over and over again. An enterprise is little more than the collective energy and capabilities of

---

*Just after the publication of *Thoughts on Man,* Matsushita told Mitsuko Shimomura: "I wanted to do the book but so many people around me discouraged its writing. I began to lose confidence. I still worry that I've made a mistake in having it published."[7]

its employees. The idea that a few individuals could build a great business only by themselves, through one or two clever strategic decisions, or with mergers and acquisitions, is absurd. Over the long term, the skill, determination, and motivation of employees is almost always key. "Collective wisdom" is essential.

Skill and wisdom are not mere commodities that you purchase. They are qualities that enterprises must nurture. The firm that aggressively develops its employees has a significant advantage over the corporation that simply exploits existing abilities.

Skills can be learned in many ways: from books, in classrooms, on the job, and through all of life's experiences. Nothing is more effective, in this regard, than delegating real authority and responsibility, even if people see it at first as a hardship. Giving orders all the time to employees denies them the opportunity to learn and grow.

Learning from one's experiences is greatly enhanced if one has sufficient information. Without information, people are simply unable to make intelligent decisions or to assess the impact of those decisions. Companies that do not openly share accounting, market, technological, and other data always restrict the growth of their personnel.

Learning from one's experiences is also enhanced greatly if one has an open mind. Teaching employees to look at life with a minimum of preconceptions is part of a leader's job. Another part is to help people believe in themselves and believe that nearly any task is doable.

Determination is especially important to an enterprise's success. A firm with less money and a smaller market share can often beat a bigger rival if its employees really believe in their capabilities. Attitudes are often central to success.

A determined group will display much motivation. A leader's

job is to enhance that motivation through an inspiring vision that is well communicated, through empowering structures, and by a good personal example.

A leader becomes a good role model when he or she is humble, respectful, open to new experiences, diligent, hardworking, and optimistic. In the final analysis, people make it happen, not the leader. But good leadership can help groups maximize their potential in the service of society.

Throughout Matsushita's management books is a most basic yet often implicit conclusion: that pessimistic world views and negative assumptions about human potential are crippling if your task is to build a successful enterprise. Gloomy beliefs undercut the ambitious goals, risk taking, humility, listening, and openness required to make both individuals and organizations grow. Hopeless attitudes become self-fulfilling prophecies. Negative philosophies that appeal narrowly to self interest or hate never inspire cooperation over a sustained period of time.

In a 1960 book entitled *The Human Side of Enterprise,* Professor Douglas McGregor at MIT's Sloan School called optimistic assumptions about human nature "Theory Y" and pessimistic assumptions "Theory X."[11] He argued that many managers have been taught to embrace Theory X and that those attitudes do not help organizations perform well, grow, or serve their communities. That observation, which is implicit throughout Matsushita's writings, was controversial when McGregor published his book thirty-five years ago, and it is still controversial today.

One other 20th-century Japanese industrialist wrote a great deal. Comparing his books to KM's is revealing.

Okochi Masatoshi was born in 1878, the son of a former lord

of a domain in the present Chiba prefecture.¹² He graduated from Tokyo Imperial University in 1903 with a major in ordinance and mechanical engineering. After further study in Germany and Austria, he obtained an engineering doctorate back in Japan and taught for a while at what had become the University of Tokyo. Starting in 1927 as head of the Institute of Physical and Chemical Research, he helped found dozens of different companies, including copier maker Ricoh. At its peak after World War II, his Riken Industrial Group was the fourteenth largest company in Japan.

Between ages fifty-five and seventy, Okochi published dozens of books and articles, some of which were best sellers in their day. The titles tell us much about his focus: *General Theory of Industrial Management* (1934), *Industrial Management as Science* (1935), *Industry and Inventions of the New Japan* (1937), *Industry and Side-Businesses in Rural Villages* (1937), *Machinery Industries in Rural Villages* (1938), *Japan: The Have Nation* (1939), *The Controlled Economy and Economic War* (1940), *Production as Primary* (1941), *The Oriental Economist* (1941), *The National Defense Economy and Science* (1942), *The Ultimate Success of Increasing Production* (1942), *Ways to Increase Aircraft Production* (1944), and *Rural Industries Combining Agriculture and Manufacturing* (1947).

Okochi was part economist, part technologist, and part military or national defense booster. As an economist, he warned about the dangers of the type of "passive capitalism" that emerged in Great Britain in the late 19th century. As a technologist, he urged his fellow businessmen to stop relying on imported Western science and to develop indigenous capabilities. As a militarist, he argued for self-sufficiency, more scientific commitment to military needs, and improved processes for increasing production.

Some of his ideas, if not the tone, sound like Matsushita, as when he talks of developing new products, lowering production costs, and thinking long term. But his biggest arguments are all centered on science. "Applying the most advanced science to industry," wrote Okochi, "will guarantee constant progress through innovation and invention."[13]

Matsushita believed so strongly in science that he founded the Japan Prize, currently the world's second biggest honor for technological achievement. Yet in his writings, it is very clear that he felt physics and chemistry were not the most important answer to humankind's problems. His management was not a scientific management. His philosophy was not a science-centered philosophy. In KM's world, peace and happiness would not come from a prosperity provided by the objective God of Science. Peace, happiness, and prosperity would come from open-minded people with humanistic values who had the courage to tackle society's most intractable problems.

Okochi seemed to be searching for the most powerful equation or formula. It is only a slight exaggeration to suggest that Matsushita longed for the most inspiring poem.

His charities funded activities that were consistent with the recommendations in the books and the PHP philosophies, and they clearly show the mark of life experiences. Much of the philanthropy was aimed at children and their education. His first gift in 1963 was to build a gym for the Kobe Canadian Academy.[14] In 1964, he funded the construction of a highway overpass as a safety measure for children. He gave still more in 1968 to help prevent traffic disasters for young people. Part of his social welfare gift in 1973 was earmarked for children. In

1975, he gave money to MIT and, in 1977, to help start the International University of Japan in Niigata.

In 1978, he donated funds for school construction in Peru. In 1979, he set aside $32 million to found his own graduate-level institution. He gave money to Harvard in 1981 and established an educational foundation in the United States in 1984. Also in 1984, a fund was created in Great Britain to train individuals to be engineers and researchers. In 1985, he gave a million dollars to Stanford University.

Just as the tragedies of his youth made him sensitive to the plight of children, the tragedies of the 1940s helped turn his attention to Japan's relationship with the rest of the world. His last two gifts reflected that orientation. One year before he died, he donated $27 million to establish the Matsushita International Foundation, an organization "to promote mutual understanding between Japan and other countries and to educate personnel capable of promoting the understanding."[15] That same year, he gave another $46 million to build an International Friendship Pavilion and Garden in Osaka.

His biggest philanthropy was the Japan Prize. Established in 1983, the award "is intended to honor scientists, of whatever nationality, whose research has made a substantial contribution to the attainment of a greater degree of prosperity for mankind."[16] Aimed at applied scientific research that is of direct benefit to humanity, the prize carries a monetary value today of about $500,000.*

The Japan Prize is pure Matsushita. It is grand in scope. It is idealistic in focus. It will probably still be having an impact at

---

*By way of contrast, a Nobel today is worth about $900,000.

least a century from now. And it is named after Japan, not its benefactor.

The world norm for large donations is very clear. We have the Nobel Prize, the Ford Foundation, the Rockefeller Foundation, and the Getty Museum. Alongside these institutions, each of which was established by an enormously generous gift, we now have the "Japan" Prize.

His philanthropies accelerated as he aged. From 1963 to 1967, he gave $360,000. During the next five years, the funding increased to $13.9 million. From '73 to '77 he donated over $21 million. During the next ten years, the gifts grew to $78 million. In '88 and '89, his charities totaled $276 million.[17]

Had he lived another decade, the gifts would have undoubtedly continued. His lifestyle was not lavish. He and Mumeno had only one child and three grandchildren. In light of his own history, the thought of passing on great wealth to his offspring must have given him mixed feelings.

One theme can be seen in virtually all the giving. He donated money to create incentives for socially useful achievements, not to save people from all hardship. Gifts to protect the weak and vulnerable were noble. Money that would encourage people to grow, even if that involved hardships, was his preference.

Many of the biggest lessons that he drew from his own life were related to growth: even the poorest can achieve much if they are willing to relentlessly stretch themselves; do not view difficult times only as threats, see them as opportunities to learn; in hardship and failure, one can be reborn stronger; success can stop personal development if it leads to arrogance and risk aversion; a willingness to humbly and honestly assess your actions is at the heart of personal development.

In many ways, almost all of his activities during his last two decades were oriented to helping others learn. He wrote to educate people. He gave money to support educational missions. And he continued, day after day, to provide an ongoing tutorial to virtually all those with whom he interacted.

He remained involved with the firm in the late 1970s and 1980s, despite heavy time commitments to PHP, writing, philanthropies, and the Matsushita Institute of Government and Management. Much of the total activity can be seen as educational in nature, teaching a new generation some of the lessons he had learned over the years.

When his managers showed him a MEI coffee maker and some competitive products in 1979, they were prepared for the kinds of questions that they and their engineers typically discussed: How many liters of water does the device hold? How many minutes does it take to make the coffee? How much energy does it use? What is the wholesale and retail price? But KM made none of those inquiries. Instead, after noticing that there were a number of different handle designs, he asked: "Which handle do you think is better?" Matsushita then proceeded to pick up each product by its handle and to pour coffee. He poured large amounts and small amounts. He poured quickly and slowly. "When our customers use this product, they spend most of the time doing just this." He looked up at his managers. "Here," he said, offering one of them the coffee pot. "Would you like to try?"[18]

Generally, he played the role of kindly professor. But when people vested with considerable power failed to implement well any of the basic precepts, Matsushita could be a harsh disciplinarian. The reservoir of anger developed early in his life could flash like lightning.

"On one occasion, I remember I had to report that, due to a variety of industry circumstances, we had gone in the red in our television manufacturing operations," reports Robert Kraft, who helped run Quasar TV in the United States. "Matsushita had been ill and the meeting was to take place in his spacious hospital room, which had been transformed into a temporary office. When I entered I found him seated at a large desk, bundled up in a heavy robe and reviewing a stack of documents. Looking thin and frail but alert, he scanned my report quickly. As he read, his eyes narrowed, his expression changed, and his face grew very dark. He virtually exploded in anger. 'If you weren't a division of a big company like Matsushita, you'd already be bankrupt!' he shouted."[19]

With all the success, after all the many accomplishments, even with hundreds of honors, the anger never went away.

16

EDUCATING FOR LEADERSHIP

T he Kennedy School of Government at Harvard University has roots that go back to 1936. Now located on the Charles River about five miles from downtown Boston, it is housed in an interconnected set of attractive ivy-covered brick buildings. Associated with what is possibly the world's most prestigious educational institution, this graduate school has seventy-five distinguished people on its faculty.[1]

The Matsushita Institute of Government and Management (MIGM) was founded in 1979 in a location about thirty miles southwest of Tokyo. The school's architecture is eclectic and international: a Norman gate, a Moorish bell tower, dormitories with cream-colored stucco walls. MIGM is associated with no university and has no full-time faculty. Administrators, part-time instructors, and students run the institute.

As this is written, the Kennedy School has seventeen people in the United States Congress among its 17,000 alumni. MIGM has fifteen people in the Japanese Diet among its 150 alumni.[2]

When Matsushita first explained his idea for MIGM to executives and politicians in 1979, more than a few politely listened in public and laughed out loud in private.[3] Fifteen years later, no one was laughing.

His introduction to the political process came in 1925 when he was elected to the district council in Nishinoda, Osaka. After winning once, he showed minimal interest in government or politics until the 1940s. Starting with the disastrous war, KM became increasingly concerned with the kind of people who were running the Japanese government. He always said that one should focus on strengths, not weaknesses, and as such he rarely criticized individuals or groups, at least in public.[4] But in a careful reading of his books and speeches, one can sense a powerful disdain for Japanese politicians.[5]

The pols, in Matsushita's view, were too short-term oriented in their thinking. They were much too willing to abandon principles for an expedient result. They often refused to tackle the big and important issues. Many were corrupt and lacked vision. Perhaps most of all, few were real leaders.

At first, he tried to reform politics by funding or backing specific candidates. This strategy had little impact, mostly because KM could find few visionary leaders seeking elected office. He thought seriously about creating a new political party, but his proposals failed to attract enough support from influential people.[6] Discouraged with his inability to achieve any reform in the short term, he adopted a long-term strategy through education.

MIGM was established in 1979 when Matsushita was eighty-five years old. His stated goal was to develop and promote leadership in government and politics for the 21st century. Like so many of his schemes, on the surface this one is preposterous. A small and distinctly odd organization, not associated with any university, would help transform politics for the next century by educating a new breed of public servant. Lest anyone get the idea that his school would promote business-as-usual in the public sector, MIGM was set up with a board of trustees, a group of advisors, and a set of counselors that included thirteen successful business executives, seven heads of nonprofit associations, five university professors, one former university president, one "commentator," and one politician (a governor from Kanagawa prefecture). The total number of Diet members, cabinet members, or high-ranking bureaucrats from Tokyo was zero.[7]

The little school was given an explicit mission and set of principles. The overall objective was to contribute to peace and prosperity by doing research on significant topics and educating a new generation of political leaders. Students would be selected and taught so as to develop in them five qualities: (1) a sincere belief that real determination can overcome nearly any obstacle, (2) a spirit of independence in thought and action, (3) a willingness to learn from all one's experiences, (4) an ability to break away from old stereotypes and traditional thinking, and (5) a capacity to cooperate and collaborate with others.[8]

The school would have only one program of two to five years for people who had already graduated from college. Traditional classroom teaching by professors would be minimal. Research projects, self-instruction, lectures by invited guests, and tutoring by fellow students would be at the core of the experience.[9]

The overall formula was, and still is, far from the educational norm anywhere on earth. In Japan in particular, with its autocratic and teacher-centered instruction, its emphasis on rote learning, and near obsession with pencil-and-paper testing, the MIGM approach was a dramatic departure from convention.

When the school began accepting applications in 1979 for its first class of twenty-three students, some observers questioned whether a sufficient number of candidates would apply. Matsushita said that they should not worry. He promised to open the school if only one student wished to attend.[10]

That first year, the total number of people who sought admission to MIGM was 904.*[11]

Reflections on his own life shaped the basic concept of the school. Hardships can be very useful, he said again and again, for building character, forging motivation, and forcing honest self-assessment. So the school would have hardships. Students would not sit in luxurious dormitories and be spoon-fed assignments and ideas. They would live in modest surroundings, work hard, and be asked to devise much of their own curriculum.

Because he believed that motivation and determination play such a crucial role in success, admission at MIGM would not be based solely on intellectual criteria. A person's goals and drive would be weighed heavily. Because an international perspective

---

*Twenty-three of 904 means an acceptance rate of 2 percent. The most prestigious universities in the world rarely have acceptance rates below 20 percent.

was so important in an increasingly global economy, all students would be given an internship out of Japan.

The overall goal would be learning, not teaching.[12] At his school, there would be few conventional classroom sessions, but much emphasis on growth. To develop a sunao mind and a merchant orientation, students would undertake humbling internships. Everyone would be required to study and empathize with other human beings and their problems. Everyone would be asked to examine not just the elite but the average fellow citizen. To develop the big and idealistic dreams from which leadership often springs, all students would learn about KM's life and philosophy.

Critics of the school have always wondered if it was meant to be the home base for a "Matsushita cult."[13] This may or may not be correct. What is undoubtedly true is that at a time when traditional education has come under increasing attack in both the United States and Japan, the institute offers an alternative model—and one that is different from the status quo in fundamental ways.

One of MIGM's graduates, Hiroyasu "Hiro" Komine, was a student at the school for two years, not the customary five, but his experiences are typical in most ways.[14]

He first heard of the institute when he was in high school. A friend showed him a brochure that had pictures of KM and of students working in a factory and on a farm. The list of part-time lecturers included well-known individuals in Japan, both in and out of academia. While attending Sophia University, Komine met a number of MIGM students and worked briefly with a few as a volunteer on an election campaign. In his senior year, he applied to MIGM himself.

The admissions process required three elaborate steps. First he filled out an application form, wrote a personal profile and a short essay on why he wanted to attend the school, and was interviewed by a staff member and an alumnus. Next he took an examination for general knowledge and English proficiency and went through a second set of interviews. Finally, after one more written examination, he was asked to meet with five members of the school's board of directors. Through this process, the institute chose Hiro and thirteen other individuals from a large applicant pool.

He moved into a Spartan MIGM dormitory in April 1989. If the admissions process had not already made clear that this was not a typical graduate school, the elaborate entrance ceremony surely did. Instead of immediately embarking on rigorous classes, Komine and other new admits participated in an induction ritual in which they were each asked to speak publicly about their hopes and plans for the future.

During their first month at MIGM, they learned about Konosuke Matsushita and his philosophy. Individuals who had known KM gave lectures which were supplemented by books and articles. In May, an assistant professor at the University of Tokyo offered a course on the Japanese economy. During this time, students also began to plan for more independent and self-directed work.

Their first internship started in June. Komine went to Karatsu City in Saga prefecture and worked in a Yoshida steel factory as a common laborer. The purpose of this activity, he and other students were told, was to help them better understand what life was like for the majority of the population and to learn what people thought about society, politics, and Japan. Upon returning to MIGM, Komine wrote a report on his internship and gave a presentation to others.

For a few weeks in the middle of the summer, all the new pupils discussed the international economy under the guidance again of their Tokyo University professor. Then from mid-August until October, they took a second internship, this time somewhere in Asia outside of Japan. Komine went to South Korea and worked for the Pohang Steel Corporation. He began at their training center where he studied the company and the country, and where he gave a lecture on modern Japanese economic history. Afterwards he went to a factory and again worked as a nonmanagerial employee. In late October, when Komine and others returned from Taiwan, Singapore, Thailand, Malaysia, Indonesia, and South Korea, they each made presentations on what they had seen and learned.

During November, a professor from Tsukuba University gave a course in domestic and international politics. Afterwards, the students worked in small teams to study specific topics. Komine's group focused on "technological strategy for Japan." Hiro looked at technology transfer to other countries from Japan and analyzed the Korean economy as a case study.

In January, most students volunteered to help MIGM alumni with their election campaigns. Komine worked with a candidate in Tokyo. In February, the students visited Kyoto for lessons on tea ceremonies from the Grand Master. At this time, they also began arranging for a third and longer internship. Komine chose to work with an MIGM graduate who was organizing a large conference on the environment. Between May and December 1990, Hiro helped create a two-day meeting which ultimately hosted over two thousand people.

Those who stayed for a third, fourth, or fifth year all focused on individually chosen projects. Many selected a place where they might center their political careers and began building a base. They conducted policy studies, met influential people, and built organizations. Some worked for politicians as secretaries. All wrote monthly reports for their supervisors at MIGM.

After graduation, most alumni keep in close contact with the school. They generate projects for students. They help each other in their election campaigns. And they hope—at least some of them do—to change the nature of Japanese politics.

In 1982, three students were asked by a visitor, "What is the most difficult aspect of the school's curriculum?"[15]

Kunihiko Okada, a University of Tokyo graduate: "We follow a process of self-planning, tailoring it to ourselves. We are responsible for deciding what we do and what we carry out. I think if we were given a particular assignment, that would be much easier. But not as pertinent."

Sumiyo Shimoyama, another University of Tokyo graduate: "I find it difficult to describe my career plan, since I have to consider whether or not the future society of Japan will accept a woman leader or not. I am a second-year student; sometimes I feel I should be specializing in a particular field. I can't always decide on the best option—that grows out of trial and error. So that's very difficult."

Toshihiko Yokoo, a graduate of Keio University: "The problem for the students in this school lies in choosing things for themselves. As Mr. Okada mentioned, we have to decide on our own curriculum, as well as a thesis. To set up the best possible program, we would have to know everything there is to know about society. But that's impossible. So we try to meet many people, and gather their arguments and wisdom, but it's still difficult. Even if we do set up such a curriculum, it is sometimes very challenging for us to keep our high ambitions.

"Sometimes we students—especially the ones who entered the school in the first year—call ourselves 'pioneers of the age.' The school is composed of people who are experimenting. In a sense, we are pioneers in society."

Judging whether MIGM is fulfilling its mission is difficult. To some degree, the same can be said for PHP and the corporation itself.

There are good reasons why one might be less than optimistic about the long-term potential of all three enterprises. Because of its small size and lack of attachment to any prestigious institution, MIGM struggles to have the impact it desires. That fact, in turn, will affect its ability to attract high-quality applicants. Now that Konosuke Matsushita is dead, PHP has to grow beyond being a publishing vehicle for his voice, which will not be easy. If the institute becomes only a KM propaganda organization, its usefulness will be limited. The company is running into all the problems that plague many big corporations today. A quick examination of the once mighty General Motors shows how difficult such problems can be.

Many factors will help determine the future of these enterprises, one of which is related to how well Matsushita institutionalized those beliefs that help organizations adapt to changing circumstances.[16] Do the cultures at MIGM, PHP, and MEI really value an open mind, a humble attitude, a customer orientation, and a desire for continuous improvement? Do the cultures value high productivity, a socially oriented mission, and the collective wisdom of others? Do important players in each of these organizations really believe in humankind's potential and in their responsibility to provide leadership to improve society? Or do they believe that KM was a man-god who should be worshiped instead of emulated? Or perhaps even more so now, do they see him as an historical relic of limited contemporary relevance?

Today, the answers to these questions are far from clear. Critics of MEI say that KM's business-building attitudes are sometimes hard to find inside the firm.[17] Instead, just like at IBM after the Watsons and General Motors after Sloane, they say one sees too much conformity pressure, inward focus, and bureaucracy.*

From society's point of view, the bigger issue is: will the Matsushita story be relevant, and thus useful, to other organizations in the future? Certainly some of his approaches to business are very much related to Japan and the specific historical circumstances in which he lived. But in an increasingly fast moving world, the capacity to adapt and grow lies at the heart of all progress—for individuals, groups, organizations, and nations. And that capability is at the very center of the Matsushita story.

"I was one of the last people to interview him before he died," says journalist Mitsuko Shimomura. "Even at that time, his passion, his energy, and his concern about Japan and the world couldn't be weakened. His curiosity remained high. He never sat down and took it easy. He was always thinking something, wanting to start something new. He was still attending meetings, writing books on various themes. He was always full of ideas. He wanted to start things and he wanted to listen. In a sense, I don't think he ever grew old."[18]

---

*Which leads, critics say, to problems like the acquisition and divestiture of U.S. motion picture maker MCA. MEI defenders point out, correctly, that rival Sony has had similar defeats and that MEI is again trying to renew itself.

Physically, Matsushita suffered from many of the problems that commonly come with advancing years. His vocal cords began to give out in 1978 and around that same time he had a brief recurrence of the lung illness, probably tuberculosis related, that had plagued him years before. Yet overall, he remained in remarkably good shape, especially for a man who had spent so much time in bed during the first half of his life. It is as if he not only conquered any corrosive feelings that ate away at his body but also generated through good works an aura that was healing.

Late in life when he said to his personal physician that he thought he would live for many more years, Dr. Yokoo respectfully pointed out that humans rarely survive beyond one hundred. According to Yokoo, Matsushita's response was: "But doctor, I am trying to undertake large tasks and to accomplish important things. If someone told you that you would live only another three, five, or even ten years, would you tackle big challenges? If we think we still have thirty or forty years left, we know there is still time to do great work."[19]

Emperor Hirohito was seven years younger than KM. The man who ruled Japan for most of the 20th century died in January of 1989. Three months later, on April 5th, Matsushita's ninety-four-year-old body developed a fever. On the 7th, his doctors warned the family that his condition was dangerous. For nearly three weeks, he was treated at the hospital, often drifting in and out of consciousness. With his condition deteriorating, fifteen members of his family arrived around 8:00 A.M. on April 27th. At 8:30, a nurse offered KM water and he took it.

"Do you want more?" she asked, but he shook his head no.

At 10:00 A.M., on April 27, 1989, he stopped breathing.[20]

EPILOGUE:
WITH A HUMBLE HEART
AND AN OPEN MIND

Two sets of questions were raised in Chapter 1, the first of which related to Matsushita's many accomplishments. How did he create a huge business enterprise, help with the postwar Japanese economic miracle, amass great wealth, and gain the admiration of millions? What role was played by specific decisions he made or specific policies he adopted? How did his childhood, character, skills, and still other factors influence his life?

That this most remarkable businessperson was a Japanese says something important about a small island nation. In some ways, KM is just an extreme version of a much broader 20th-century story. But the Japanese context cannot explain why Matsushita's legacy completely dwarfs all but a few of his fellow countrymen's. To understand KM's remarkable achievements, one needs to go beyond national culture and examine the specific details of his life. Although we will never know as much about his experiences as we would like, the story as it has been told here highlights a number of factors that are closely associated with his many accomplishments.

Success during his early years in business is directly related to the entrepreneurial strategies and practices that differentiated his little firm from the competition. A strong customer orientation, obsession with productivity and low costs, willingness to take risks to improve products invented by others, innovative marketing, speedy product development, after-sales service, drive for continuous improvement, faith in his employees, specialized retail distribution system, and limited business focus all helped his enterprise to grow rapidly and profitably. Decades before most other Japanese firms recognized the power of mass production and mass marketing, KM was leading the way. Decades before most corporations anywhere realized that one could dominate product categories by leaving basic invention to others while being bold in production and marketing, MEI was a role model. Fully sixty years before the publication of *In Search of Excellence,* Matsushita was discovering and using many of the practices that Peters and Waterman would describe in their 1982 book.

Like so many great entrepreneurs, he embraced methods that enabled his firm to compete against bigger and better financed rivals, strategies that produced a stream of superior or less costly products that appealed to customers. Such an approach to business demanded risk taking, but unlike Morita and Sony, Matsushita left the product invention or basic R&D to others while being bold in production, marketing, and after-sales service, an approach which often *reduced* the risk for his customers. The value of these methodologies became particularly clear in the 1929–1931 economic downturn. Those who wished to start businesses couldn't find the capital to back their ventures. Bureaucratic, cautious, and inwardly focused competitors often struggled to survive. Yet despite dismal economic conditions, Matsushita's enterprise expanded.

After MEI came to employ over a thousand people in the early 1930s, his success continued because KM grew with his organization. Going beyond being just a clever entrepreneur, he created visions that were idealistic and compelling. He worked relentlessly to help his employees understand and believe in those principles. He empowered people to act with a divisionalized structure and a relatively open sharing of financial information. Matsushita expected near miracles from his employees, and they responded accordingly, becoming stronger in the process. People with little formal education grew into inventors, supervisors, managers, and entrepreneurs. The ultimate test of this leadership came after the horror of World War II when, in spite of terrible circumstances, he inspired his work force to rebuild the company.

When his enterprise came to employ over 10,000 in the 1950s, it continued to succeed largely because Matsushita helped nurture a remarkably adaptive corporate culture. After World War II, in addition to an emphasis on customers, productivity, speed, teamwork, and empowerment, he also stressed international expansion and extremely bold five-year goals. Globalization and ambitious plans forced employees to search constantly for superior methods and to keep growing themselves. To reinforce these tendencies and to ensure that the company's success did not create a rigid and arrogant environment, he tried tirelessly to inculcate the kind of continuous improvement that is driven by humble hearts and open minds.

After his official retirement, instead of pausing to rest and enjoy the vast wealth he had accumulated, Matsushita took on new challenges that went far beyond the usual domain of business. He became an author, a philanthropist, an educator, and a philosopher of sorts. His ultimate success as a public figure is directly related to his willingness to reflect on his life and the condition of humankind and then to act on those observations.

From apprentice to merchant entrepreneur, to business leader, to institution builder, to educator and philosopher, the single biggest theme that runs throughout his life is associated with growth—as a human being, a businessperson, and a leader. Young Matsushita was not highly educated, rich, charismatic, or well connected. The man who worked side by side with him for thirty years, Toshio Iue, actually said that young KM was not especially talented. Yet from this humble beginning, he grew and grew. In a world where riches often lead to arrogance and apathy, he was remarkably unaffected by the forces of corruption. While so much of humanity stagnates relatively early in life, he took on a whole new career in education at age eighty-five. Because he kept learning and reinventing himself with the times, he peaked very late in life and declined only in his last few years. In the final analysis, it is this remarkable growth that appears to be most closely related to his achievements, more so than IQ, charisma, privilege, luck, or dozens of other factors we normally associate with great success.

Had Matsushita stayed at the bicycle shop, he would probably be unknown today. Had he stopped growing after becoming a successful entrepreneur, his list of accomplishments would be one tenth as long. Had he given up after World War II, the gigantic firm, MIGM, PHP, and the Japan Prize would not exist.

Actions that facilitated his development were simple but

nevertheless powerful. Again and again, he pushed himself and others out of comfortable routines, took risks, reflected humbly on successes and failures, listened carefully, viewed life with an open mind, and tried to draw from the collective wisdom of others. As a result, he and his company became stronger and stronger despite few resources initially or few unique product breakthroughs later on. Even after attaining great success in the late 1950s, instead of becoming arrogant, closed to new ideas, and risk averse, KM maintained his growth-inducing habits, and they took both him and MEI to new heights.

Of all the factors that fostered those habits in Matsushita, none appears to have been more important than his ambitions and beliefs. Starting with vague aspirations to restore family honor, his goals developed over the years until they became grand in scope and broadly humanistic in focus. The objective of regaining family wealth evolved into becoming a successful entrepreneur, then expanding a company, then creating a prosperous nation through that company, then helping to build a wealthy and peaceful world. Self-centered and personal economic goals became increasingly social in focus and vast in scope. These phenomenally ambitious and highly motivating aspirations spurred him on, put all his actual accomplishments in a humbling perspective, helped him to endure the pain associated with ongoing growth, and provided the basis for his principled leadership.

Beliefs operated in a similar way. Optimism in his youth may have been only a defense mechanism against depression: yes, life is difficult now, but it will surely get better. As he evolved, so did an idealistic philosophy that gained depth and character as it was tested and refined. That philosophy, in turn, said that risk taking, openness, listening, and humility were all rational actions.

His background clearly helped create these beliefs and aspirations. Many people were influential, none more so than his parents. The emotionally ravaged couple placed all of their hopes and dreams on their only remaining son. Those ideals and ambitions were subsequently shaped and strengthened by Matsushita himself, by the opportunities he encountered, and, most of all, by a string of tragedies.

Plunging into poverty at age four, starting work at age nine, losing his entire family before he was thirty, the death of his son, the Great Depression, and World War II cumulatively had an immense impact on this man. Tragic events created enormous hardships, but with support coming from parents, siblings, a master, a wife, a mistress, and others, those events also encouraged a degree of self-examination and questioning which influenced his goals, strategies, and philosophies. Hardships encouraged him to reevaluate and to learn. Difficult times produced a degree of insecurity which kept him ever alert and far from complacent. Living through tragedy taught him that he could survive failure and thus take risks. All of this evoked vast and difficult feelings—pain, anger, shame, humiliation—which became a powerful source of energy.

Simple diagrams can never capture the complexity of real life, but the exhibit on page 244 tries to summarize the relationships among Matsushita's tragedies, beliefs, growth, and accomplishments. It says, in essence, that to understand this man's unusual achievements, one needs to appreciate his phenomenal development over a lifetime, the mental habits used to foster that development, the set of ideals that helped support those habits, and the series of hardships from which those ideals emerged. In this remarkable flow of events, tragedies that often either destroy people or lead to sociopathic lives are turned into a source of great deeds.

The causal flow shown in the exhibit could be idiosyncratic to Matsushita's life, but that is unlikely. There is a certain logic to the pattern it traces that could easily apply in varying degrees to others. Successful businesspeople in America, Europe, and Asia who read drafts of this book have commented that they could see something of themselves here. KM himself demonstrated the broader applicability of those ideas by helping others to grow in a similar way. By fostering big and idealistic dreams and the habits associated with growth, he encouraged hundreds of people to develop into inventors, managers, entrepreneurs, and leaders. In the final analysis, all these others, not Matsushita, turned the little MEI enterprise into a 20th-century phenomenon.

The second set of questions in Chapter 1 asked what KM's experiences tell us about business and leadership. Can any generalizations be made that travel well beyond Japan and the specific time in which he lived? As we look to the 21st century and a myriad of economic and industrial challenges, what can be learned from this story that is potentially important?

If conditions in the next few decades were going to be easy, one might question the relevance of most of Matsushita's experiences. But with the continuing globalization of the economy, competition and change will make life challenging for thousands of businesses and billions of people. Under these circumstances, generalizations from more benign times become suspect while insights from the tumultuous Matsushita story may take on new meaning.

His life seems to say: forget about the typical mid-20th-century corporation with its centralized structure, many levels,

A Series of Tragedies

- Which led his parents to "pin all their hopes" on him
- Which taught him to reject the status quo and desire something better
- Which demonstrated that he could survive difficult times
- Which evoked powerful dreams

Evolving Goals and Beliefs

- Which were optimistic about human nature and human potential
- Which grew to be vast in scope and humanistic in focus
- Which made all his actual accomplishments look modest

Actions that Facilitated Growth

- Moving out of comfort zones
- Taking risks
- Reflecting humbly on experiences
- Observing with an open mind
- Listening carefully
- Drawing on the collective wisdom of others

Growth Over a Lifetime as a Person and Leader

- From apprentice
- To merchant entrepreneur
- To business leader
- To institution builder
- To philosopher and educator

Matsushita's Extraordinary Achievements

bureaucratic approach, internal focus, high costs, and slow response time. Such a company is no longer a useful role model. That organization flourished in a less globalized, more oligopolistic, and slower moving world. In the highly competitive economy of the next few decades, winning corporations may look more like Matsushita Electric of the 1920s, '30s, '50s, and '60s. The customer will be king. Productivity will be constantly improving. Employees will feel empowered and be committed to corporate goals. A premium will be placed on speed. Standards will be exceptionally high.

Forget also about the typical mid-20th-century executive. To fit into his organizational context, he was a cautious manager who often had little impact and who sometimes excelled only at pleasing his boss. In a competitive and faster-changing environment, the successful executive will have to be more entrepreneurial, more of a leader, and more of an institution builder. Like Matsushita, he or she will need to become customer and cost focused, to embrace optimistic and ethical goals, to communicate those visions widely, and to help others to perform to the highest of standards.

Forget, too, naive notions about success being a simple linear journey upward. KM's economic fortunes crashed twice, in 1899 and 1946. His health, psychological well-being, and personal happiness also fluctuated many times. In a volatile 21st century, this pattern could become more common.

Most of all, forget the mid-20th-century model of learning, careers, and growth. If current trends continue, the success stories of the next few decades will not be about people who are educated from age five to twenty-five and who then apply that schooling until they retire forty years later. Winners will be those who are both willing and able to grow throughout their lifetimes.

If there is any single lesson from his life that Matsushita himself seems to have thought would be particularly applicable and important in the future it was this: don't assume that we cannot continue to develop, and develop greatly, as we age. Yes, it is true that most people become more closed to new ideas as they become older. Success often creates arrogance and complacency. Failure often undermines one's willingness to take risks. But there is nothing biologically determinant about these tendencies.

His favorite poem says it all:

Youth is not a time of life, it is a state of mind, it is not a
matter of rosy cheeks, red lips and supple knees; it is a
matter of the will, a quality of the imagination, a vigor
of the emotions; it is the freshness of the deep springs
of life.

Youth means the temperamental predominance of courage
over timidity, of the appetite for adventure over the
love of ease. This often exists in a man of sixty more
than a boy of twenty. Nobody grows old merely by
a number of years. We grow old by deserting our
ideals.

Years may wrinkle the skin, but to give up enthusiasm
wrinkles the soul. Worry, fear, self-distrust bows
the heart and turns the spirit back to dust.
Whether sixty or sixteen, there is in every human
being's heart the lure of wonder, the unfailing
childlike appetite of what's next, and the joy of
the game of living.

In the center of your heart and my heart there is a wireless station; so long as it receives messages of beauty, hope, cheer, courage and power from men and from the Infinite, so long are you young. When the aerials are down, and your spirit is covered with snows of cynicism and the ice of pessimism, then you are grown old, even at twenty. But as long as your aerials are up, to catch waves of optimism, there is hope you may die young at eighty.

Sentiments about beauty, hope, cheer, and courage are often viewed with great suspicion in a world of escalating ethnic conflicts, huge disparities in wealth, and cold scientific rationalism. Yet the available evidence suggests that these ideals played an enormously important role in Matsushita's life and are directly connected to his powerful leadership and his extraordinary achievements. They gave direction to difficult emotions, especially sadness and anger. They kept him thinking like a young man, open to change and eager to learn.

It is hard to say how much of this overall pattern is uniquely Japanese or Eastern. Certainly some aspects of this story do not sound like the Americas or Europe. But KM's ideas did help transform a disastrous Quasar television operation in the United States into a moneymaker. His products have attracted customers everywhere around the globe. His practices, having been discovered by Western Japanologists, are now helping corporations in many lands.

On the surface, he was very much an Asian. But it is telling that the poem he loved so dearly was written by a European-born Jew who lived most of his life in Birmingham, Alabama.

Konosuke Matsushita's most basic and potentially most powerful ideas are about the roots of lifelong learning. A privileged background and degrees from the University of Tokyo (or Harvard or Oxford) are nice, he would say, but they are not essential. The same is true of unusually high intelligence, good looks, and a dramatic personality. More important than any of these factors are certain habits and a set of ideals that help support those habits. With a humble heart and an open mind, he told people again and again, one can learn from any experience and at any age. With ideals that are big and humanistic, one can conquer success and failure, learn from both, and continue to grow.

His extraordinary life stands as a powerful testimony to these propositions.

LESSONS FOR THE 21ST CENTURY

In a changing environment, lifelong learning may be more related to great success or unusual achievements than IQ, parental socioeconomic status, charisma, and formal education.

Lifelong learning is closely associated with humility, an open mind, a willingness to take risks, a capacity to listen, and honest self reflection.

Big idealistic/humanistic goals and beliefs are not incompatible with success in business. They may even foster achievements, at least in a rapidly changing context, by supporting those habits which encourage growth.

Hardships are not necessarily career or life killers. Under the right conditions, tough times can nurture big idealistic goals, continuous growth, and great accomplishments.

A COMMENT ON SOURCES

Much written material exists on Konosuke Matsushita and Matsushita Electric. Most of the paperwork is in Japanese and can be found in libraries at MEI (Osaka), PHP (Kyoto), and MIGM (Chigasaki City). In addition to drawing extensively on these sources, a research assistant and I interviewed seventy people in Japan. These discussions were used to confirm the validity of the written record, to collect additional anecdotes, and to gather opinions about the man and his enterprise.

Because KM's autobiography, *Quest for Prosperity,* is closer to an historical record than many similar works, and because interviewees uniformly testified to its basic validity, I have relied on that publication more extensively than would normally be prudent in this kind of undertaking. Instead of being created from memory late in life, the autobiography is a compilation of reports written between 1934 and 1976. Over half was first published in Matsushita Electric's company bulletins in the late 1930s and early 1940s. Most of the rest is based on two series of articles written for the *Nihon Keizai Shimbun* in 1956 and 1976.

Drafts of this book were given to MEI, PHP, and MIGM, as well as more independent sources, to check for factual errors and to critique the presentation and conclusions. A list of specific individuals who helped in this way can be found in the Preface.

NOTES

Chapter 1. The Legacy

1. Height and weight estimates provided by Mototaka Yoshitani, Associate Councilor in the Office of Corporate History, Matsushita Electric, May 12, 1993.
2. Based on a report published in Ogawa's book *Pana Management* (Kyoto: PHP Institute, 1991), pp. 133–135.
3. From "Thirty Important Points for People in Sales," Matsushita Electric Monthly Report, January and February 1936. These ideas were developed during Matsushita's first fifteen years in business (1917–1932).
4. Quote from Matsushita's autobiography *Quest for Prosperity* (Kyoto: PHP Institute, 1988), pp. 202, 203.
5. Konosuke Matsushita, *Not For Bread Alone: A Business Ethos, A Management Ethic* (Kyoto: PHP, 1984), pp. 87 and 88.
6. All taken from an interview with Mukasa on February 19, 1992.
7. See *In Search of Excellence* (New York: Harper & Row, 1982).
8. See Warren Bennis and Burt Nanus, *Leaders* (New York: Harper & Row, 1985), Noel Tichy and Mary Anne Devanna,

The Transformational Leader (New York: John Wiley, 1986), and John P. Kotter, *A Force for Change: How Leadership Differs from Management* (New York: Free Press, 1990).

9. See Ogawa, *Pana Management* (Kyoto: PHP Institute, 1991), pp. 134, 135, and 136.
10. See, for example, Richard A. Kraft, "Great Patience!" *Intersect,* June 1994, pp. 17 and 18.
11. From an interview with Masaharu Matsushita on February 19, 1992.
12. Ibid. The man who knew him best, son-in-law Masaharu, believes he was very lonely at times.
13. He had three sons and a daughter by this woman. He acknowledged all the children and provided for them economically.
14. Katsuhiko Eguchi, who worked with KM after 1967, says he would regularly get phone calls in the middle of the night from his restless boss. (Interview on February 18, 1992.) Sadayoshi Yokoo, KM's physician during his last two decades, says that Matsushita took a sleeping pill every night. (Interview on November 4, 1993.)
15. From an interview on September 7, 1994.
16. I considered a number of alternatives to a chronological presentation before deciding that they all had serious drawbacks. A non-chronological structure can focus on key findings, and thus give the book a more "how-to" feel, but it lacks the power of chronology in allowing readers to assess for themselves the conclusions drawn by the author.

Chapter 2. Early Loss and Its Consequences

1. See *Quest for Prosperity,* p. 105.
2. Family history supplied by the Office of Corporate History, Matsushita Electric.

3. See Konosuke Matsushita, *Michi wa Ashitani* (Tokyo: Mainichi Shinbunsha, October 30, 1974), pp. 9 and 10.

4. Interviews with Wasamura residents.

5. Other crops included wheat, mandarin oranges, and persimmons.

6. Oxen made the work somewhat less onerous, but agriculture back then in Japan was an exhausting endeavor.

7. From an interview with Yutaka Tsujimoto on October 31, 1993.

8. Nangaku Hatano, *Wasa 5,000 Nen Shi* (Self-published, March 20, 1966), pp. 128–129. Masakusu was one of twelve elected in 1889 and one of six elected in 1892.

9. According to Matsushita, the family had a "good reputation." See his *Michi wa Ashitani* (Tokyo: Mainichi Shinbunsha, October 30, 1974), p. 9.

10. One source who lived in Wasamura at the end of the last century says that "KM's father was influential. If people saw him, they snapped to attention." Interview with Shizue Sekimoto on November 2, 1993.

11. When talking about his childhood, Matsushita often spoke of his "nurse."

12. Tokue has been described by one source who knew her as "a very kind person." Interview with Shizue Sekimoto on November 2, 1993.

13. Kazuo Hatano's father was four years older than Matsushita and knew the Matsushita family at the turn of the century. According to Kazuo, his father told him "KM's brothers and sisters loved him very much. They often carried KM on their backs when they played." From an interview with Hatano on November 1, 1993.

14. From *Quest for Prosperity,* p. 3.

15. Ibid.

16. Ibid.

17. Well-educated Japanese in 1868 were aware of technological developments in the West, often reading scientific texts in

Dutch. But the industrial revolution had not yet made its way into Japanese life.

18. See note 8.

19. Silk and cotton examples from Taichi Sakaiya, *What Is Japan?* (New York: Kodansha America Inc., 1993).

20. Number of spindles and railroad data from R. H. P. Mason and J. G. Caiger, *A History of Japan* (Tokyo: Charles E. Tittle, 1972), pp. 228–230.

21. Army, navy, and education information from W. Scott Morton, *Japan: Its History and Culture* (New York: McGraw-Hill, 1984), p. 154.

22. For a discussion of the late 20th-century business environment, see John P. Kotter, *The New Rules: How to Succeed in Today's Post-Corporate World* (New York: Free Press, 1995), Chapter 3.

23. See Wakayama Kenseishi Hensan Iinkai, *Wakayama Kenseishi Dai Ikkan, Johen Meijihen* (Wakayama: Wakayama Prefecture, 1967), p. 584.

24. See Makoto Sakurai, *Kome Sono Seisaku to Undo Jo* (Noson Kyoson Bunk Kyokai, August 10, 1989), pp. 35–36.

25. Four years of education became compulsory in 1886.

26. I am making inferences here based on available data.

27. See Konosuke Matsushita, *Michi wa Ashitani* (Tokyo: Mainichi Shinbunsha, October 30, 1974), pp. 9 and 10.

28. From a 1993 interview in Wakayama prefecture with Yutaka Tsujimoto, a long-time friend of KM who lived near the house where Matsushita was born.

29. Konosuke Matsushita, *Watashi no Ikikata Kangaekata* (Tokyo: Jitsugyo no Nihonsha, 1968), p. 13.

30. Victor Showers, *World Facts and Figures, Third Edition* (New York: a Wiley-International Publication, 1989), p. 160.

31. An estimate based on all available evidence is that they lived in three rooms. Interview with Kazuo Hatano and others.

32. *Quest for Prosperity*, p. 4.

33. Konosuke Matsushita, *Michi wa Ashitani* (Tokyo: Mainichi Shinbunsha, October 30, 1974), p. 1.

34. Matsushita Seikei Juku Hen, *Matsushita Seikeijuku Jukucho Kowaroku* (Kyoto: PHP, April 1981), pp. 56–58.

35. Date of death from the Office of Corporate History, Matsushita Electric.

36. Ibid.

37. *Quest for Prosperity,* p. 5.

38. Ibid.

39. Date of death from the Office of Corporate History, Matsushita Electric.

40. *Quest for Prosperity,* p. 5. In the English version, Matsushita says "the loss of the three oldest children." This is incorrect. The oldest daughter did not die until 1921.

41. Ibid.

42. Ibid.

43. Interview with Magobei Tamura (who was ninety-nine years old at the time) on November 1, 1993.

44. From an interview with Satoshi Nakajima, March 24, 1993.

45. See *Quest for Prosperity,* p. 6.

46. Ibid.

47. Ibid.

48. Ibid.

49. Ibid.

50. The residential population of Osaka in 1900 was 881,344. See *Twenty-Fifth Annual Statistics of the City of Osaka,* 1926, pp. 2–4.

51. *Quest for Prosperity,* p. 6.

52. PHP Sogokenkyusho Kenkyuhonbu "Matsushita Konosuke Hatsugenshu" Hensanshitsu, *Matsushita Konosuke Hatsugenshu 16* (Kyoto: PHP Institute, November 27, 1991), p. 124.

53. *Quest for Prosperity,* p. 6.

54. Ibid., p. 7.

55. Konosuke Matsushita, *Watashi no Ikikata Kangaekata* (Tokyo: Jitsugyou no Nihonsha, August 1, 1968), p. 16.
56. Konosuke Matsushita, *Michi wa Ashitani* (Tokyo: Mainichi Shinbunsha, October 30, 1974), p. 13.
57. *Quest for Prosperity,* p. 7.

Chapter 3. Growth Through Hardship

1. An early 20th-century book called *The Study of the Apprentice System* claims there were 75,000 apprentices in Osaka at the time and that about one hundred of the city's richest people had started as apprentices. From Tokio Yoshida, in an interview on June 16, 1992.
2. *Quest for Prosperity,* pp. 7 and 8.
3. Ibid., p. 8.
4. "Shashi Sumitomo Denki Kogyo Kabushiki Kaisha" (A company history of Sumitomo Electric Industrial Company, 1961), p. 95.
5. *Matsushita Seikeijuku Hen Jukucho Kowaroku* (Kyoto: PHP, April 1981), pp. 58 and 59.
6. Konosuke Matsushita, *Wakasa ni Okuru* (Tokyo: Kodansha, April 1966), p.19.
7. *Matsushita Seikeijuku Hen Jukucho Kowaroku* (Kyoto: PHP, April 1981), pp. 58 and 59.
8. Some reports say that the shop ran into financial difficulty. See the internal MEI publication *Konosuke Matsushita: His Life and Thoughts* (Hirakata, Japan: The Overseas Training Center, Matsushita Electric, February 1983), p. 2.
9. Kinya Ninomiya, *Matsushita to Sony* (Tokyo: Kodansha, October 1968), p. 15.
10. Konosuke Matsushita, *Watashi no Ikikata Kangaekata Waga Hansei no Kiroku* (Kyoto: PHP, September 16, 1986), p. 23.
11. Godai Gohei Kotoku-Kai, *Godai Gohei Den* (Osaka: Godai Gohei Kotoku-Kai, February 15, 1937), p. 149.

12. *Quest for Prosperity,* p. 12.

13. Konosuke Matsushita, *Wakasa ni Okuru* (Tokyo: Kodansha, April 1966), p. 20.

14. He talked much about learning during these years. See, for example, *Wakasa ni Okuru* (Tokyo: Kodansha, April 1966), pp. 22–26, and "My Childhood," *Asahi Shogakusei Shinbun* (Asahi Shogakusei Shinbun, June 23, 1939).

15. From an interview with Masaharu Matsushita conducted on February 19, 1992.

16. *Quest for Prosperity,* pp. 8 and 9.

17. At times, Matsushita has said not three but five days' wages. See *Mono no Mikata Kangaekata* (Kyoto: PHP, May 16, 1986), p. 106.

18. *Quest for Prosperity,* pp. 8 and 9.

19. Konosuke Matsushita, *Watashi no Ikikata Kangaekata Waga Hansei no Kiroku* (Kyoto: PHP Institute, September 16, 1986), p. 26.

20. *Quest for Prosperity,* pp. 13 and 14. In Godai's book, he says that KM broke a rib (instead of a collarbone). See *Godai Gohei Den* (Osaka: Godai Gohei Kotoku-Kai, February 15, 1937), pp. 151–152.

21. Konosuke Matsushita, *Mono no Mikata Kangaekata* (Kyoto: PHP, May 16, 1986), p. 107.

22. See *Quest for Prosperity,* p. 16.

23. Ibid.

24. See Konosuke Matsushita, *Wakasa ni Okuru* (Tokyo: Kodansha, April 1966), pp. 27–31 and *Quest for Prosperity,* pp. 14–16.

25. *Quest for Prosperity,* p. 15.

26. Ibid., pp. 15 and 16.

27. Ibid., p. 16.

28. Konosuke Matsushita, *Watashi no Ikikata Kangaekata Waga Hansei no Kiroku* (Kyoto: PHP, September 16, 1986), pp. 28–29.

29. Most reports claim that KM saw little of his mother during his apprentice days. See, for example, *Konosuke Matsushita: His*

Life and Thoughts (Hirakata, Japan: The Overseas Training Center, Matsushita Electric, February 1983), p. 3.

30. *Quest for Prosperity*, p. 18.
31. Konosuke Matsushita, *Not For Bread Alone: A Business Ethos, A Management Ethic* (Kyoto: PHP Institute, June 1984), p. 116.
32. Konosuke Matsushita, *Watashi no Ikikata Kangaekata Waga Hansei no Kiroku* (Kyoto: PHP, September 16, 1986), pp. 33–34.
33. Office of Corporate History, Matsushita Electric.
34. *Godai Gohei Kotoku-Kai, Godai Gohei Den* (Osaka: Godai Gohei Kotoku-Kai, February 15, 1937), p. 155.
35. Some of the old-timers in Wasamura believe that Tokue came home and remarried. So do people like Seinosuke Takahashi, a longtime secretary to both KM and his wife Mumeno (from an interview on November 4, 1993). I was unable to confirm this.
36. *Quest for Prosperity*, p.19.
37. Ibid.
38. See John C. Beck, "The Change of a Lifetime: Individuals, Organizations, and Environment in Japan's Employment System," Ph.D. thesis, Harvard University, 1989.
39. See *Made in Japan: Akio Morita and Sony* (New York: Signet, 1988), p. 53.
40. (1) Kokudocho, *Kokudo Riyo Hakusho* (Tokyo: Okurasho Insatsukyouko, 1982); (2) *World Almanac* (New York: Press Publishing, 1901); (3) B. R. Mitchell, *European Historical Statistics 1750–1975* (New York: Facts on File, 1981); (4) B. R. Mitchell, *International Historical Statistics, Africa and Asia* (New York: NYU Press, 1982); (5) B. R. Mitchell, *International Historical Statistics, America and Australia* (London: Macmillan, 1983).
41. Kinya Ninomiya, *Matsushita to Sony* (Tokyo: Kodansha, October 1968), p. 15.
42. Konosuke Matsushita, *Mono no Mikata Kangaekata* (Kyoto: PHP, May 16, 1986), pp. 109–110.

43. Konosuke Matsushita, *Watashi no Ikikata Kangaekata* (Kyoto: PHP, September 16, 1986), p. 37.

44. *Quest for Prosperity,* p. 21.

45. See, for example, Morgan W. McCall, Jr., Michael M. Lombardo, and Ann M. Morrison, *The Lessons of Experience* (Lexington, MA: Lexington Books, 1988), Chapter 4.

Chapter 4. Responsibility and Exposure at an Early Age

1. *Quest for Prosperity,* p. 22.

2. Ibid., pp. 23–24.

3. Ibid., p. 25.

4. Ibid.

5. Konosuke Matsushita, *Matsushita Seikeijuku Hen Jukucho Kowaroku* (Kyoto: PHP, April 1981), p. 65.

6. Ibid., p. 66.

7. Ibid., p. 65.

8. Konosuke Matsushita, *Wakasa ni Okuru* (Tokyo: Kodansha, April 1966), p. 38.

9. *Quest for Prosperity,* p. 27.

10. Ibid., pp. 31 and 32.

11. Ibid., pp. 32 and 33.

12. In his autobiography, he says that he paid the Kanayamas seven or eight yen per month. His salary at Osaka Light probably averaged about twelve yen a month.

13. *Quest for Prosperity,* p. 33.

14. Ibid., p. 34.

15. Ibid.

16. Ibid., pp. 28 and 29.

17. Ibid., pp. 31 and 32.

18. Ibid., p. 30.

19. Office of Corporate History, Matsushita Electric.

20. *Quest for Prosperity,* pp. 34 and 35.

21. Office of Corporate History at MEI.

22. *Quest for Prosperity,* p. 35.

23. Ibid., pp. 36 and 37.

24. Source of Mumeno's age: Office of Corporate History, Matsushita Electric.

25. Konosuke Matsushita, *Watashi no Ikikata Kangaekata* (Kyoto: PHP, September 16, 1986), pp. 58–59.

26. See Mitsuko Shimomura, *Matsushita Konosuke Kongen o Kataru* (Tokyo: Diamond-sha, March 5, 1981), pp. 177, 178, and 188. Also Katsuhiko Eguchi, *Kokorowa Itsumo Kokoniaru; Matsushita Konosuke Zuibunroku* (Kyoto: PHP, October 1990), pp. 120, 121, and 216. Seinosuke Takahashi, a longtime secretary to Mumeno, also describes her as "never losing a competition" and as "having a violent temper." From an interview on November 4, 1993.

27. An official Matsushita history written by his company says he was the youngest inspector. See *Konosuke Matsushita: His Life and Thoughts* (Hirakata, Japan: The Overseas Training Center, Matsushita Electric, February 1983), p. 3.

28. *Quest for Prosperity,* p. 39.

29. Matsushita Seikeijuku, *Matsushita Seikeijuku Jukucho Kowaroku* (Kyoto: PHP, April 1981), pp. 70–72.

30. *Quest for Prosperity,* pp. 40–41.

31. Ibid., pp. 39 and 40.

32. Ibid., p. 41.

33. Ibid.

34. Office of Corporate History, Matsushita Electric.

Chapter 5. Risk Taking, Perseverance, and the Launching
          of a Business

1. See Barbara Molony, "Noguchi Jun and Nitchitsu: Investment Strategies of a High-Tech Enterprise," in *Managing Industrial*

Enterprise: Cases from Japan's Prewar Experience, edited by William D. Wray (Cambridge, MA: Harvard University Press, 1989), Chapter 7.

2. See *Toyota: A History of the First 50 Years* (Toyota City: Toyota Motor Corporation, 1988), and Yukiyasu Togo and William Wartman, *Against All Odds: The Story of the Toyota Motor Corporation and the Family That Created It* (New York: St. Martin's Press, 1993).

3. See *Quest for Prosperity,* p. 42.

4. Because there appears to be no record of the entire employment histories for Hayashi and Morita, the assertion that neither had worked at a start-up is an educated guess.

5. *Quest for Prosperity,* p. 43.

6. This account of the first months of Matsushita Electric comes from verbal reports from Matsushita himself (on numerous occasions) and from his autobiography.

7. *Quest for Prosperity,* pp. 43 and 44.

8. Ibid., pp. 44 and 45.

9. Ibid., p. 45.

10. Ibid.

11. Office of Corporate History, Matsushita Electric.

12. "In the early days of the business, there were times when KM couldn't sell his products and when he worried that the company would fail. On such occasions, she encouraged him very much to continue the business." From an interview with Masaharu Matsushita on February 19, 1992.

13. From MEI company records.

14. *Quest for Prosperity,* p. 46.

15. Ibid., p. 47.

16. Ibid.

17. MEI company records.

18. *Quest for Innovation—75 Years of Matsushita Electric,* Office of Corporate History, Matsushita Electric, 1994, pp. 8–9.

19. Office of Corporate History, Matsushita Electric.

20. See *Quest for Prosperity,* pp. 49–50.
21. MEI company records.
22. See Barbara Molony, "Noguchi Jun and Nitchitsu: Investment Strategies of a High-Tech Enterprise," in *Managing Industrial Enterprise: Cases from Japan's Prewar Experience,* edited by William D. Wray (Cambridge, MA: Harvard University Press, 1989), Chapter 7.
23. See James C. Collins and Jerry I. Porras, *Built to Last* (New York: Harper Business, 1994), Chapter 2.
24. *Quest for Prosperity,* p. 52.
25. Ibid., p. 56.
26. See Takeshi Asozu, *Matsushita Konosuke no Hitozukai no Shinzui* (Tokyo: Nihon Jitsugyo Shuppansha, April 1977), pp. 42, 43, and 94. Also Kuniji Matsumoto, *Matsushita Denki no Joshi Shain Kyoiku* (Tokyo: Diamond Inc., March 1982), p. 31.
27. Tatsuhiko Hayashi, *Jitsuroku Iue Gakko* (Tokyo: Diamond Inc., October 13, 1985), p. 8.
28. Ibid., p. 9.
29. "The Osaka custom is 'Customer is King.' Tokyo has a different tradition, one that focuses more on progress and the advancement of technology for its own sake. Working as an apprentice in Osaka undoubtedly influenced Matsushita." Interview with Professor Tsunehiko Yui, Meiji University, September 6, 1994. "The Osaka market was very competitive, much more so than Tokyo. That affected how people did business [e.g., customer as king]. The lessons KM learned during his apprenticeship years pervaded his career." Interview with Professor Yasuo Okamoto, Aoyamagakuin University, September 7, 1994.
30. See the commentary in John P. Kotter, *The New Rules: How to Succeed in Today's Post-Corporate World* (New York: Free Press, 1995), Chapter 5, especially the data on p. 75.
31. Tatsuhiko Hayashi, *Jitsuroku Iue Gakko* (Tokyo: Diamond Inc., October 13, 1985), p. 9.

32. Yasuo Okamoto, *Hitachi to Matsushita (Ge) Nihon-Keiei no Genkei* (Tokyo: Chuokoronsha, April 1979), p. 4.

33. See *Quest for Prosperity,* pp. 60–61.

34. Ibid., pp. 23 and 24.

35. MEI company records.

Chapter 6. Unconventional Strategies

1. See, for example, Michael Yoshino's discussion of this in his book *Japan's Managerial System: Tradition and Innovation* (Cambridge, MA: MIT Press, 1968), Chapter 2.

2. Taro Nawa, *Matsushita Konosuke Keiei no Shinzui o Kataru* (Tokyo: Kokusai Shogyo Shuppan Kabushiki Kaisha, January 1983), p. 36.

3. *Quest for Prosperity,* p. 62.

4. Ibid., p. 67.

5. Office of Corporate History, Matsushita Electric.

6. Ibid. In his autobiography, KM gives slightly different dates: construction started in March 1922 and completed in July 1922.

7. *Quest for Prosperity,* p. 70.

8. Ibid.

9. Office of Corporate History, Matsushita Electric.

10. Ibid.

11. *Quest for Prosperity,* pp. 74 and 75.

12. From Seiichi Goto, who was one of those workers. Interview on November 5, 1993.

13. *Quest for Prosperity,* p. 75.

14. From the Office of Corporate History, Matsushita Electric, and *Quest for Prosperity,* p. 77.

15. *Quest for Prosperity,* p. 78.

16. Ibid.

17. Ibid., p. 79.

18. Ibid.
19. Ibid.
20. Ibid., pp. 80 and 81.
21. Ibid., p. 82.
22. Ibid.
23. Office of Corporate History, Matsushita Electric.
24. Ibid.
25. *Quest for Prosperity,* pp. 115–118.
26. Ibid., p. 118.
27. Ibid., p. 119.
28. Ibid.
29. Ibid., p. 122.
30. Doi was interviewed on November 8, 1993, Goto on November 5.
31. Office of Corporate History, Matsushita Electric.
32. *Quest for Prosperity,* p. 125.
33. Ibid., pp. 125–130.
34. Akio Morita, *Made in Japan* (New York: Signet, 1988), p. 86.
35. *Quest for Prosperity,* pp. 130–134.
36. Rowland Gould, *The Matsushita Phenomenon* (Tokyo: Diamond Sha, 1970), p. 23.
37. All figures from the Office of Corporate History, Matsushita Electric.
38. Toshihiko Yamashita, the president of Matsushita from 1977 to 1986, gives this figure in his book *The Panasonic Way* (Tokyo: Kodansha International, 1989), p. 28.
39. Yasuo Okamoto, *Hitachi to Matsushita (Jo) Nihon-Keiei no Genkei* (Tokyo: Chuokoronsha, April 1979), p. 39.
40. *Quest for Innovation—75 Years of Matsushita Electric,* Office of Corporate History, Matsushita Electric, 1994, pp. 18–19.
41. *Quest for Prosperity,* p. 138.
42. According to Okamoto, the business lost 10,000 yen. See Yasuo Okamoto, *Hitachi to Matsushita (Jo) Nihon-Keiei no Genkei* (Tokyo: Chuokoronsha, April 1979), p. 39.

43. Ibid.
44. All statistics from the Office of Corporate History, Matsushita Electric.
45. *Quest for Prosperity,* p. 149.
46. Ibid.
47. Ibid.
48. Kazuo Noda, *Matsushita Konosuke Sono Hito to Jigyo* (Tokyo: Jitsugyo no Nihonsha, July 25, 1968), p. 131.

Chapter 7. Coping with Economic Hard Times

1. Office of Corporate History, Matsushita Electric.
2. Ibid.
3. Sidney Fine, *Sit Down: The General Motors Strike of 1936–1937* (Ann Arbor: University of Michigan Press, 1969), p. 21.
4. MEI company records.
5. B. R. Mitchell, *International Historical Statistics, Africa and Asia* (New York: New York University Press, 1982), pp. 728–729.
6. Kenji Fukuda, *Iue Tohio no Jigyo to Jinsei* (Tokyo: Nihon Jitsugyo Shoppansha, November 5, 1969), pp. 139–140.
7. According to Seiichi Goto, there were many rumors at that time that there would be a layoff. From an interview with Goto on November 5, 1993.
8. See *Quest for Prosperity,* p. 156.
9. Ibid.
10. Ibid., pp. 156–157.
11. Akio Morita's discussion of this in his autobiography is particularly interesting. See his chapter on "Management" in *Made in Japan* (New York: Signet, 1988), pp. 144–189.
12. See *Quest for Prosperity,* p. 157.
13. Office of Corporate History, Matsushita Electric.
14. Ibid.
15. See Kuniji Matsumoto, *Matsushita Denki no Joshi Shain Kyoiku*

(Tokyo: Diamond, Inc., March 1982), p. 31, and Takeshi Asozu, *Matsushita Konosuke no Hitozukai no Shinzui* (Tokyo: Nihon Jitsugyo Shuppansha, April 1977), pp. 42–43.

16. Matsushita Denkisangyo Kabushikikaisha Sogyo 50 Shunen Kinen Gyoji Junbi Iinkai, *Matsushita Denki Gojunen no Ryakushi* (Osaka: Matsushita Denkisangyo Kabushikikaisha Sogyo 50 Shunen Kinen Gyoji Junbi Iinkai, May 5, 1968), pp. 81–89. The entire discussion of the radio business in this chapter draws heavily from this document.

17. MEI company records.

18. See *Quest for Prosperity*, p. 170.

19. Ibid., p. 171.

20. Two versions of these events can be found in corporate historical documents. In one, KM bought a radio factory. In another, he set up a joint venture with Kokudo Electric.

21. MEI company records.

22. *Quest for Prosperity*, p. 173.

23. Ibid.

24. MEI company records.

25. *Quest for Prosperity*, pp. 174–176.

26. Ibid.

27. Ibid., pp. 176–177.

28. MEI company records.

29. Ibid.

30. *Quest for Prosperity*, pp. 177–178.

31. MEI company records.

32. Shiro Ishiyama, *Matsushita Konosuke Zenkenkyu Series 2 Meichi no Kokusaikeiei* (Tokyo: Gakushukenkyusha, December 1, 1981), p. 306. The Office of Corporate History, Matsushita Electric, does not have these figures on radio production and cannot confirm that they are accurate.

33. *Quest for Prosperity*, p. 181.

34. MEI company records

35. Ibid.

36. *Quest for Prosperity,* pp. 186 and 187.
37. Ibid., p. 188.
38. MEI company records.
39. Ibid.
40. MEI company records.
41. *Quest for Prosperity,* p. 190.
42. See, for example, the discussion of this in John P. Kotter, *The New Rules: How to Succeed in Today's Post-Corporate World* (New York: Free Press, 1995), Chapter 3.

Chapter 8. A Mission for the Corporation

1. This account comes mostly from his autobiography. Matsushita told this story on many occasions.
2. *Quest for Prosperity,* pp. 191 and 192.
3. Ibid., p. 193.
4. Ibid., pp. 193 and 194.
5. Ibid., pp. 194–196.
6. The lumber mill is gone and a few other buildings have been added.
7. *Quest for Prosperity,* pp. 196–198.
8. Ibid., p. 198.
9. Ibid.
10. Journalist Mitsuko Shimomura says that after talking with KM on many occasions, she concluded that he was very much interested in money when he started the company, but that after ten to fifteen years, "he realized that making money was not enough to buy happiness." From an interview on February 17, 1992. Son-in-law Masaharu says that when he first met KM in 1939 "he was not eager to accumulate personal wealth." From an interview on February 19, 1992.
11. Author, journalist, and publishing executive Tokio Yoshida: "When Matsushita started to grow and develop more and

more business, he wondered whether he was forcing his competitors into difficult predicaments, even bankruptcy. He felt responsible. But because his products were enjoyed so much by the public, he considered it was destiny that he continue manufacturing them. In order to relieve his earlier guilt, he decided that he needed to return something to society. In this sense, making social contributions was how he cleaned his mind of the guilt he felt about driving his competitors out of business." From an interview on June 16, 1992.

12. People who suffer hardships often search deeply for meaning in their lives. See Victor E. Frankez, *Man's Search for Meaning* (New York: Touchstone, 1984).

13. *Quest for Prosperity,* pp. 198 and 199.

14. Time, date, and place from the Office of Corporate History, Matsushita Electric.

15. This account of the events on May 5, 1932 comes mostly from his autobiography.

16. *Quest for Prosperity,* p. 202.

17. Ibid., p. 203.

18. Ibid., pp. 203 and 204.

19. Shigeo Nishiki knew Matsushita for nearly forty-five years. In a 1992 interview he told me: "In the beginning, he was not very good at speaking to people. He was never eloquent, but his speech was always very candid and earnest. The epitome of his speaking style was demonstrated in the 'Sense of Mission' speech in 1932. Again, he was not eloquent. But he spoke with great sincerity and honesty."

20. One of those in the audience claims that by the end of the session people were very emotional. From an interview with Seiichi Goto on November 5, 1993. Matsushita says the same in his autobiography, *Quest for Prosperity,* p. 206.

21. As Rowland Gould puts it, the maxim at Matsushita became: "Profit is the reward accorded management by consumers sat-

isfied with the quality and service of a product." See *The Matsushita Phenomenon* (Tokyo: Diamond Sha, 1970), p. 17.

22. See Byron K. Marshall, *Capitalism and Nationalism in Prewar Japan: The Ideology of the Business Elite 1868–1941* (Stanford, CA: Stanford University Press, 1967).

23. Ibid., p. 50.

24. Ibid., p. 31.

25. I started collecting these statements in the mid-1980s until three file folders overflowed. My sense is that the majority of large corporations in the United States now have some type of value/principle/mission statement.

26. See "Johnson and Johnson (A)," a Harvard case, #384–053, written by Professor Francis J. Aguilar and Arvind Bhambri (Boston: HBS Press, 1983).

27. Office of Corporate History, Matsushita Electric.

28. *Konosuke Matsushita: His Life and Thoughts* (Hirakata, Japan: The Overseas Training Center, Matsushita Electric, February 1983), pp. 17 and 18.

29. See Toshihiko Yamashita, *The Panasonic Way* (Tokyo: Kodansha International, 1989), p. 89.

30. Yasuo Okamoto, *Hitachi to Matsushita (Jo) Nihon-Keiei no Genkei* (Tokyo: Chuokoronsha, April 1979), p. 36.

31. MEI company records. The organization was called Hoichi Kai (One Step Society).

32. Office of Corporate History, Matsushita Electric.

33. Tetsuo Sakiya, *Honda Motor: The Men, the Management, the Machines* (Tokyo: Kodansha International, 1987), p. 195.

34. Matsushita Denkisangyo Kabushikikaisha Sogyo 50 Shunen Kinen Gyoji Junbi Iinkai, *Matsushita Denki Gojunen no Ryakushi* (Osaka: Matsushita Denkisangyo Kabushikikaisha Sogyo 50 Shunen Kinen Gyoji Junbi Iinkai, May 5, 1968), p. 127.

35. Ibid., pp. 127 and 128.

36. *Konosuke Matsushita: His Life and Thoughts* (Hirakata, Japan:

The Overseas Training Center, Matsushita Electric, February 1983), pp. 18 and 19.

37. Most of those who have studied Matsushita Electric have concluded that the sales network did become an important source of advantage. "KM developed wonderful relationships with retailers. His business advice constantly led them to earn healthy profits. This fact fostered strong loyalty between KM and retailers." From an interview with Professor Moriaki Tsuchiya, University of Tokyo, September 5, 1994. Also see, for example, Yasuo Okamoto, *Hitachi to Matsushita (Ge) Nihon-Keiei no Genkei* (Tokyo: Chuokoronsha, April 1979), pp. 24–25.

38. Office of Corporate History, Matsushita Electric.

39. During KM's last two decades, he worked closely with Katsuhiko Eguchi. Eguchi told me in a 1992 interview: "In 1932, his company had two major competitors that weren't faring nearly as well as Matsushita Electric. KM didn't revel in his comparative success. In fact, he felt guilty. He wondered if it was right for him to be so successful when his competitors were struggling. He suffered a spiritual agonizing of this issue." The mission he formulated helped him resolve this "spiritual agony," says Eguchi.

40. From an interview with Nawa on February 17, 1992.

Chapter 9. Creating "The Division System"

1. Office of Corporate History, Matsushita Electric.
2. Ibid.
3. See Alfred P. Sloan Jr., *My Years With General Motors* (New York: Doubleday, 1963). For a more general discussion of the switch to divisionalization at GM and elsewhere see Alfred Chandler, *Strategy and Structure* (Cambridge MA: MIT Press, 1962).
4. Noel M. Tichy and Stratford Sherman, *Control Your Destiny or*

Someone Else Will; How Jack Welch Is Making General Electric the World's Most Competitive Corporation (New York: Currency and Doubleday, 1993), p. 257.

5. *Quest for Innovation—75 Years of Matsushita Electric,* Office of Corporate History, Matsushita Electric, 1994, p. 33.

6. Rowland Gould, *The Matsushita Phenomenon* (Tokyo: Diamond Sha, 1970), p. 21.

7. Hiroshi Majima, *Matsushita Denki no Jigyobusei* (Tokyo: Nihon Jitsugyo Shuppansha, November 10, 1978), p. 79.

8. *Quest for Prosperity,* p. 225.

9. Kazuo Noda, *Matsushita Konosuke Sono Hito to Jigyo* (Tokyo: Jitsugyo no Nihonsha, July 29, 1968), p. 197.

10. *Quest for Prosperity,* p. 225.

11. *Konosuke Matsushita: His Life and Thoughts* (Hirakata, Japan: The Overseas Training Center, Matsushita Electric, February, 1983), p. 17.

12. Hiroshi Majima, *Matsushita Denki no Jigyobusei* (Tokyo: Nihon Jitsugyo Shuppansha, November 10, 1978), pp. 79 and 80.

13. See Toshihiko Yamashita, *The Panasonic Way* (Tokyo: Kodansha International, 1989), p. 28.

14. Ibid., pp. 58 and 59.

15. Ibid., p. 59.

16. According to one of his division managers. Interview with Yasuharu Nakagawa on February 20, 1992.

17. From an interview with Professor Tsunehiko Yui, Meiji University, on September 6, 1994. This idea comes up repeatedly in our interviews. "KM was very unusual in the way he trusted subordinates," said Professor Moriaki Tsuchiya, Tokyo University, September 5, 1994.

18. See Rowland Gould, *The Matsushita Phenomenon* (Tokyo: Diamond Sha, 1970), p. 21.

19. "Some people think Takahashi was a better businessman than his boss." Interview with Kazuo Noda on September 6, 1994.

20. MEI company records.

21. In his classic study of Matsushita Electric, Yasuo Okamoto wrote: "KM's vision permeated the entire organization. This unified vision facilitated harmonious relations among divisions and thereby fostered the company's growth." From Yasuo Okamoto, *Hitachi to Matsushita (Jo) Nihon-Keiei no Genkei* (Tokyo: Chuokoronsha, April 1979), p. 33.

22. Two thirds of those interviewed who talked about divisionalization gave the "health" answer.

23. MEI company records.

24. *Quest for Prosperity,* pp. 217 and 218.

25. See Rowland Gould, *The Matsushita Phenomenon* (Tokyo: Diamond Sha, 1970), p. 23.

26. Ibid., p. 50. Also, Toshihiko Yamashita, *The Panasonic Way* (Tokyo: Kodansha International, 1989), p. 87.

27. From multiple interviews with current and former Matsushita executives.

28. Office of Corporate History, Matsushita Electric.

29. According to son-in-law Masaharu (interview on February 19, 1992).

30. The *Time* cover story on Matsushita of February 23,1962 says that his schedule "brings him home only on weekends to his wife Mumeno."

31. See Mitsuko Shimomura, *Matsushita Konosuke Kongen o Kataru* (Tokyo: Diamond-sha, March 5, 1981), pp. 177, 178, and 188. Also Katsuhiko Eguchi, *Kokorowa Itsumo Kokoniaru; Matsushita Konosuke Zuibunroku* (Kyoto: PHP, October 1990), pp. 120, 121, and 216. Seinosuke Takahashi, a longtime secretary to Mumeno, also describes her as "never losing a competition" and as "having a violent temper." From an interview on November 4, 1993.

32. Mitsuko Shimomura, *Matsushita Konosuke Kongen o Kataru* (Tokyo: Diamond-sha, March 5, 1981), p. 187.

33. Lesley Downer, *The Brothers: The Hidden World of Japan's Richest Family* (New York: Random House, 1994), pp. 54 and 55.

34. MEI company records.
35. From an interview with Masaharu Matsushita on February 19, 1992.
36. Morikawa Hidemasa, "The Increasing Power of Salaried Managers in Japan's Large Corporations," Chapter 2 in *Managing Industrial Enterprise,* edited by William D. Wray (Cambridge, MA: Harvard University Press, 1989), p. 32.
37. From an interview with Masaharu Matsushita on February 19, 1992.

Chapter 10. World War II

1. See R. H. P. Mason and J. G. Caiger, *A History of Japan* (Tokyo: Charles E. Tuttle Co., 1973), Chapters 16–17; also W. Scott Morton, *Japan: Its History and Culture* (New York: McGraw-Hill, 1984), Chapters 14–15; and Milton W. Meyer, *Japan: A Concise History, Third Edition* (Lanham, Maryland: Rowman and Littlefield, 1993), Chapters 14–15.
2. Ibid.
3. Ibid.
4. Ibid.
5. Hitoshi Misono, *Nihon no Dokusen* (Tokyo: Shiseido, 1965), pp. 41 and 42.
6. See Tetsuo Sakiya, *Honda Motor: The Men, the Management, and the Machines* (Tokyo: Kodansha International, 1987), p. 55.
7. *Quest for Prosperity,* pp. 231–234. Also, "The Matsushita Chronicle, 1894–1989," Office of Corporate History, Matsushita Electric, April 1990.
8. *Quest for Prosperity,* p. 236.
9. Shiro Ishiyama and Michio Koyanagi, "Watashi no Keieishi Sono Hikari to Kage 'Yaru' to 'Yareru' no Aida, Matsushita Konosuke Kaisoroku Ge," in *President,* July 1973, pp. 71 and 72.
10. Ibid. Also, Arataro Takahashi, *Kataritsugu Keiei* (Kyoto: PHP, October 1983), pp. 72 and 73.

11. Ibid., p. 72.
12. *Quest for Prosperity,* p. 239.
13. Hiroshi Majima, *Matsushita Denki no Jigyobusei* (Tokyo: Nihon Jitsugyo Shuppansha, November 10, 1978), p. 82.
14. Office of Corporate History, Matsushita Electric.
15. Ibid.
16. *Quest for Prosperity,* p. 239.
17. Ibid.
18. Fellow entrepreneur Yasuharu Nakagawa's interpretation of this change: "For people like KM and me, when the company is running very well, sometimes we feel not worthwhile. I need something to struggle with. Without a problem to fight, I sometimes feel disappointed." From an interview with Nakagawa on February 20, 1992.
19. Konosuke Matsushita, *Matsushita Seikeijuku Jukucho Kowaroku,* (Kyoto: PHP, April 1984), p. 114.
20. *Quest for Prosperity,* p. 242.
21. Michael Yoshino, *Japan's Managerial System* (Cambridge, MA: MIT Press, 1968), p. 86.
22. MEI company records.

Chapter 11. Up from Ashes

1. G. C. Allen, *Japan's Economic Expansion* (London: Oxford University Press, 1965), p. 5.
2. Akio Morita, *Made in Japan: Akio Morita and Sony* (New York: Signet, 1988), p. 46.
3. Shiro Ishiyama and Michio Koyanagi, *Kyu, Matsushita Konosuke Keiei Kaiso Roku* (Tokyo: Diamond Time Inc., May 1974), p. 164.
4. *Quest for Prosperity,* pp. 241 and 242.
5. Ibid., p. 242.

6. Ibid., p. 243.

7. Ibid.

8. Michael Yoshino, *Japan's Managerial System: Tradition and Innovation* (Cambridge, MA: MIT Press, 1968), pp. 97 and 98.

9. Ibid., p. 98.

10. Shiro Ishiyama and Michio Koyanagi, *Kyu, Matsushita Konosuke Keiei Kaiso Roku* (Tokyo: Diamond Time Inc., March 1974), pp. 174–180.

11. Yasuo Okamoto, *Hitachi to Matsushita (Ge) Nihon-Keiei no Genkei* (Tokyo: Chuokoronsha, April 1979), p. 8.

12. Shiro Ishiyama and Michio Koyanagi, *Kyu, Matsushita Konosuke Keiei Kaiso Roku* (Tokyo: Diamond Time Inc., March 1974), pp. 174–180.

13. MEI company records.

14. Hitoshi Misono, *Nihon no Dokusen* (Tokyo: Shiseido, 1965), pp. 38 and 39.

15. *Quest for Prosperity,* pp. 244 and 245.

16. Ibid., p. 245.

17. Ibid., p. 253.

18. Company records.

19. Ibid.

20. Yasuo Okamoto, *Hitachi to Matsushita (Ge) Nihon-Keiei no Genkei* (Tokyo: Chuokoronsha, April 1979), pp. 4 and 5.

21. Office of Corporate History, Matsushita Electric.

22. Arataro Takahashi, "Matsushita Konosuke no Jinsei: Gareki no Naka kara 'Kaden Gannen' e," in *Matsushita Konosuke no Kenkyu,* edited by President (Tokyo: President-sha, December 5, 1980), pp. 78 and 79.

23. Ibid., pp. 79 and 80.

24. *Quest for Prosperity,* p. 246.

25. Yasuo Okamoto, *Hitachi to Matsushita (Ge) Nihon-Keiei no Genkei* (Tokyo: Chuokoronsha, April 1979), p. 10.

26. *Quest for Prosperity,* pp. 249 and 250. Also, Shiro Ishiyama and

Michio Koyanagi, *Kyu, Matsushita Konosuke Keiei Kaiso Roku* (Tokyo: Diamond Time Inc., March 1974), pp. 77–79.

27. *Quest for Prosperity,* p. 250.

28. MEI company records.

29. See Arataro Takahashi, "Matsushita Konosuke no Jinsei: Gareki no Naka kara 'Kaden Gannen' e," in *Matsushita Konosuke no Kenkyu,* edited by President (Tokyo: President-sha, December 5, 1980), p. 81.

30. MEI company records.

31. In his autobiography, Akio Morita says, "The black market was the place everyone had to shop." See *Made in Japan: Akio Morita and Sony* (New York: Signet, 1988), p. 57.

32. Shiro Ishiyama and Michio Koyanagi, *Kyu, Matsushita Konosuke Keiei Kaiso Roku* (Tokyo: Diamond Time Inc., March 1974), pp. 168–172.

33. Arataro Takahashi, "Matsushita Konosuke no Jinsei: Gareki no Naka kara 'Kaden Gannen' e," in *Matsushita Konosuke no Kenkyu,* edited by President (Tokyo: President-sha, December 5, 1980), pp. 80 and 81.

34. MEI company records.

35. Office of Corporate History, Matsushita Electric.

36. MEI company records.

37. Ibid.

38. *Quest for Prosperity,* p. 253.

39. Ibid., p. 254.

40. Ibid.

41. MEI company records.

42. "In the days when he was designated one of the Zaibatsu families, he had nothing to do. He just drank a lot." From an interview with Masaharu Matsushita on February 19, 1992.

43. *Quest for Prosperity,* p. 255.

44. The young man was Shigeo Nishiki. From an interview with Nishiki on February 20, 1992.

45. The idea here of something beyond good business leadership is similar to what Philip Selznick has called "institutional leadership." See his *Leadership in Administration* (New York: Harper & Row, 1957).

Chapter 12. The Globalization of an Enterprise

1. B. R. Mitchell, *International Historical Statistics, Africa and Asia* (New York: New York University Press, 1982), p. 732.
2. Office of Corporate History, Matsushita Electric.
3. Arataro Takahashi, "Matsushita Konosuke no Jinsei: Gareki no Naka kara 'Kaden Gannen' e," in *Matsushita Konosuke no Kenkyu,* edited by President (Tokyo: President-sha, December 5, 1980), p. 82.
4. *Quest for Prosperity,* pp. 258 and 259.
5. Arataro Takahashi, "Matsushita Konosuke no Jinsei: Gareki no Naka kara 'Kaden Gannen' e," in *Matsushita Konosuke no Kenkyu,* edited by President (Tokyo: President-sha, December 5, 1980), pp. 82 and 83.
6. Ibid., pp. 83 and 84.
7. Ibid., pp. 82–84.
8. Ibid., pp. 83–85.
9. *Quest for Prosperity,* p. 259.
10. Office of Corporate History, Matsushita Electric.
11. *Quest for Prosperity,* pp. 259 and 260.
12. Ibid., p. 260.
13. From an interview with Toshihiko Yamashita on February 18, 1992. "We could see that that first trip to the United States had a very strong impact on him."
14. Office of Corporate History, Matsushita Electric.
15. *The Japanese Economic Journal,* October 24, 1967, p. 7.
16. Office of Corporate History, Matsushita Electric.

17. *Quest for Prosperity,* p. 262.

18. Arataro Takahashi, "Matsushita Konosuke no Jinsei: Gareki no Naka kara 'Kaden Gannen' e," in *Matsushita Konosuke no Kenkyu,* edited by President (Tokyo: President-sha, December 5, 1980), pp. 90 and 91.

19. *Quest for Prosperity,* p. 263.

20. Ibid.

21. MEI company records.

22. Ibid.

23. Office of Corporate History, Matsushita Electric.

24. Toshihiko Yamashita claims that the real starting point for the success of Matsushita Electric today was the venture with Philips. From an interview on February 18, 1992.

25. *Quest for Prosperity,* p. 264.

26. Ibid., p. 267.

27. Arataro Takahashi, "Matsushita Konosuke no Jinsei: Gareki no Naka kara 'Kaden Gannen' e," in *Matsushita Konosuke no Kenkyu,* edited by President (Tokyo: President-sha, December 5, 1980), p. 95.

28. MEI company records.

29. Yasuo Okamoto, *Hitachi to Matsushita (Ge) Nihon-Keiei no Genkei* (Tokyo: Chuokoronsha, April 1979), p. 290.

30. Ibid., pp. 24 and 25.

31. Matsushita Electric Industries Sogyo 50 Shunen Kinen Gyoji Junbi Iinkai, *Matsushita Denki Gojunen no Ryakushi,* Matsushita Electric Industries, May 5, 1968, pp. 247–249.

32. Rowland Gould, *The Matsushita Phenomenon* (Tokyo: Diamond Sha, 1970), p. 59.

33. This discussion of Sony and Matsushita is based on Morita's autobiography, *Made in Japan* (New York: Signet, 1988), a book by Nick Lyons, *The Sony Vision* (New York: Crown, 1976), and interviews with half a dozen people who knew both Matsushita and Morita.

Chapter 13. Fighting Arrogance and Complacency

1. MEI company records.
2. From an interview with Nakagawa on February 20, 1992.
3. *Quest for Prosperity,* p. 269.
4. Matsushita Denkisangyo Kabushikikaisha Sogyo 50 Shunen Kinen Gyoji Junbi Iinkai, *Matsushita Denki Gojunen no Ryakushi* (Osaka: Matsushita Denkisangyo Kabushikikaisha Sogyo 50 Shunen Kinen Gyoji Junbi Iinkai, May 1968), p. 273.
5. Konosuke Matsushita and Goro Tagawa, *Asu wo Hiraku Keiei* (Tokyo: Yomiuri Shinbun Sha, December 30, 1982).
6. An interview with Shigeo Nishiki, February 20, 1992.
7. Matsushita Denkisangyo Kabushikikaisha Sogyo 50 Shunen Kinen Gyoji Junbi Iinkai, *Matsushita Denki Gojunen no Ryakushi* (Osaka: Matsushita Denkisangyo Kabushikikaisha Sogyo 50 Shunen Kinen Gyoji Junbi Iinkai, May 1968), pp. 249 and 250.
8. Ibid., pp. 261 and 262.
9. *Quest for Prosperity,* p. 274.
10. Ibid.
11. Matsushita Denkisangyo Kabushikikaisha Sogyo 50 Shunen Kinen Gyoji Junbi Iinkai, *Matsushita Denki Gojunen no Ryakushi* (Osaka: Matsushita Denkisangyo Kabushikikaisha Sogyo 50 Shunen Kinen Gyoji Junbi Iinkai, May 1968), pp. 257–261.
12. From an interview with Shinya on June 15, 1992.
13. Ibid.
14. Ibid.
15. Ibid.
16. Ibid.
17. *Quest for Prosperity,* pp. 281 and 282.
18. Ibid.
19. Ibid., p. 301.
20. Ibid., p. 303.

21. Office of Corporate History, Matsushita Electric.

22. For a discussion of the problems in this period, see Chapter 3 in Yasuo Okamoto, *Hitachi to Matsushita (Ge) Nihon-Keiei no Genkei* (Tokyo: Chuokoronsha, April 1979).

23. *Quest for Prosperity,* p. 281. I have changed the verb forms in this quote from past to present tense so as to better fit the narrative flow.

24. Nearly everyone I interviewed as background for the book stressed KM's emphasis on a "fair" profit. Again and again he told his people that neither high profits from a monopoly nor low prices to buy market share were acceptable.

25. Matsushita Denkisangyo Kabushikikaisha Sogyo 50 Shunen Kinen Gyoji Junbi Iinkai, *Matsushita Denki Gojunen no Ryakushi* (Osaka: Matsushita Denkisangyo Kabushikikaisha Sogyo 50 Shunen Kinen Gyoji Junbi Iinkai, May 1968), p. 258.

26. From Junnosuke Shinya, a former senior managing director at Matsushita Communication Industrial. Interview on June 15, 1992.

27. Matsushita Denkisangyo Kabushikikaisha Sogyo 50 Shunen Kinen Gyoji Junbi Iinkai, *Matsushita Denki Gojunen no Ryakushi* (Osaka: Matsushita Denkisangyo Kabushikikai-sha Sogyo 50 Shunen Kinen Gyoji Junbi Iinkai, May 1968), p. 246.

28. Toshihiko Yamashita, *The Panasonic Way* (Tokyo: Kodansha International, 1989), p. 89.

29. From Katsuhiko Eguchi, who was at the meeting. Interview on February 18, 1992.

30. *Quest for Prosperity,* p. 307.

31. Ibid.

32. See Rowland Gould, *The Matsushita Phenomenon* (Tokyo: Diamond Sha, 1970).

33. MEI company records.

34. *Yearbook of Labour Statistics 1972* (Geneva: International Labour Office, 1972), p. 606.

35. Industrial Relations Department, MEI.

36. Toshihiko Yamashita, *The Panasonic Way* (New York: Kodansha International, 1989), p. 19.

37. From an interview with Professor Hideo Ishida, Keio Business School on September 6, 1994. Ishida adds: "His lack of subservience is maybe why KM liked him."

38. Toshihiko Yamashita, *The Panasonic Way* (New York: Kodansha International, 1989), p. 7.

39. Ibid., p. 24.

40. Ibid., p. 32.

41. Ibid., pp. 37 and 38.

42. Ibid., p. 42.

43. Ibid., p. 60.

44. Ibid., p. 95.

45. Ibid., p. 41.

46. From an interview with Yamashita on February 18, 1992.

47. Toshihiko Yamashita, *The Panasonic Way* (New York: Kodansha International, 1989), p. 34. For a most interesting analysis of this episode, see Michael Cusumano, Yiorgos Mylonadis, and Richard Rosenbloom, "Strategic Maneuvering and Mass Market Dynamics: The Triumph of VHS over Beta," *Business History Review,* Volume 66 (Spring 1992), pp. 51–94.

48. "At the time [1964], it was considered to be a very wise decision. In retrospect, it is now clear it was a very bad decision." Interview with Professor Hideo Ishida, Keio Business School, on September 6, 1994.

49. "Matsushita believed it would be too difficult to get funding from MITI for the development of computers because MITI was biased against Matsushita." Interview with Professor Tsunehiko Yui, Meiji University, on September 6, 1994.

50. Toshihiko Yamashita, *The Panasonic Way* (New York: Kodansha International, 1989), p. 64.

Chapter 14. The Study of Human Nature

1. MEI company records.
2. PHP historical records.
3. Ibid.
4. Taro Nawa, *Matsushita Konosuke Keiei no Shinzui o Kataru* (Tokyo: Kokusai Shogyo Shuppan Kabushiki Kaisha, January 1983), pp. 100 and 101.
5. *Quest for Prosperity,* pp. 255 and 256.
6. Taro Nawa, *Matsushita Konosuke Keiei no Shinzui o Kataru* (Tokyo: Kokusai Shogyo Shuppan Kabushiki Kaisha, January 1983), pp. 99–101.
7. Ibid.
8. *Quest for Prosperity,* p. 256.
9. PHP records.
10. The Research Division, PHP Institute, *Matsushita Konosuke Hatsugenshu IV* (Kyoto: PHP, October 27, 1991), p. 69.
11. Office of Corporate History, Matsushita Electric.
12. *Time,* February 23, 1962.
13. PHP records.
14. *Quest for Prosperity,* pp. 335 and 336.
15. PHP records.
16. Ibid.
17. From Jeffrey Cruikshank, *Matsushita* (Boston: HBS Bulletin 1983), p. 50.
18. "KM's habit was to assemble theories that, in total, were contradictory, while the parts were all independently true. The key to understanding his philosophy is to understand this paradoxical nature of his thinking. His mind was a disorganized whole, yet everything was somehow in harmony. Most religions are made up of contextual stories filled with contradictions. KM's philosophy was the same way. Unlike Western Cartesian thinking, KM thought in terms of contradictions and therefore his

thinking was much closer to religion than Western thought."
From an interview with Professor Tadao Kagono, Kobe University, on September 12, 1994.

19. *The PHP Group* (Kyoto: PHP, 1994), p. 3.
20. Ibid.
21. Ibid.
22. Ibid.
23. Konosuke Matsushita, *My Management Philosophy* (Kyoto: PHP, 1978), p. 63.
24. *Imadakara Matsushita Konosuke, THE21 7 Gatsu Tokubetsu Zokan Go* (Kyoto: PHP, July 1, 1993), p. 34.
25. Professor Moriaki Tsuchiya of the University of Tokyo: "From all the evidence I've seen, I'd say his philosophy, 'Peace Through Prosperity,' pervaded every aspect of his life. This philosophy was manifest in the way he conducted himself both inside the company and out." Interview conducted on September 5, 1994.
26. This is a summary compilation based on over a dozen interviews.
27. Interview with Masaaki Arai in June of 1992.

Chapter 15. Books and Philanthropies

1. Books written by Konosuke Matsushita:

    PHP no Kotoba (Kyoto: Kocho Shorin, April 1953).

    Watashi no Ikikata Kangaekata (Tokyo: Jitsugyo no Nihonsha, May 1954).

    Shigoto no Yume Kurashi no Yume (Tokyo: Jitsugyo no Nihonsha, February 1960).

    Mono no Mikata Kangaekata (Tokyo: Jitsugyo no Nihonsha, April 1963).

    Minnade Kangaeyo: Keiei no Kachi Jinsei no Myomi (Tokyo: Jitsugyo no Nihonsha, September 1963).

Han-ei no Tame no Kangaekata (Tokyo: Jitsugyo no Nihon-sha, September 1964).

Naze (Tokyo: Bungeishunju, May 1965).

Wakasa ni Okuru (Tokyo: Kodansha, April 1966).

PHP Michi o Hiraku (Kyoto: PHP Institute, May 1968).

Ichi Nihonjin Toshiteno Watashi no Negai (Kyoto: PHP Institute, October 1968).

PHP Omoumama (Kyoto: PHP Institute, January 1971).

Sono Kokoroikiya Yoshi (Kyoto: PHP Institute, July 1971).

Ningen o Kangaeru, Atarashii Ningenkan no Teisho (Kyoto: PHP Institute, August 1971).

Shobai Kokoroe Cho (Kyoto: PHP Institute, February 1973).

Kaerimite Asu o Omou, Shinsei Nihon eno Ishikikaikaku o (Kyoto: PHP Institute, March 1973).

Keiei Kokoroe Cho (Kyoto: PHP Institute, July 1974).

Shain Kagyo, Shigoto no Kotsu Jinsei no Aji (Kyoto: PHP Institute, October 1974).

Kuzureyuku Nihon o Do Sukuuka (Kyoto: PHP Institute, December 1974).

Matsushita Konosuke Jitsugoroku (Tokyo: Ushio Shuppansha, November 1974).

Ningen o Kangaeru Dai Ikkan, Atarashii Ningenkan no Teisho Shin no Ningendo o Motomete (Kyoto: PHP Institute, February 1975).

Michi wa Mugenni Aru (Kyoto: PHP Institute, May 1975).

Wakai Kimitachi ni Tsutaetai (Tokyo: Kodansha, October 1975).

Kiki Nihon eno Watashi no Uttae (Kyoto: PHP Institute, December 1975).

Shidosha no Joken, Jinshin no Myomi ni Omou (Kyoto: PHP Institute, December 1975).

Shin Kokudo Sosei Ron (Kyoto: PHP Institute, June 1976).

Sunao na Kokoroni Narutameni (Kyoto: PHP Institute, September 1976).

Keizaidangi (Kyoto: PHP Institute, December 1976).

Watashi no Yume Nihon no Yume, 21seiki no Nihon (Kyoto: PHP Institute, January 1977).

Waga Keiei o Kataru (Kyoto: PHP Institute, March 1977).

Seiji o Minaoso (Kyoto: PHP Institute, March 1977).

Jinji Mange Kyo, Watashi no Hito no Mikata Sodate Kata (Kyoto: PHP Institute, September 1977).

Zoku PHP Michi o Hiraku (Kyoto: PHP Institute, January 1978).

Nihon wa Yomigaeruka, Megurikuru Han-ei (Kyoto: PHP Institute, February 1978).

Ketsudan no Keiei (Kyoto: PHP Institute, March 1979).

Jissen Keiei Tetsugaku (Kyoto: PHP Institute, June 1978).

Hito o Ikasu Keiei (Kyoto: PHP Institute, September 1979).

Keiei no Kotsu Kokonarito Kizuita Kachi wa Hyakumanryo (Kyoto: PHP Institute, March 1980).

Matsushita Seikeijuku Jukucho Kowaroku (Kyoto: PHP Institute, April 1981).

Shain Kokoroe Cho (Kyoto: PHP Institute, September 1981).

Nihon no Dento Seishin, Nihon to Nihonjin Nitsuite, Ningen o Kangaeru Dai Nikan (Kyoto: PHP Institute, August 1982).

Matsushita Konosuke Keiei Goroku, Riida no Kokoroe 38 Kajo (Kyoto: PHP Institute, March 1983).

Oriori no Ki, Jinsei de Deatta Hitotachi (Kyoto: PHP Institute, July 1983).

Jinsei Kokoroe Cho (Kyoto: PHP Institute, September 1984).

Yume o Sodateru (Tokyo: Nihon Keizai Shinbun Sha, May 1989).

Ningen Toshiteno Seiko (Kyoto: PHP Institute, September 1989).

Jinsei Dangi (Kyoto: PHP Institute, June 1990).

2. Data on gifts from PHP Institute, *Imadakara Matsushita Konosuke, THE 21 7 Gatsu Tokubetsu Zokan Go* (Kyoto: PHP, July 1, 1993), p. 31, and from Corporate Citizenship Department of MEI.

3. Konosuke Matsushita, *Shin Kokudo Sosei Ron* (Kyoto: PHP, June 1976).

4. See *Quest for Prosperity,* pp. 332 and 333.

5. Konosuke Matsushita, *Kuzureyuku Nihon o Do Sukuuka* (Kyoto: PHP, December 1974).

6. From Konosuke Matsushita (translated by Charles S. Terry), *Japan at the Brink* (Tokyo: Kodansha International; distributed by New York: Harper & Row, 1976), p. 92.

7. From an interview with Shimomura on February 17, 1992.

8. Konosuke Matsushita, *My Management Philosophy* (Kyoto: PHP, 1978), p. 9.

9. Ibid., p. 42.

10. See, for example, Matsushita's *A Piece of the Action* (Kyoto: PHP, 1993), and *Not For Bread Alone: A Business Ethos, A Management Ethic* (Kyoto: PHP, 1984). This summary of key ideas also comes from discussions with Katsuhiko Eguchi.

11. Douglas McGregor, *The Human Side of Enterprise* (New York: McGraw-Hill, 1960), pp. 45–49.

12. The material on Okochi is from Michael A. Cusumano, "Scientific Industry: Strategy, Technology, and Entrepreneurship in Pre-war Japan," Chapter 8 in *Managing Industrial Enterprise: Cases from Japan's Pre-war Experience,* edited by William Wray (Cambridge, MA: Harvard University Press, 1989).

13. Ibid., quoted on p. 284.
14. Data on the gifts from PHP Institute, *Imadakara Matsushita Konosuke, THE 21 7 Gatsu Tokubetsu Zokan Go* (Kyoto: PHP, July 1, 1993), p. 31 and from the Corporate Citizenship Department of MEI. Average exchange rate from IMF, *International Financial Statistics Yearbook* ,Vol. XIV, 1992.
15. From the brochure announcing the foundation.
16. From the brochure entitled "The Science and Technology Foundation of Japan, 1991," p. 5.
17. See note 14.
18. From an interview with Junnosuke Shinya on June 15, 1992.
19. Richard A. Kraft, "Great Patience!" *Intersect,* June 1994, pp. 17 and 18.

Chapter 16. Educating for Leadership

1. Information on the Kennedy School is from its Facilities and Services Department and its Office of the Registrar.
2. Data on alumni supplied by the schools.
3. Even Japanese businessmen, individuals who were clearly sympathetic to KM, often questioned his vision of MIGM. See, for example, the interview with Tsutsumi Yoshiaki in *Gekkan Keieijuku Rinjizokango Issatsu Marugoto Matsushita Konosuke,* by Gekkan Keieijuku (Tokyo: Keieijuku, December 1994), pp. 24 and 25. See also the interview with Jiro Ushio, pp. 29–31.
4. "Emphasis on a person's good qualities was at the heart of Mr. Matsushita's philosophy": Toshihiko Yamashita, *The Panasonic Way* (Tokyo: Kodansha International, 1989), p. 55.
5. When asked what made Matsushita mad, Tomomi Doi (who knew KM for nearly thirty years) said, "He always got angry about politics." From an interview on November 8, 1993.

6. He tried on at least two occasions to interest others in a new political party, but failed. Interview with Katsuhiko Eguchi on November 5, 1993.

7. MIGM records and interviews with MIGM staff.

8. Ibid.

9. Ibid.

10. Jeffrey Cruikshank, *Matsushita* (Boston: HBS Bulletin, 1983), p. 42.

11. MIGM records.

12. For a discussion of this distinction, see Richard Boyatzis, Scott Cowen, David Kolb and Associates, *Innovation in Professional Education* (San Francisco: Jossey-Bass, 1995), Chapters 1 and 10.

13. "Many people did not like the idea of MIGM and felt it was just a 'rich man's hobby.'" From an interview with Professor Hideo Ishida, Keio Business School, conducted on September 6, 1994.

14. Komine helped in the preparation of this book.

15. Jeffrey Cruikshank, *Matsushita* (Boston: HBS Bulletin, 1983), p. 47.

16. See the discussion of the more general issue in John P. Kotter and James L. Heskett, *Corporate Culture and Performance* (New York: Free Press, 1992).

17. "MEI has been losing touch with KM's philosophy." From an interview in September 1994 with someone who wished not to be quoted as being critical of MEI.

18. Interview with Shimomura, February 17, 1992.

19. Interview with Dr. Yokoo on November 4, 1993.

20. Ibid.

INDEX

ABOUT THE AUTHOR

John P. Kotter is the Konosuke Matsushita Professor of Leadership at the Harvard Business School. He is a graduate of MIT and Harvard and has been on the Business School faculty since 1972. In 1980, at the age of thirty-three, he was voted tenure and a full professorship, making him one of the youngest people in the history of the University to be so honored.

Professor Kotter is the author of *The General Managers* (1982), *Power and Influence: Beyond Formal Authority* (1985), *The Leadership Factor* (1987), *A Force for Change: How Leadership Differs from Management* (1990), *Corporate Culture and Performance* (1992, with Jim Heskett), *The New Rules: How to Succeed in Today's Post-Corporate World* (1995), and *Leading Change* (1996), all of which have been best-sellers among business books in the United States. He has also created two highly acclaimed executive videos, one on *Leadership* (1991) and one on *Corporate Culture* (1993), as well as an educational CD-ROM on *Initiating Change* (1997). His articles written over the past twenty years for the *Harvard Business Review* have sold a million and a half reprints.

The many honors won by Professor Kotter include an Exxon Award for Innovation in Graduate Business School Curriculum Design, a Johnson, Smith & Knisely Award for New Perspectives in Business Leadership, and a McKinsey Award for best *Harvard Business Review* articles.

Professor Kotter has taught in both MBA and Executive programs at Harvard and is a frequent speaker at top management meetings around the world. He lives in Cambridge, Massachusetts, and Ashland, New Hampshire with wife Nancy Dearman, daughter Caroline, and son Jonathan.